FAIRFIELD PARK, STOTFOLD, BEDFO~~~~
LATER PREHISTORIC SETTLEM~~~
IN THE EASTERN CHILTERNS

By Leo Webley, Jane Timby and Martin Wilson

with contributions by

Leigh Allen, John Crowther, Rebecca Devaney, Emily Edwards, Robert Francis, Matilda Holmes, Lynne Keys, Sylvia Peglar, Ruth Pelling, Ruth Shaffrey, Elizabeth Stafford, Gill Thompson and Annsofie Witkin

Illustrations by

Georgina Slater, Helen Crossman, Sarah Lucas, Julia Moxham, Mercedes Planas and Elin Sundman

Bedfordshire Archaeology Monograph 7

Published Jointly by The Oxford Archaeological Unit and The Bedfordshire Archaeological Council

© 2007 Bedfordshire County Council

ISBN 978-0-9531531-3-8

Figure 1.1 is reproduced from the Ordnance Survey on behalf of the controller of Her Majesty's Stationery Office, © Crown Copyright, AL 100005569
Figure 1.2 by permission of the British Geological Survey, © NERC. All rights reserved.

Contributions to the monograph series should be sent to
Michael Dawson, Ragsdale, 1 Church Lane, Great Cransley, Kettering, NN14 1PX

Contents

List of Figures

CHAPTER 4

CHAPTER 5

CHAPTER 6

APPENDIX

List of Plates

List of Tables

Summary

This volume reports upon the excavation of late Bronze Age to middle Iron Age remains at Fairfield Park, Stotfold, Bedfordshire, by Oxford Archaeology in 2002–3. The excavations took place at two separate locations (Sites A and B) within the grounds of the former Fairfield Hospital, which lies on a prominent hilltop. The earliest features at Site A were datable to the late Bronze Age and included a large, apparently empty enclosure and an adjacent cluster of pits. Three late Bronze Age cremation burials also occurred, one at Site A and two at Site B. After a possible hiatus in occupation, substantial settlements were laid out at both sites in the latter stages of the early Iron Age, around the 5th-4th centuries BC. Features at both settlements included small enclosures, roundhouses, four-post structures and numerous storage pits. There was some limited continuity of occupation into the middle Iron Age at Site B. Post-Iron Age activity was limited to agricultural use of the hilltop.

The site is significant as it represents one of the first large-scale modern excavations of early Iron Age settlement remains within the region. Extensive assemblages of artefacts and faunal remains were recovered, along with good environmental evidence. A number of unusual artefacts occurred, including pottery with unique forms of decoration, a group of atypically early rotary querns, a set of 49 bone weaving tools from a single pit, and a range of metal objects including an involuted pin with coral studs. Human remains and articulated animal skeletons had been deposited in several of the pits. The richness of the data is such that detailed analyses have been possible of spatial patterning both within and between the two settlements.

Acknowledgements

Oxford Archaeology would like to thank Fairfield Redevelopments Ltd for funding the work, and Mike Hutchinson at Mills Whipp Projects Ltd for acting as the archaeological consultant. Martin Oake, County Archaeological Officer of Bedfordshire County Council, also played an important role in facilitating the project.

The various stages of fieldwork were directed by Annie Bingham, Dave Score, Andy Simmonds and Dave Thomason, and were managed by Martin Wilson. The post-excavation work was managed by Jane Timby. Support was provided by Leigh Allen (finds management), Nicky Scott (archives management) and Dana Challinor and Rebecca Nicholson (environmental management). The authors are also grateful to the many other OA staff who worked on the project, both in the field and at the post-excavation stage.

Many thanks are due to J D Hill for reading and commenting on the text. Valery Rigby and Ian Stead are also thanked for their assistance in identifying the metalwork and facilitating access to comparanda at the British Museum. Drew Shotliff and Holly Duncan at Albion Archaeology and Anwen Cooper at Cambridge Archaeological Unit kindly provided information on unpublished excavations. Jim Inglis assisted with access to archive material held at Bedford Museum, and GSB Prospection Ltd kindly allowed reproduction of their geophysical survey results.

Rebecca Devaney would like to acknowledge the work undertaken by Kate Cramp on the evaluation of the flint and her valuable assistance during the production of the flint report in this volume.

Emily Edwards would like to acknowledge the work undertaken by Edward Biddulph and Jane Timby on the evaluation of the pottery, and Anna Slowikowski's assistance with access to the Bedfordshire Pottery Type Series.

Ruth Shaffrey would like to acknowledge the assistance of Professors John Allen and Bruce Sellwood of the School of Human and Environmental Sciences at the University of Reading.

The archive

The finds, paper records and digital archive are to be deposited at Bedford Museum (accession code BEDFM.2002.98). The archive includes all records made on site; evaluation and watching brief reports; post-excavation assessment reports; original versions of the final artefact, bone and environmental reports; pottery and animal bone databases; pottery recording sheets; human bone recording sheets; full radiocarbon results; and digital CAD plans of the site.

Chapter 1: Introduction

Fairfield Park is an area of modern residential development located in Stotfold parish in south Bedfordshire. It occupies the grounds of the former Fairfield Hospital, originally a Victorian asylum. Oxford Archaeology (OA) undertook excavations at two separate locations in the hospital grounds, referred to as Sites A and B, in 2002–3. The work was carried out on behalf of Fairfield Redevelopments Ltd in advance of road and housing construction.

The excavations in both areas revealed extensive settlement remains, dating mainly to the early Iron Age. As one of the first modern, large-scale investigations of a site of this period in eastern England, the results are of considerable significance. Substantial assemblages of artefacts and animal bone were recovered, along with a range of environmental evidence. The richness of the data has allowed detailed analyses of spatial patterning both within and between the two settlement areas.

SITE LOCATION AND GEOLOGY

Fairfield Park lies on a north-facing spur of the Chiltern Hills, with a maximum height of 75 m OD (Fig. 1.1). To the north and west, the hilltop commands good views over the valleys of the Rivers Ivel and Hiz respectively. To the east, the ground slopes down gently to the valley of the Pix Brook, a minor tributary of the Ivel. To the south, the hilltop is connected to the Chiltern ridge by a 'neck' of fairly level, raised ground. The geology consists of Letchworth Gravels and Anglian Glacial Till, overlying Lower Chalk (Fig. 1.2). The soils are characteristic of the Wantage 2 Association (well-drained, calcareous, silty: Hodge et al. 1984). The prevailing wind is from the south-west (Pettigrew et al. 1998, 30).

Of the two excavated areas, Site A was located on the eastern side of the spur, centred at TL 204 348, while Site B lay 550 m further north, at TL 204 354. Prior to excavation, both sites were under grass, although Site A had been ploughed in the recent past.

ARCHAEOLOGICAL AND HISTORICAL BACKGROUND

Before the evaluation fieldwork described below, there had been no knowledge of any archaeology at the site itself, although the surrounding landscape had produced significant evidence for later prehistoric activity. This included excavated Iron Age settlements at Groveland Way/Norton Road, Stotfold (2 km to the north-east: Steadman forthcoming) and

Blackhorse Road, Letchworth (3 km to the east-south-east: Moss-Eccardt 1988). The late Bronze Age to Iron Age 'hillfort' at Wilbury lies 2.5 km to the south (Applebaum 1933; 1949; Moss-Eccardt 1964). The nature of later prehistoric settlement in the area around Fairfield Park will be considered in more detail below (Chapter 6).

Documentary evidence indicates that from the later medieval period onwards, the hilltop formed part of the open fields of Stotfold parish. The site straddles the boundary between two of these fields, namely Marshfield to the north and Highfield to the south (Doggett 1983). The present layout of field boundaries in the area dates from the enclosure award of 1848. Fairfield Hospital (originally the Three Counties Asylum) was founded in the late 1850s and remained in operation until 1998 (Pettigrew et al. 1998).

EVALUATION FIELDWORK

The first phase of evaluation fieldwork was carried out by the Bedfordshire County Archaeology Service (BCAS) in 1997, involving gradiometer survey and surface collection of artefacts, focussed on the area to the south of the main hospital buildings (Table 1.1). The gradiometer survey (commissioned from GSB Prospection Ltd.) was carried out over four discrete areas totalling 4.8 ha in area. The most significant discovery was a pair of substantial, parallel, curvilinear ditches that could be traced for a distance of c 325 m along the eastern edge of the hilltop (Fig. 1.3 and Pl. 1.1). Meanwhile, the artefact collection produced a concentration of Iron Age and Roman pottery from the north-western part of the surveyed area. The Roman pottery forms included jars and mortaria; two Roman brick or tile fragments were also retrieved from the same area. Sparse quantities of worked flint, medieval/post-medieval pottery and ceramic building material were also recovered from across the survey area, with no concentrations apparent.

Following the geophysical survey and artefact collection, a total of 46 evaluation trenches were excavated to the south of the hospital (Fig. 1.4; BCAS 1997). A further 16 evaluation trenches were subsequently excavated by Oxford Archaeology in 2001–2 to the north and east of the hospital (OA 2001; 2002). Whilst the majority of the trenches contained no evidence for activity other than post-medieval agriculture, three concentrations of archaeological features were identified. These will be referred to in this report as Sites A–C (Fig. 1.3).

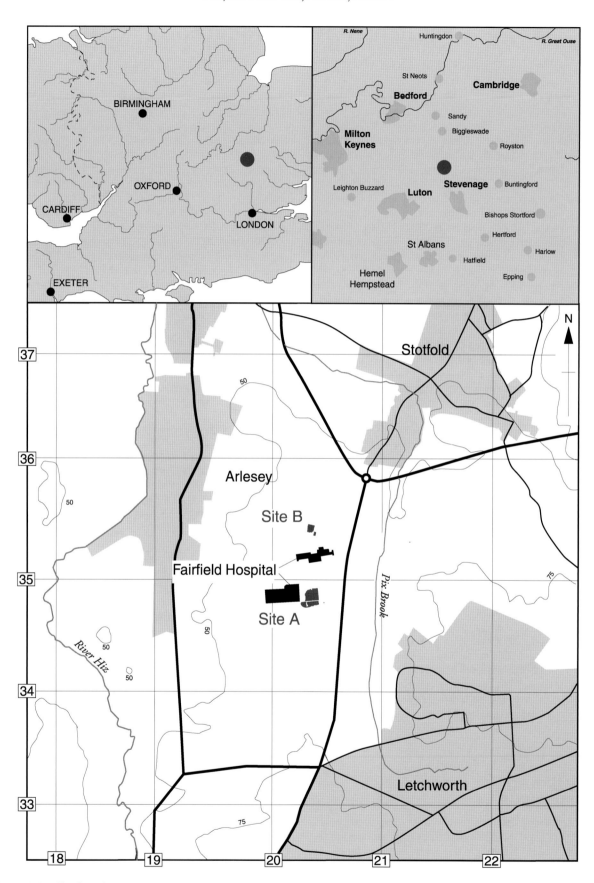

Figure 1.1   Site location.

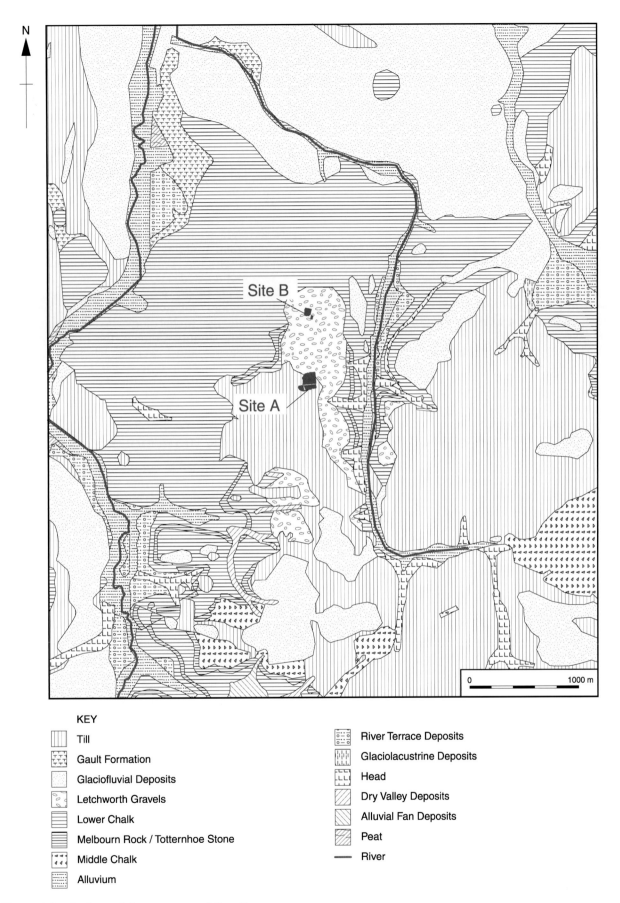

KEY

Till		River Terrace Deposits	
Gault Formation		Glaciolacustrine Deposits	
Glaciofluvial Deposits		Head	
Letchworth Gravels		Dry Valley Deposits	
Lower Chalk		Alluvial Fan Deposits	
Melbourn Rock / Totternhoe Stone		Peat	
Middle Chalk		—— River	
Alluvium			

Figure 1.2   Geology of the area around the site.

Table 1.1   Summary of fieldwork events.

Year	Event
1997	Gradiometer survey, fieldwalking and evaluation trenching to south of Hospital (BCAS)
2001	Evaluation trenching to east of Hospital
2002	Evaluation trenching to north of Hospital; excavation of Site A (central area)
2003	Excavation of Site A (northern and southern areas) and Site B; watching brief near Hospital building

Site A consisted of Iron Age settlement remains (ditches, pits and postholes) uncovered within Trenches 8, 9, 19, 20, 43 and 44 of the BCAS evaluation (Fig. 1.4). The features within Trenches 9 and some of the features within Trench 43 were sample excavated, producing a total of 2.3 kg of early to middle Iron Age pottery.

Site B consisted of a further concentration of Iron Age ditches, pits and postholes lying 550 m to the north of Site A, within Trenches 1–4 and 7 of the 2002 OA evaluation. All of the features were sample excavated, yielding 300 g of early Iron Age pottery and 450 g of animal bone.

Site C consisted of features uncovered within Trenches 10, 16, 17 and 21 of the BCAS evaluation (Fig. 1.4), corresponding to the spread of Iron Age and Roman pottery identified during the surface artefact collection. The features within Trench 10 were sample excavated, producing evidence for at least two phases of activity (Fig. 1.5). The earliest phase took the form of a group of postholes and pits, containing pottery broadly datable to the late Bronze Age/early Iron Age (see Chapter 3). Post-dating these were a series of ditches on an approximately N-S/E-W axis, containing small amounts of late Iron Age to early Roman pottery. Placed adjacent to the intersection of two of these ditches was a rich cremation burial dating to *c* AD 75–120. The grave cut was rectangular, and a scatter of nails and a band of organic staining suggested that the burial had been interred inside a wooden casket. The ashes were contained within a blue glass amphora, and accompanying grave-goods included three smaller glass vessels, four samian cups, three samian dishes, a ring-necked flagon, a copper alloy toilet spoon, a copper alloy brooch and bone hairpin fragments (BCAS 1997).

In addition to these three sites, archaeological features were also encountered in Trench 22 of the BCAS evaluation (Fig. 1.4). This trench had been placed to investigate the parallel ditches identified through geophysical survey on the eastern side of the hill. Three parallel ditches on a NE-SW alignment were in fact present (Fig. 1.6). The easternmost ditch (499 under the evaluation numbering system) was the smallest of the three, measuring 1.36 m wide and 0.50 m deep. Lying

1.50 m to the east was ditch 497, 2.70 m wide and more than 0.80 m deep (base not reached). It contained two fills, the lower of which had slumped in from the eastern edge, perhaps indicating that a bank lay on that side. Small quantities of early Anglo-Saxon pottery (5th–7th centuries AD) and residual later prehistoric sherds were recovered from each of the fills. The third ditch (494) was placed a further 2.50 m to the east. Unlike the other two ditches, this feature may have cut the subsoil, which could suggest a relatively recent date.

Subsequent to the evaluation trenching, a watching brief was carried out in 2003 on geotechnical test pits and light wells in the immediate vicinity of the main hospital building. Only modern disturbance associated with the construction of the hospital was encountered (OA 2004a).

As a result of the various phases of evaluation fieldwork, and following consultation with the clients and the archaeological representatives of Bedfordshire County Council, the Iron Age settlements at Sites A and B were targeted for open area excavation. Site C has been left to be preserved *in situ*, and no further work has been carried out on the Anglo-Saxon boundary feature.

EXCAVATION METHODOLOGY

Site A was excavated in two separate stages. An east-west aligned strip 25 m wide was excavated across the centre of the site in advance of road construction in Autumn 2002, while the remaining areas to the north and south were excavated between June and November 2003 (Fig. 1.7). A combined area of 2.2 ha was stripped. The excavation of Site B took place during Spring 2003. Two discrete areas were stripped, a larger area of 3600 m² and a smaller detached area of 450 m² to its south-east. The zone between these two areas could not be excavated due to the presence of service ducts.

All work followed procedures laid down in the *OA Fieldwork Manual* (OA 1992). The overburden was stripped under archaeological supervision using a 360° tracked mechanical excavator with a toothless ditching bucket. The hand-excavation of archaeological features then followed. All discrete features were half-sectioned, and some completely excavated. A minimum of 10% of all linear ditches and gullies was excavated. All archaeological deposits were allocated a unique context number (Site A: context numbers 1–600 and 3000–5300; Site B: 1000–2400). Plans and sections of individual features were drawn at a scale of 1:20, and tied into the overall digital site plan using a Leica TC705. Features were also recorded using colour and monochrome photography. Finds were recorded by context, with objects of special interest additionally being given a unique small find number (eg SF 10).

A large number of environmental bulk samples were taken from both sites, following standard OA

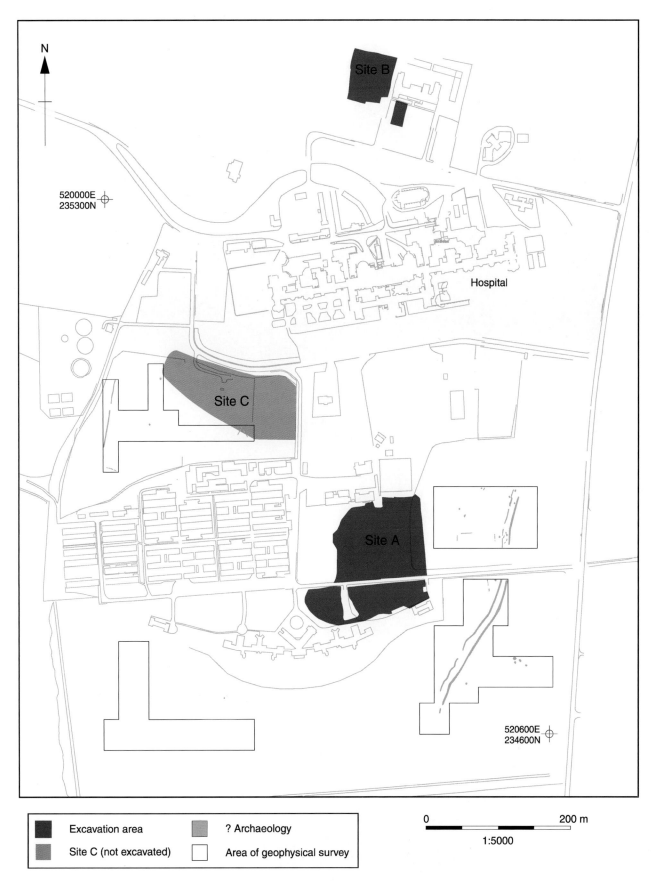

Figure 1.3 Location of excavation areas and areas of geophysical survey. Geophysical data used courtesy of GSB Prospection Ltd.

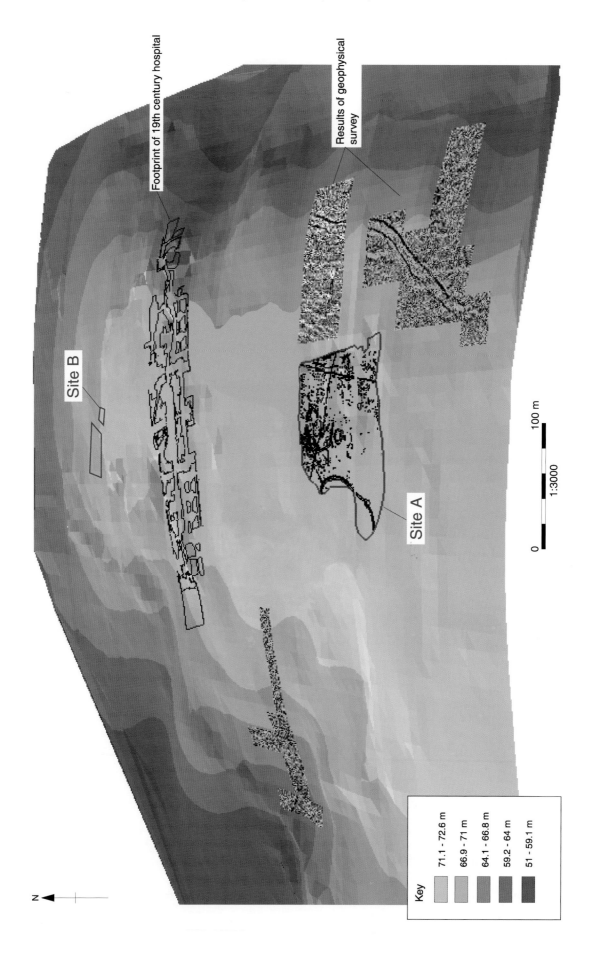

Footprint of 19th century hospital

Results of geophysical survey

Site B

Site A

N

Key	
	71.1 - 72.6 m
	66.9 - 71 m
	64.1 - 66.8 m
	59.2 - 64 m
	51 - 59.1 m

0   1:3000   100 m

Plate 1.1 Location of excavation areas and areas of geophysical survey in relation to topography. Geophysical data used courtesy of GSB Prospection Ltd.

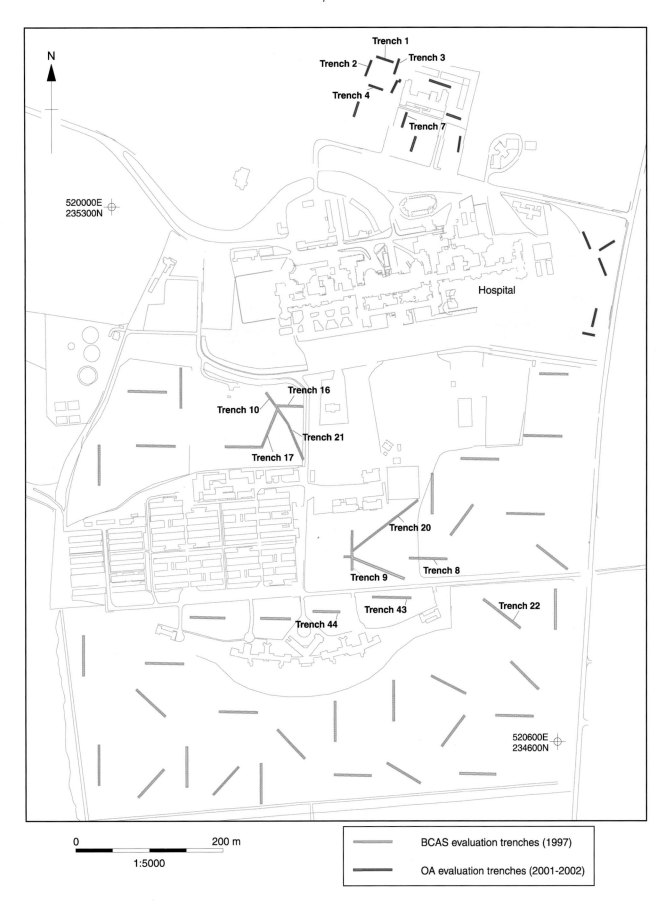

Figure 1.4   Evaluation trenches (numbered where mentioned in text).

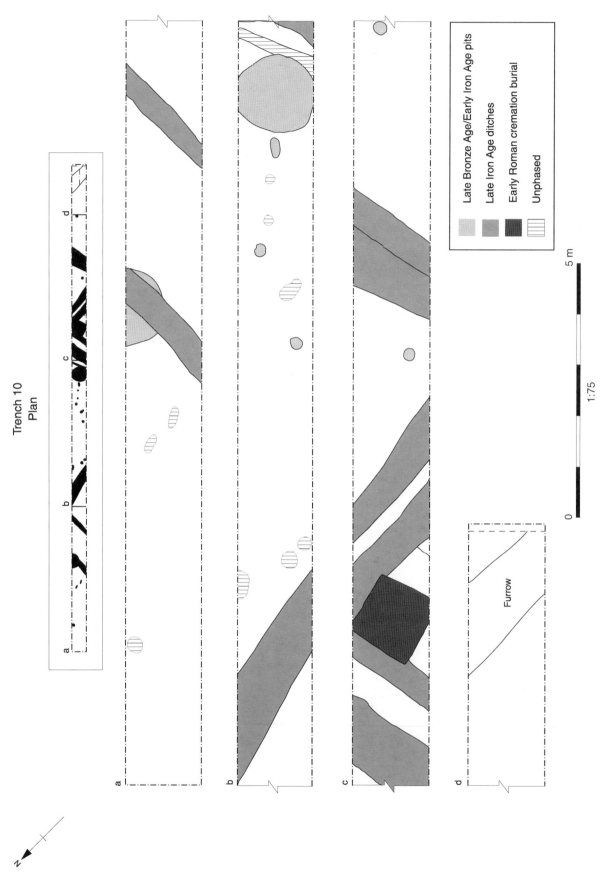

Figure 1.5   Plan of BCAS evaluation Trench 10 (Site C).

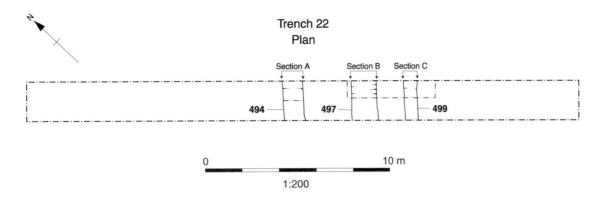

Trench 22
Plan

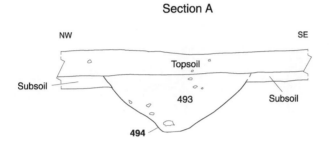

Section A

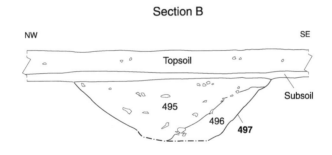

Section B

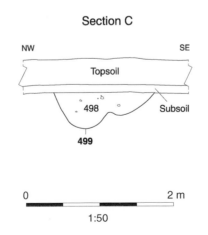

Section C

Figure 1.6   Plan of BCAS evaluation Trench 22 and sections of Anglo-Saxon ditches.

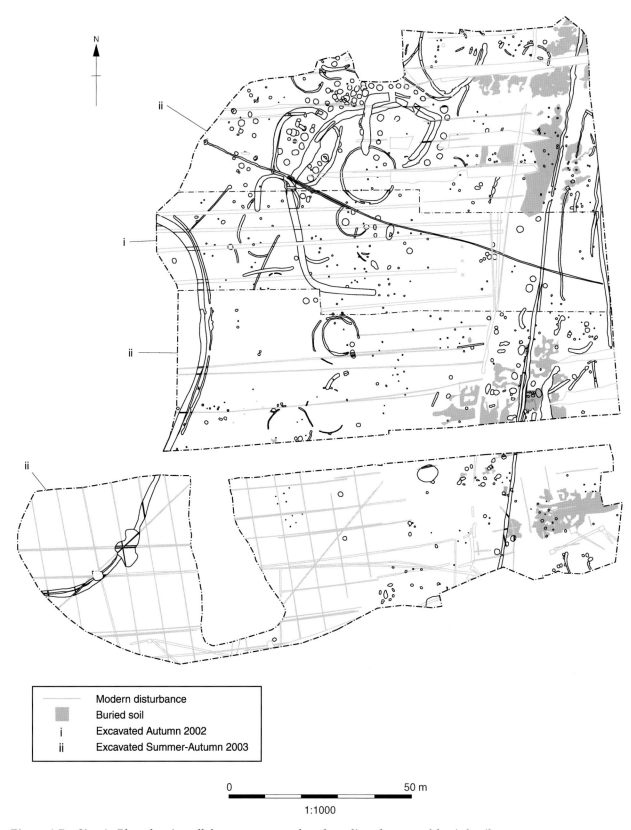

N

ii

i

ii

ii

Modern disturbance
Buried soil
i   Excavated Autumn 2002
ii Excavated Summer-Autumn 2003

0   50 m

1:1000

Figure 1.7   Site A. Plan showing all features, extent of modern disturbance and buried soil.

procedures. Priority was given to the basal fills of features and to those contexts showing visible charred plant remains. For features such as postholes, sampling was limited to those that could be firmly attributed to a datable structure.

A programme of phosphate sampling was additionally carried out at Site A. Secondary deposits within features were targeted, with control samples taken from the topsoil, subsoil and natural geology at various locations across the site.

Chapter 2:   The Archaeological Sequence

INTRODUCTION

Significant medieval and post-medieval agricultural truncation of archaeological features had clearly occurred at both sites. The extent of the truncation cannot be accurately estimated, but it may have been similar to the depth of the topsoil and subsoil overlying the archaeological levels, which varied from *c* 0.30–0.50 m. In addition to this 'blanket' truncation, Site A was covered by a network of furrows and field drains (see Fig. 1.7), which cut on average around 0.10 m into the archaeological levels.

Despite this, a buried soil (3074/3133) survived patchily across much of the eastern half of Site A, where the ground surface began to slope downwards. This consisted of dark brown silty clay with an average depth of 0.08 m. It directly overlay the natural geology, and was cut by all archaeological features in the area. The deposit had a disturbed appearance, and it is uncertain whether it represents a ploughsoil. It produced artefacts of varying dates, including early prehistoric worked flint, early to middle Iron Age pottery and one sherd of Roman pottery. No buried soil survived at Site B.

Although limited early prehistoric activity is evinced at both sites by small amounts of residual worked flint, the earliest features belong to the later prehistoric period. The features have been divided into six phases of activity, as follows:

Phase 1: late Bronze Age
Phase 2: early Iron Age
Phase 3: middle Iron Age
Phase 4: Romano-British period
Phase 5: medieval period?
Phase 6: medieval/post-medieval period

EARLY PREHISTORIC ACTIVITY

Sites A and B both yielded small amounts of worked flint dating to periods prior to the 1st millennium BC (see Devaney, Chap. 3). All was recovered as residual material from later deposits.

At Site A, low densities of flintwork were recovered from the buried soil (3074/3133) and from Iron Age features dispersed across the excavated area. These included a broken arrowhead, which may date to either the earlier Neolithic or the early Bronze Age.

Diagnostically early finds from Site B consisted of four blades dating to the Mesolithic or early Neolithic, and a flake from a Neolithic polished flint implement. Notably, these were all recovered from features clustered tightly together in the north-western corner of the site, in and around Structure

34 (Fig. 2.29). This discrete spread of material suggests a single small-scale episode of occupation.

PHASE 1: LATE BRONZE AGE

Site A (Fig. 2.1)

Dominating the crest of the ridge in Site A was a substantial curvilinear enclosure (Enclosure I). While the dating of this enclosure is slightly problematic, it seems likely that the initial cut of the ditch was created during the late Bronze Age, although it was reworked and finally infilled during the early Iron Age. The enclosure showed no evidence of internal occupation, but a small cluster of pits and postholes containing late Bronze Age pottery occurred immediately to its east. Meanwhile, an un-urned cremation burial (407) to the north-east of the enclosure can probably be dated to the late Bronze Age by analogy with a similar feature from Site B.

Enclosure I

Enclosure I was partially exposed at the western edge of the excavated area (Pl. 2.1). It appears to have been roughly oval in form, with an internal area of 100 m NNE-SSW by at least 30 m ESE-WNW. While the southern half of the enclosure circuit was defined by only a single ditch, in the northern half there was also a second concentric ditch placed 0.35–1.50 m to the east.

The main enclosure ditch had been remodelled at least once, with a relatively shallow initial cut (3500) later replaced by a more robust cut (3450). Ditch 3500 was only sporadically visible around the enclosure circuit, where it had not been truncated away by the later cut. It was up to 0.80 m wide and 0.14–0.35 m deep (Table 2.1), with pale, naturally-deposited silty clay fills. The only finds consisted of two sherds of flint-tempered late Bronze Age pottery and a few small fragments of animal bone from fill 4346 (Fig. 2.2). The later ditch, 3450, was up to 2.14 m wide and 1.00 m deep (Table 2.1). Evidence for a recut of 3450 was visible in one intervention, but not elsewhere. The southern half of the ditch circuit was characterised by naturally-formed fills containing very few finds. In the northern half of the circuit, however, these fills were interleaved with darker layers containing pottery, animal bone, charcoal and burnt stone. The dating evidence from these fills is difficult to interpret. In intervention 4339 (Fig. 2.2), the finds from middle fill 4342 included a small amount of flint-tempered late Bronze Age pottery, and charred cereal grain from this layer produced a radiocarbon date of 1250–1230 cal BC/1220–1010

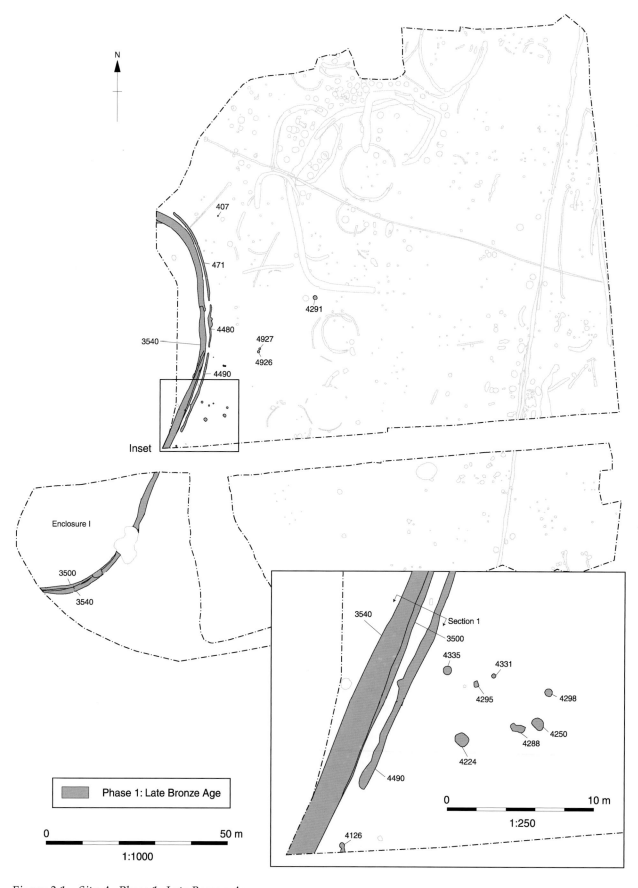

Figure 2.1   Site A. Phase 1: Late Bronze Age.

Plate 2.1 Site A during the 2002 season of excavation, looking east. Enclosure I can be seen in the foreground, with Enclosure III (under excavation) beyond. The view in the background stretches across the valley of the Pix Brook to the hill beyond.

cal BC (NZA-21952: 2916 ± 25 BP; Table 2.12). However, in interventions further to the north the pottery appears to be of early Iron Age character, including some sherds from the lower fills of the ditch. It is possible that the presence of this early Iron Age material is due to episodes of recutting or cleaning out of the ditch at the northern end of the circuit. Alternatively, it may be that ditch 3450 was indeed first created in the early Iron Age, with the late Bronze Age material from intervention 4339 merely being residual.

The outer ditch of the enclosure (471/4480/4490) was up to 0.70 m wide and 0.36 m deep (Table 2.1), becoming increasingly shallow towards the south (Fig. 2.2). It had a single, naturally-deposited silty fill, which yielded a few sherds of pottery of both late Bronze Age and early Iron Age character and some small fragments of animal bone.

Table 2.1   Summary of Enclosure 1.

Ditch cut		Width (m)	Depth (m)
Main ditch	3500	0.31–0.80	0.14–0.35
	3540	0.93–2.14	0.40–1.00
Outer ditch	471	0.50–0.70	0.20–0.36
	4480	0.26–0.40	0.10–0.14
	4490	0.20–0.64	0.06–0.13

All of the ditches described above had essentially U-shaped profiles. The direction from which the fills had entered the ditches seems to have varied, thus giving no clear evidence for the location of any upcast bank.

Occupation features

The exposed part of the interior area of Enclosure I was entirely devoid of late Bronze Age features. However, a small group of shallow features containing flint-tempered late Bronze Age pottery was found immediately to the east of Enclosure 1, clustered within an area of *c* 55 m across.

The core of the occupation area, where most of the artefacts were recovered, comprised a group of eight features (Table 2.2) including a posthole (4295), two shallow pits (4224 and 4250), a small bell-shaped pit (4126), two small pits or postholes (4335 and 4351), and two tree throw holes (4288 and 4298). Each of these features possessed a single fill of sandy silt. Posthole 4295 had vertical sides and contained sandstone cobbles which may have been disturbed post-packing. In contrast, the two neighbouring pits or postholes 4335 and 4351 both had concave profiles. They yielded the largest quantity of pottery of any of the Phase 1 features, although this still amounted to less than 200 g each. A copper alloy awl (SF 135; see Fig. 3.19.1) was recovered from

Section 1

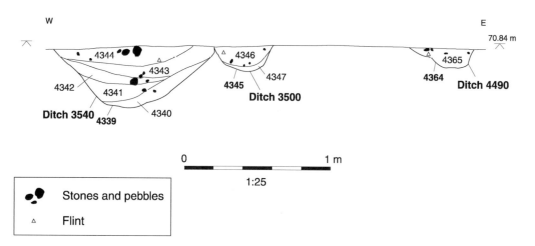

Figure 2.2   Section of Enclosure I.

shallow pit 4250. Further features containing small amounts of late Bronze Age pottery lay to the north of this core of activity. These consisted of a pair of tree throw holes (4926 and 4927) and a shallow flat-based pit (4291; Table 2.2).

Cremation burial

Un-urned cremation burial 407 was located to the north of the 'occupation area' and to the north-west of Enclosure 1 (Fig. 2.1). It consisted of a single homogeneous deposit of charcoal and burnt bone. It was contained within a small, irregular cut measuring 0.32 m across and 0.06 m deep. Although no artefacts were recovered, this feature is likely to date to the late Bronze Age due to its similarity to cremation burial 2094 from Site B (see below).

Site B

Un-urned cremation burials 2094 and 2361 were placed 72 m apart within Site B (Fig. 2.26). Both were contained within circular, concave cuts, burial 2094 measuring 0.50 m in diameter and 0.28 m deep, while 2361 measured 0.36 m in diameter and 0.12 m deep. Their homogeneous fills of charcoal and burnt bone contained no artefacts. However, a radiocarbon date of 920–790 cal BC (NZA-22062; 2687±40 BP)

was obtained on charcoal (*Prunus* sp.) from burial 2094 (Table 2.12).

PHASE 2: EARLY IRON AGE

Site A (Fig. 2.3)

Following a possible hiatus in activity, Site A was reoccupied during the latter stages of the early Iron Age. Settlement features were densest in the north-western part of the excavated area, and included a series of successive enclosures. One of the enclosures appears to have contained a pair of roundhouses, which formed part of a swathe of at least seven buildings following a NNE-SSW alignment across the site. To the east of the roundhouses, features included pits, two large hollows, and numerous four-post 'granaries'. The south-western part of the excavated area was almost devoid of features.

The pottery from this phase overwhelmingly belongs to the later part of the early Iron Age, *c* 5th–4th centuries BC (see Edwards, Chap. 3). Other closely datable artefacts were few, but included a La Tène I brooch from Site A dating to the 4th–mid 3rd centuries BC (SF 44; Fig. 3.17.3). The artefactual evidence concurs with the radiocarbon dates for this phase, all of which are compatible with occupation during the 4th century BC (see *Radiocarbon dating* below).

Table 2.2   Phase 1 pits and postholes, Site A.

Feature	Interpretation	Diameter (m)	Depth (m)	Finds
4126	Pit	0.21	0.20	Pottery, bone
4224	Pit	1.00	0.25	Pottery
4250	Pit	0.85	0.10	Pottery, bone, bronze awl
4291	Pit	1.10	0.25	Pottery
4295	Posthole	0.35	0.38	Pottery
4335	Pit or posthole	0.55	0.21	Pottery, bone
4351	Pit or posthole	0.30	0.10	Pottery, bone

Figure 2.3   Site A. Phase 2: Early Iron Age.

Enclosure I

As discussed above (see *Phase 1*), Enclosure I may have been recut during this phase. Certainly, the bulk of the pottery recovered from the later cut of the enclosure ditch dates to the early Iron Age. It is notable that almost all of this material derives from the northern part of the enclosure circuit, the part adjacent to the early Iron Age settlement core. There is thus little evidence that the enclosure itself was a focus for activity during this phase. The only early Iron Age feature located within the enclosure was a single bell-shaped pit (364; see below).

Enclosures II–V

The enclosures in the north-western part of the excavated area show a stratigraphic sequence as follows (Fig. 2.4):

(i) Enclosure II and ditch 473
(ii) Enclosure III
(iii) Enclosure IV (with pit row 3530) and Enclosure V

Enclosure II seems to have post-dated at least some early Iron Age activity, as it cut two pits, 4457 and 4556. At the other end of the sequence, the upper layers of the ditches of Enclosures IV and V contained middle Iron Age material, indicating that the final in-filling of these features occurred during Phase 3 (see below). The enclosures are described in chronological order below.

Enclosure II and ditch 473

Enclosure II (Figs 2.5–9) was sub-oval in form, measuring c 18 m NE-SW by 15.1 m NW-SE (c 225 m^2), with a NE-facing entranceway. Much of the southern side of the enclosure had been obliterated by the later Enclosures III and V. The western side exhibited two cuts, the first (4410) measuring 0.56–1.40 m wide and 0.33–0.70 m deep, while the subsequent recut (4610) was shallower at 0.60–1.90 m wide and 0.18–0.40 m deep. The eastern side of the enclosure showed only a single cut for most of its length (4400), measuring 0.65–1.16 m wide and 0.46–0.50 m deep, with a series of fills suggesting separate episodes of natural silting. However, it had been reworked at its terminal end by recut 4790, 0.70 m wide and 0.12–0.20 m deep. The combined effect of the recuts at the western and eastern terminal ends was to markedly reduce the width of the entranceway from 5.90 m to 2.90 m. The fills consisted of silty clays, most of which were probably deliberate back-fill deposits. The interior of the enclosure contained several pits of varying forms.

Ditch 473 was also cut by Enclosure III (Fig. 2.9). This ditch was a short curvilinear feature, lying 18 m to the south of Enclosure II. It was 6.2 m long, with a notably steep-sided and deep cut (0.70–0.76 m wide and 0.60–0.70 m deep). It contained a sequence of three clay back-fill deposits, which produced small amounts of pottery and animal bone.

Enclosure III (Fig. 2.7 and Pl. 2.2)

Enclosure III took the form of an irregular sub-oval, open on its eastern side, measuring 50 m NNE-SSW by 28 m WNW-ESE (c 1080 m^2). It was demarcated by a substantial ditch (4700), 1.66–2.80 m wide and 0.70–1.38 m deep, with steep sides and a flat base. In most places, only a single cut was evident. However,

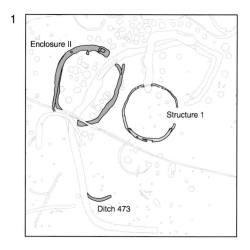

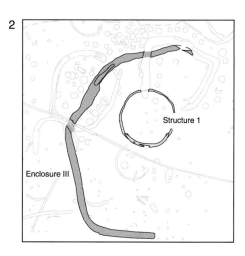

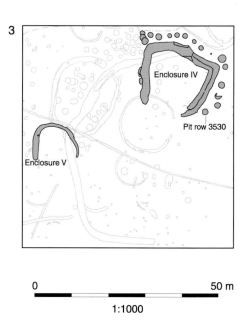

Figure 2.4 Site A. Sequence of enclosures in north-western part of early Iron Age settlement.

18

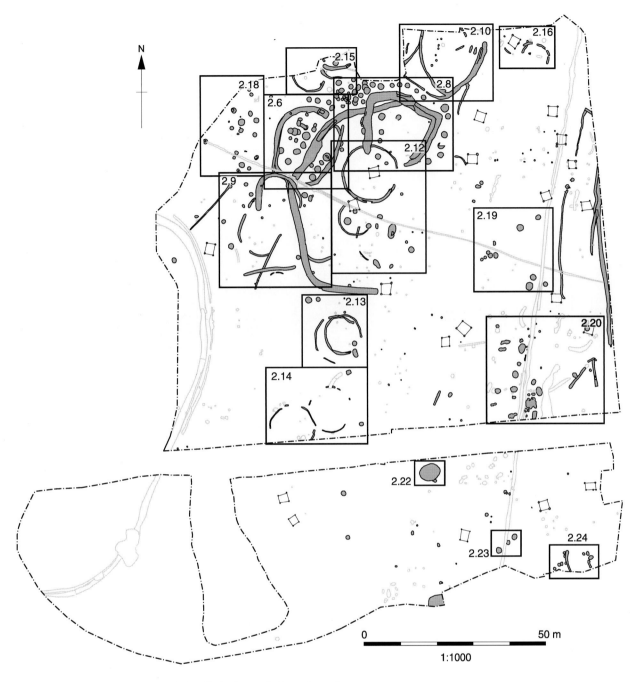

Figure 2.5   Site A. Location of detailed plans of Phase 2 settlement.

the final 8 m of the circuit at the northern butt end showed a shallower recut, at least 1.10 m wide and 0.70–0.80 m deep. The enclosure ditch was characterised by a series of silty clay back-fill deposits interleaved with natural erosion layers, at least some of which seem to have been deposited from the inner side of the enclosure. The middle and upper fills tended to be the richest in finds, with the greatest quantities of pottery and animal bone occurring in the interventions at and near the terminal ends of the ditch. Features within the enclosure (Fig. 2.3) included three roundhouses (Structures 1, 2 and 8) and two four-post 'granaries' (Structures 20 and 29).

Enclosure IV and pit row 3530 (Fig. 2.8)

Enclosure IV took the form of a trapezium, open on its shortest, SSW-facing side. This open side was 9.5 m long, while the northern side was 14.3 m long and the eastern and western sides were 15.0 m long (*c* 190 m^2). The ditch exhibited a series of recuts and had thus clearly been maintained over a significant period of time.

On the eastern side of the enclosure, the initial cut was up to 1.40 m wide and 0.45–0.60 m deep, with a V-shaped profile (3080). This was truncated along its outer edge by a recut 0.95–1.40 m wide and

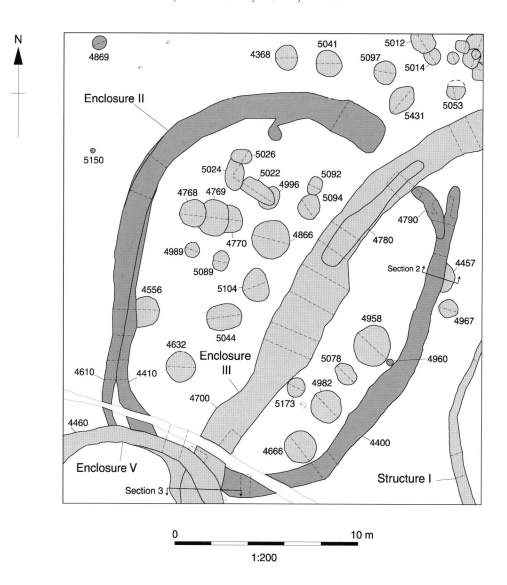

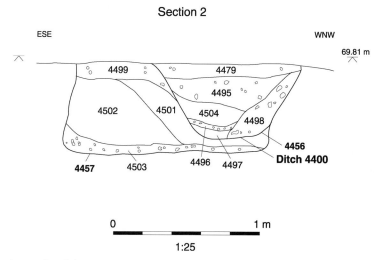

Figure 2.6   Enclosure II and associated features.

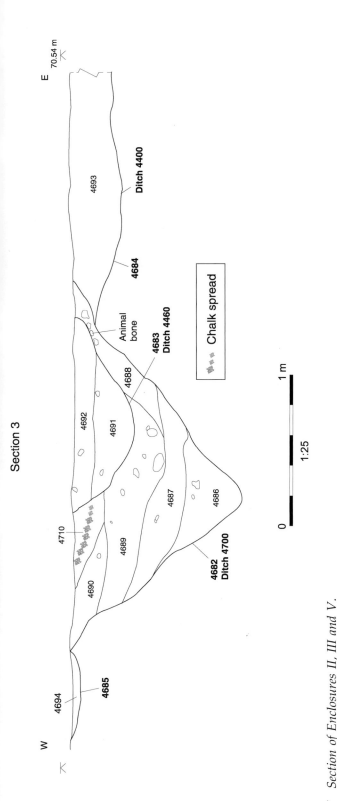

Section 3

Figure 2.7 Section of Enclosures II, III and V.

Plate 2.2   Enclosure III, southern terminal end of ditch looking west.

0.55–0.72 m deep (3070). The northern and western sides of the enclosure showed more complex sequences, with as many as five cuts visible in some of the excavated slots. These cuts were generally shallower, reaching a maximum depth of 0.62 m. The exception was the western terminal end of the enclosure, which showed only a single cut, much broader and deeper than those elsewhere (1.96 m wide and 1.13 m deep). It seems probable that the butt end saw a particularly robust final cut which completely truncated away all earlier cuts.

The fills of the enclosure ditch seemed in general to be deliberately deposited, being dark and finds-rich, although there was no consistency in the direction from which the material was dumped. The greatest quantities of pottery and animal bone occurred at the terminal ends of the ditch. A worked human femur was recovered from a middle fill (3068) of the recut of ditch 3070.

Pit row 3530 surrounded and respected the northern and eastern sides of Enclosure IV in a manner which strongly suggests contemporaneity. The row was made up of fourteen pits, set 0.7–3.3 m apart, all with similar profiles and fills. They were roughly circular, ranging between 1.06 m and 2.10 m in diameter (Table 2.3), with sheer sides and flat bases. Most of the pits were 0.05–0.50 m deep, but

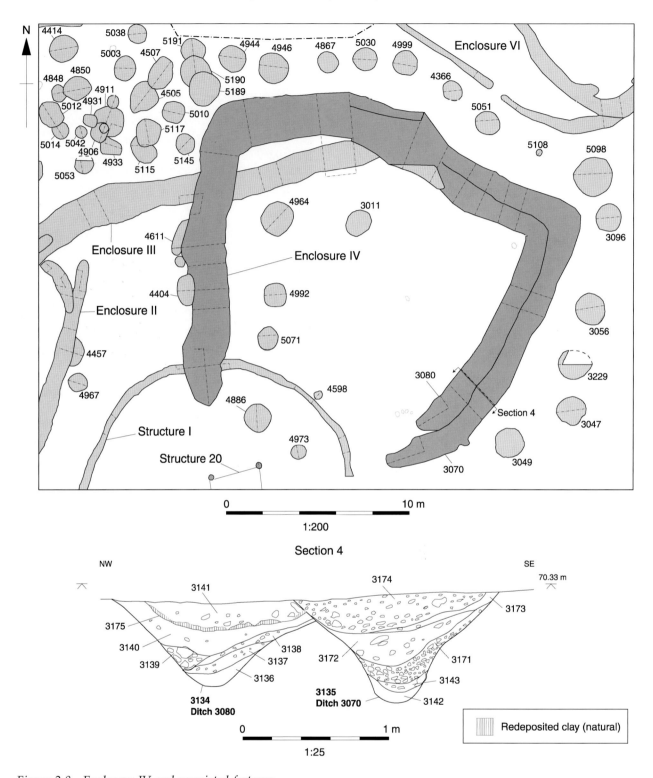

Figure 2.8 Enclosure IV and associated features.

the pits near the terminal ends (3056 and 5189) were deeper at 0.65–0.70 m. Most seem to have been deliberately back-filled with silty clay. Artefacts were generally sparse, the exception being terminal pit 3049, which contained large amounts of pottery and animal bone.

The most notable finds from the pit row, however, were two sub-adult human skeletons. The middle fill of terminal pit 5189 contained the crouched burial (5144) of a child aged 10–13 years, possibly male (Pl. 2.5). The body lay in the eastern half of the pit, on its right side facing west, and was placed on a slope so that its feet were higher than its head. Meanwhile, pit 4867 contained a heavily truncated skeleton (4885) of a child aged 6–10 years. This had been placed near the top of the single fill of the pit,

Table 2.3 Pit row 3530. Pits listed in sequence from north-west to south-east.

Pit	Diameter (m)	Depth (m)	Pottery (g)	Animal bone (g)	Other finds
5191*	1.38	0.22	56	15	Fired clay
5190*	1.70	0.64	225	91	
5189	1.79	0.65	374	266	Human burial 5144
4944	1.40	0.10	21	42	
4946	1.50	0.35	173	158	
4867	1.10	0.30	66	90	Human burial 4885
5030	1.30	0.05	3	17	
4999	1.15	0.30	158	262	
4366	1.06	0.11	23	8	
5051	1.30	0.26	23	74	
5098	2.10	0.50	113	200	
3096	1.35	0.30	51	6	Fired clay
3056	1.65	0.47	18	6	
3229	1.84	0.44	137	83	
3047	1.70	0.20	66	16	
3049	1.89	0.70	1315	3465	Iron object SF 101, slag

* = pit stratigraphically earlier than pit 5189.

in the southern part of the feature. Only the lower legs survived, and the posture of the burial is thus unclear.

Most of the pits in the row show no stratigraphic relationships to other features. However, terminal pit 5189 cut an earlier pit, 5190, which in turn cut pit 5191. Both of these stratigraphically earlier pits had steep-sided and flat-based profiles, and might have served as previous termini of the row.

A dense cluster of pits occurred immediately to the west of 'terminal' pits 5189/5190/5191 (see below), and it could be argued that at least some of these continued the course of row 3530 westwards. However, the profiles and fills of these features were much more variable, suggesting that they did not belong to the same episode of pit digging and back-filling.

Enclosure V (Figs 2.7 and 2.9)

Enclosure V was a horseshoe-shaped feature open on its southern side, measuring 10.25 m E-W by 8.70 m N-S (c 70 m²). The ditch was 0.70–1.70 m wide and 0.32–0.50 m deep, with a U-shaped cut which became broader and deeper towards the western butt end. It contained apparently naturally deposited silty clay fills, yielding fewer finds than the other enclosures in this area. The only features within the enclosure were a pair of small pits or postholes (98 and 253).

Other enclosures

Two further enclosures were encountered at the margins of the main north-western enclosure group. Enclosure VI was only partially exposed at the northern limit of excavation, while the heavily truncated Enclosure VII lay to the west of Enclosure III.

Enclosure VI (Fig. 2.10)

Enclosure VI underwent two distinct phases of differing forms, although its overall layout is unclear as it continued beyond the limit of excavation. The initial phase seems to have been subrectangular, measuring at least 18 m NE-SW by c 13.5 m NW-SE. It was demarcated on its southern and eastern sides by gully 3260, which measured 0.20–0.55 m wide and 0.05–0.35 m deep, with a U-shaped cut. A clear butt-end was present at the northern terminus of the eastern side. A narrow interruption of 0.56 m was present in the southern side, but this may have been the result of truncation, as the gully was very shallow on either side. The western side of the enclosure may be represented by gully 3050, although the supposed intersection with the southern side lay outside the area of excavation. Gully 3050 was 0.22–0.44 m wide and 0.10–0.18 m deep.

The second phase of the enclosure followed the same alignment on its eastern side, recutting gully 3260. The western side was realigned, however, so that the enclosure was reduced in size and took on a more sub-oval form, measuring at least 15.5 m NE-SW by 16.4 m NW-SE. The western gully (3060) was 0.50–0.66 m wide and 0.09–0.20 m deep, with straight sides and a flat base. The eastern gully had a U-shaped cut, and was more substantial at 1.07–1.35 m wide and 0.42–0.60 m deep, becoming broader and deeper towards the butt end. All of the gullies of both phases of the enclosure were characterised by silty clay fills that were probably naturally deposited.

A shallow, irregular gully, 5159, ran off from the eastern side of the enclosure, although no stratigraphic relationship could be observed between the two. This was 8.7 m long, 0.44 m wide and 0.06 m deep.

A possible subdivision within Enclosure VI was observed in the form of a 7.3 m-long row of six postholes on a NNE-SSW alignment (3911). The individual postholes were set 0.3–1.3 m apart, and ranged from 0.24–0.58 m in diameter and from 0.04–0.21 m deep. Stone cobbles were present in some of the postholes, possibly representing disturbed post packing, but no post-pipes were apparent. Other features within the enclosure included a possible roundhouse (Structure 11, see below).

Enclosure VII and neighbouring gullies (Fig. 2.9)

Enclosure VII was sub-oval in form, measuring at least 12 m NE-SW by 10 m NW-SE. It was demarcated on its southern and western sides by a very shallow gully, 0.20–0.50 m wide and 0.06–0.14 m deep, which had been entirely truncated away by plough furrows in two places. This gully had a single, naturally deposited silty clay fill containing very few finds.

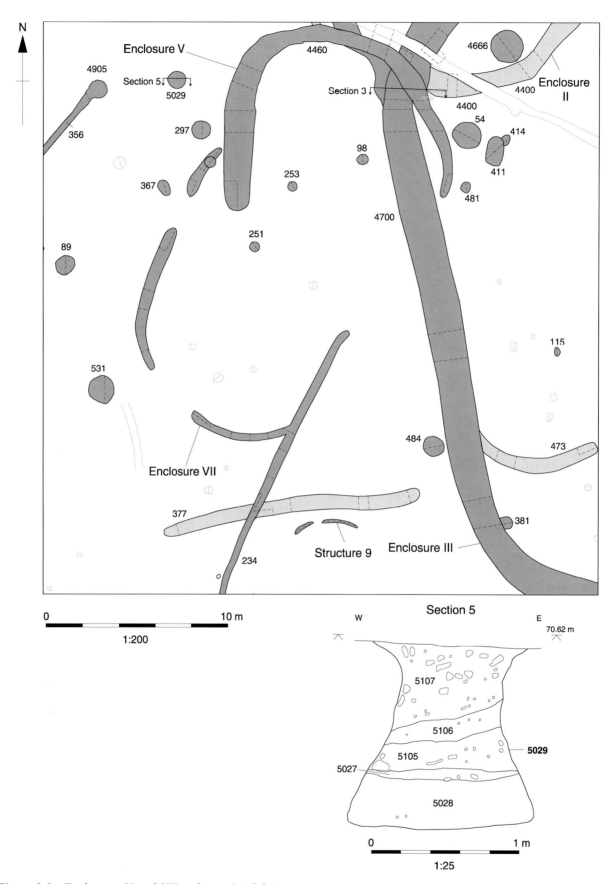

Figure 2.9   Enclosures V and VII and associated features.

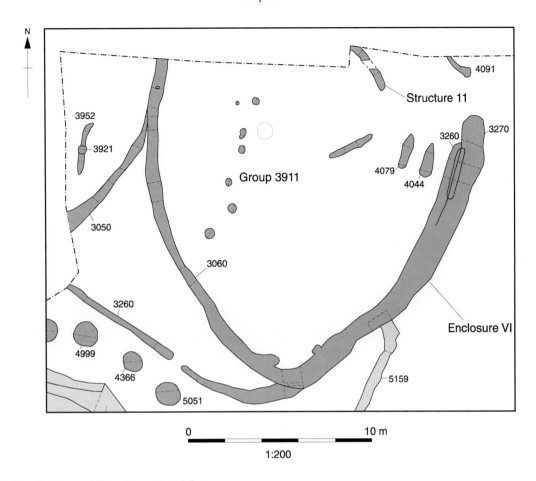

Figure 2.10   Enclosure VI and associated features.

Three further linear gullies lay close to Enclosure VII, although it is unclear whether they were associated with it. Gully 234 ran for 9 m on a SE-NW alignment, merging with the eastern side of Enclosure VII, although no relationship between the two could be observed. It measured 0.56 m wide and 0.30 m deep. Gully 234 cut a further, E-W aligned linear, 377, which measured 14 m long, 0.67 m wide and 0.36 m deep. Meanwhile, 8 m to the north-east of Enclosure VII, gully 356 ran for 16 m on a SE-NW alignment. It was 0.50 m wide and 0.23 m deep, and terminated to the north-west in a possible sump pit (4905), 1 m in diameter and 0.36 m deep. All three of these gullies had silty clay fills containing few finds.

Eastern boundary features (Fig. 2.11)

A group of linear gullies at the eastern edge of the site may relate to further enclosures lying beyond the limit of excavation, although they can only be tentatively ascribed to this period. Gully 3280 and its continuation 3290 ran for a total length of 50 m on a NNE-SSW alignment. The northern end of 3290 made an acute turn towards the south-east before disappearing beyond the eastern limit of excavation. Lying 8 m to the east of this feature and approximately parallel to it was gully 3100, 23 m long. This was recut and extended in the form of gully 3110,

44 m long. These features were characterised by U-shaped profiles, up to 0.42 m deep, and had naturally deposited silty fills. Small quantities of early Iron Age pottery were recovered, although the fragments were often abraded, raising the possibility that they were residual.

Roundhouses

A total of seven certain and five possible roundhouses can be attributed to Phase 2 (Structures 1–3 and 5–12; Table 2.4). All were defined by shallow penannular gullies with internal diameters of between 6.0–13.9 m. Where an entranceway was clearly apparent, it always faced between east and south-east. Stratigraphic relationships indicate that a maximum of seven of the identified roundhouses could have stood at any one time.

The gullies had U-shaped cuts, 0.15–0.65 m wide and up to 0.35 m deep, in many cases interrupted as a result of plough truncation. They were characterised by silty fills that appear to have been naturally accumulated, and none contained any evidence of postholes or beam-slots. It is thus likely that these were eaves-gullies, rather than structural foundations for walls. Evidence from other Iron Age sites in southern England indicates that the diameters of the roundhouses themselves are likely to

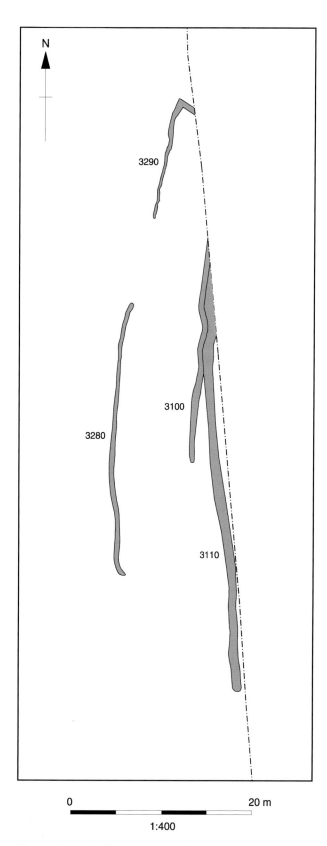

Figure 2.11   Gullies at eastern edge of site (other features not shown).

have been in the order of 1–2 m less than that of the eaves-gullies. In all but one case the gullies show only a single cut, perhaps suggesting that the individual structures were not particularly long-lived. Finds from the gullies generally consisted only of modest quantities of pottery and bone, although a saddle quern (SF 1) was recovered from Structure 1. Although a few postholes were sometimes encountered within the areas enclosed by the eaves-gullies, in no case are there any grounds to assume that these formed part of the roundhouse or its internal fittings. In fact, the only internal feature that seems very likely to be associated with one of the roundhouses is a clay-lined pit within Structure 1.

Structure 1 (Fig. 2.12)

Structure 1 was the largest and best preserved of the roundhouses at Site A, measuring 13.9 m in diameter. It had an entrance 4.1 m wide, oriented a little to the south of due east. Uniquely for the roundhouses at this site, the southern half of the gully showed clear evidence for recutting. The initial cut (25) measured 0.40–0.50 m wide and 0.21–0.33 m deep, with steep sides and a fairly flat base. The recut (23), which truncated the southern edge of the first gully, was of similar dimensions (0.30–0.53 m wide and 0.11–0.25 m deep) and form. The northern half of the eaves-gully showed only a single phase, and was generally narrower and shallower (0.20–0.35 m wide and 0.07–0.09 m deep) with a more gently rounded cut. Fills throughout the eaves-gully consisted of grey-brown silty clays. More finds were found than in any of the other roundhouse gullies at Site A or B, in terms of both overall quantities and relative density (92 g of pottery and 120 g of animal bone per metre length of gully excavated). These were distributed along the whole of the circuit, with no notable concentrations.

The eaves-gully shows stratigraphic relationships to both earlier and later features. The northern side of the gully was cut by the ditch of Enclosure IV, while the recut of the southern side of the gully truncated one of the postholes of a four-post 'granary', Structure 29. A second 'granary', Structure 20, was located within the area enclosed by the eaves-gully and so cannot have been contemporary with the roundhouse.

Although no certain structural elements of the building survive, two undated postholes placed 2.5 m apart in the southern half of the structure are possible candidates. One internal feature almost certainly related to the roundhouse was clay-lined pit 4973, which was placed in the north-eastern part of the structure, just to the north of the entrance. Its relationship with the building seems very likely as similar features have been found in an identical location within early and middle Iron Age roundhouses at a number of other sites across the region. This pit will be discussed in more detail below (see *Clay-lined pits*). The only other feature within the area enclosed by the eaves-gully was pit 4886. This may

Table 2.4   Roundhouses, Site A.

Structure	Phase	Internal diameter (m)	Area (m²)	Eaves-gully dimensions		Finds from eaves-gullies	
				Width (m)	Depth (m)	Pottery (g)	Animal bone (g)
1	2	13.9	152	0.20–0.53	0.07–0.33	1003	1315
2	2	8.3	54	0.22–0.60	0.09–0.24	78	10
3	2	11.5	104	0.38–0.50	0.10–0.18	57	89
4	3	9.2	66	0.32–0.53	0.09–0.26	435	212
5	2	11.0	95	0.18–0.46	0.07–0.16	353	634
6	2	11.2	98	0.15–0.40	0.02–0.25	7	15
7	2	8.3	54	0.30–0.40	0.10–0.35	314	453
8*	2	c 13–14	?	0.20–0.50	0.09–0.19	98	13
9*	2	c 6	?	0.16	0.07	–	–
10*	2	7.3	42	0.45–0.65	0.15–0.20	206	187
11*	2	c 5–6	?	0.31–0.37	0.11–015	41	264
12*	2	c 7	?	0.30–0.50	0.09–0.20	23	41

* = uncertain roundhouse.

not be contemporary with the roundhouse as it appears to form part of a group of pits aligned along the western side of the later Enclosure IV.

Structure 2 (Fig. 2.12)

Located immediately to the south of Structure 1, Structure 2 consisted of the southern and western sides of an eaves-gully, 8.3 m in diameter. The southern side of the gully cut the eaves-gully of Structure 8, while the northern butt end of the gully was truncated by Phase 5 ditch 4450. 'Granary' Structure 29 overlaps with the area of the building and so cannot have been contemporary.

It is unclear whether Structure 2 was coeval with Structure 1, but if so then the two buildings would have been in close proximity to each other. If a northern side to the eaves-gully of Structure 2 is extrapolated, it would lie only c 0.30 m from the gully of Structure 1. Alternatively, of course, the Structure 2 gully may only ever have formed a partial circuit around the building which it enclosed.

The only possible remnant of the building itself was a single shallow posthole, 209, which could perhaps represent one of the entrance posts. Two concave pits were placed within the rear of the area enclosed by the ring gully, one shallow (48) and one fairly deep (149; see *Pits* below). Pit 383, which was placed across the presumed east-facing entrance to the ring gully, contained middle Iron Age material (see below).

Structure 3 (Fig. 2.13)

Structure 3 was demarcated by a discontinuous eaves-gully of 11.5 m diameter. The gully ring was open on its eastern and south-eastern sides, where the entrance presumably lay. It was cut by the eaves-gully of Structure 4 (see Phase 3). Three postholes (4922, 4930 and 4971) could have formed part of the post-ring to this house, although they could equally

well have been associated with Structure 4. Clay-lined pit 4565 lay within the eastern side of the building and may have been an internal feature of the roundhouse. It is possible that it was situated just inside and to the north of the entrance, in a similar way to the clay-lined pit within Structure 1. This must remain conjectural, however, given that the precise location of the entrance to this structure is unknown. Pit 4565 and its parallels are discussed in more detail below (see *Clay-lined Pits*).

Structures 5 and 6 (Fig. 2.14)

Structure 5 was a truncated eaves-gully of 11.0 m diameter, with its eastern and north-western sides surviving. The southern side of the structure lay beyond the limit of excavation. Three possible stakeholes occurred in the eastern part of the enclosed area (4121, 4381 and 4383), and three probable tree throw holes in its southern part.

Heavily truncated eaves-gully Structure 6 measured 11.2 m in diameter. The gully survived sporadically on its northern and southern sides, but could not be traced on the western side. If a western side to the gully is extrapolated, it would overlap with the eaves-gully of Structure 5. This may indicate that the two buildings were not contemporaneous, although it is possible that they did coexist with their eaves-gullies conjoined.

The eaves-gully to Structure 6 cut shallow undated pit 4108, and was in turn cut by Phase 4 gully 4360 (see below). The only feature within the area enclosed by the eaves-gully was a single small posthole, 4399.

Structure 7 (Fig. 2.15)

The eaves-gully of Structure 7 was only partially exposed, as it extended beyond the northern limit of excavation. It measured 8.3 m in diameter and had a 5.0 m-wide, east-facing entranceway. The southern

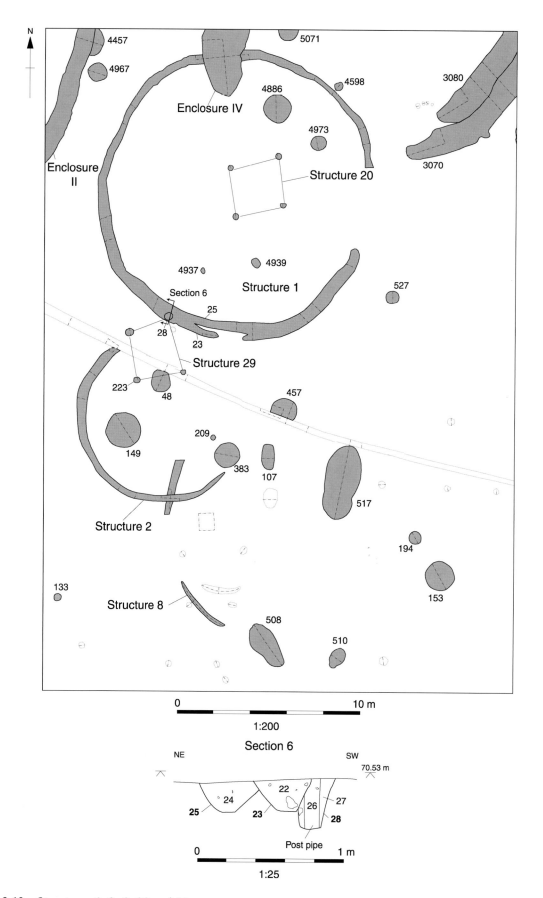

Figure 2.12   Structures 1, 2, 8, 20 and 29.

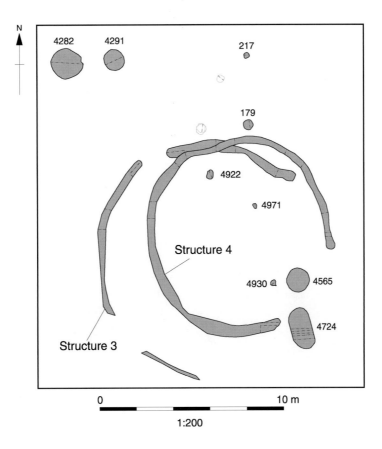

Figure 2.13   Structures 3 and 4.

butt end of the gully was truncated by a modern posthole. Two features were present within the area enclosed by the gully. Placed just inside the entrance-way, posthole 4593 was 0.50 m in diameter and 0.06 m deep, and contained sandstone cobbles that might have represented disturbed post-packing. Pit 5167, meanwhile, measured 0.80 × 0.67 × 0.39 m, with sheer sides and a flat base.

Structures 8 and 9

Structures 8 and 9 were two possible roundhouses in the vicinity of the main north-western enclosure group. Structure 8 (Fig. 2.12) measured *c* 13–14 m diameter, with only the western side of the gully being extant. It was cut by the eaves-gully of Structure 2. Structure 9 (Fig. 2.9) was located to the west of Enclosure III, with only a short section of the northern side of the gully surviving. It measured *c* 6 m in diameter.

Structures 10–12

Structures 10, 11 and 12 were possible roundhouses situated in the north-eastern corner of the excavated area. Structure 10 (Fig. 2.16) was extant on its northern and eastern sides, measuring 7.3 m in diameter. It had a segmented appearance resulting from modern truncation. It cut the eaves-gully of possible roundhouse Structure 12. Features located

within the area enclosed by the eaves-gully comprised a pair of inter-cutting postholes, 4036 and 4038, and an amorphous feature probably of natural origin.

Structure 11 (Fig. 2.10) was a possible roundhouse of *c* 5–6 m diameter defined only on its eastern side by two sections of gully. The southern section measured 2.5 m long, while the northern section was at least 2.8 m long, continuing beyond the northern limit of excavation. The 2.3 m-wide gap between these two sections may well represent the entrance to the roundhouse, facing a little to the south of due east.

Structure 12 (Fig. 2.16) consisted of two sections of gully which may have formed the southern part of a roundhouse eaves-gully of *c* 7 m diameter, although an alternative interpretation would be that they formed part of a drainage ditch or enclosure around 'granary' Structure 31. The western gully section measured 2.2 m long, 0.30–0.33 m wide and 0.09–0.11 m deep, while the eastern section was more robust at 3.6 m long, 0.40–0.50 m wide and 0.12–0.20 m deep. Both were filled with grey-brown clay. The outward kink made by 3350 at its western end may indicate that the entrance to the eaves-gully or enclosure lay here, between the two gully sections. If so, then this entrance had a SSE orientation and measured 3.0 m wide. As noted above, gully 3350 was cut by the eaves-gully of Structure 10.

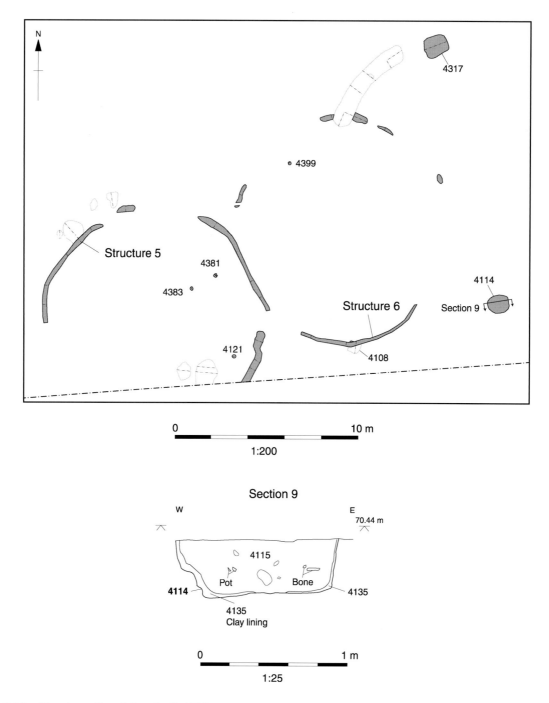

Figure 2.14   *Structures 5 and 6 and pit 4114.*

Four-post structures

A total of twenty four-post structures of square or subsquare form have been identified at Site A (Structures 13–32; Figs 2.16–17), mainly in a swathe to the east and south of the roundhouses (Fig. 2.3). Their lengths varied from 2.00 to 3.30 m, within the accepted range for such structures (Table 2.5). Their alignments tended to fall around the cardinal points (Fig. 6.5). Four-post structures are traditionally interpreted as raised granaries (Gent 1983).

Only two of the four-post structures showed any evidence of rebuilding in the form of recut or replaced postholes. Structure 17 appears to have been rebuilt on the same spot but on a slightly different alignment, as three of the four corners of the structure were marked by a pair of closely adjacent postholes. These two phases of building have been referred to as Structures 17a and 17b respectively, although it is unclear which came first. Structure 18, meanwhile, had a pair of inter-cutting postholes marking its north-west corner (4226 and 4268). The general absence of evidence for the rebuilding of four-post structures suggests that they may have been relatively short-lived, and thus that only a few may have stood at any one time.

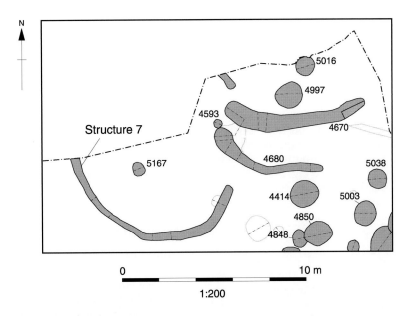

Figure 2.15   Structure 7 and associated features.

Few four-post structures showed clear strati-graphic relationships to other features. One posthole of Structure 29 was cut by the eaves-gully of roundhouse Structure 1, and the placing of Structure 20 shows that it too cannot have been contemporary with this roundhouse (Fig. 2.12). At the eastern edge of the site, meanwhile, one posthole of Structure 30 cut pit 3274. Nearby, only three postholes of Structure 32 were evident, and it is probable that the 'missing' posthole had been obliterated by gully 3280 (Fig. 2.3).

The individual postholes of these structures averaged 0.34 m in diameter and 0.20 m deep, with a maximum depth of 0.56 m. They typically showed a single fill of silt or clay. A post-pipe was only evident in three cases, suggesting that the posts were generally not left to rot *in situ* but were pulled out from the ground upon abandonment of the struc-ture. One post-pipe occurred in Structure 15 (post-hole 3341) and measured 0.33 m diameter. The other two were found in Structure 29 (postholes 28 and 223; Fig. 2.12), measuring 0.10 m and 0.30 m diameter respectively, and were both surrounded by a packing of sandstone and flint cobbles. Similar stone packing was also observed in posthole 3094 of

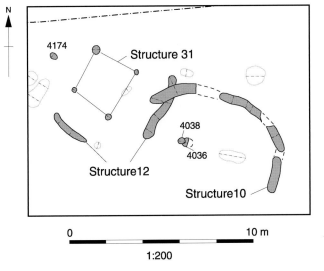

Figure 2.16   Structures 10, 12 and 31.

Table 2.5   Four-post structures, Site A.

Structure	Dimensions (m)		Posthole diameters (m)	Posthole depths (m)
	Min	*Max*		
13	2.45	2.55	0.26–0.31	0.10–0.23
14	2.35	2.50	0.35–0.45	0.32–0.56
15	2.45	2.65	0.39–0.60	0.20–0.29
16	2.35	2.50	0.45–0.52	0.21–0.30
17a	1.75	2.25	0.28–0.58	0.30–0.49
17b	1.65	2.00	0.20–0.58	0.16–0.38
18	2.15	2.30	0.28–0.42	0.05–0.22
19	2.25	2.75	0.26–0.30	0.10–0.20
20	2.55	2.65	0.33–0.35	0.10–0.20
21	2.55	3.00	0.35–0.40	0.05–0.17
22	2.00	2.40	0.20–0.35	0.07–0.17
23	2.35	3.00	0.35–0.75	0.15–0.30
24	2.00	2.40	0.20–0.25	0.06–0.14
25	1.85	2.15	0.16–0.26	0.06–0.13
26	2.15	2.75	0.13–0.26	0.06–0.26
27	2.35	2.50	0.23–0.45	0.09–0.34
28	2.30	2.90	0.30–0.40	0.05–0.15
29	2.45	2.60	0.25–0.40	0.34–0.50
30	2.10	2.40	0.28–0.40	0.08–0.36
31	2.30	2.75	0.25–0.43	0.07–0.22
32	2.15	2.50	0.20–0.40	0.14–0.30

Structure 14, although here no post-pipe could be seen. Randomly distributed sandstone and flint cobbles also occurred in the postholes of many other four-post structures, and could potentially represent packing that was disturbed by the removal of the post. Charcoal flecks could be seen in some postholes, but in no case were the quantities sufficient to suggest that the structure had burned down. Artefacts from the postholes were generally sparse, although one notable find was a fragment of a La Tène copper alloy brooch (SF 44; see Fig. 3.17.3) from Structure 17a (posthole 3574). None of the sampled postholes produced significant quantities of charred plant remains (see Chap. 5, *Charred plant remains*).

Structure 33 (Fig. 2.17)

Situated in the south-eastern corner of the excavated area, Structure 33 was a rectangular arrangement of five postholes, measuring 2.8 m E-W by 1.9 m N-S. The individual postholes were 0.28–0.33 m in diameter and 0.12–0.24 m deep. Small amounts of pottery and animal bone were recovered. The role of this structure is unclear, although it is possible that it was simply a variant on the four-post 'granary'.

Clay-lined 'cooking' pits

Five features belonged to a distinctive category of small clay-lined pits (4114, 4565, 4967, 4973 and 5006; Table 2.6). These pits could be either bowl-shaped or have vertical sides and a flat base, and were between 0.57–1.26 m wide and 0.20–0.40 m deep. The bases and sides were lined with a layer of clean yellow or orange clay, between 0.03 m and 0.10 m thick. The fills of pits 4565, 4967 and 5006 contained substantial quantities of burnt and fire-cracked stones. In the case of pit 4565, the stone included four burnt rotary quern fragments lying at the base of the pit (Pl. 2.3). However, in no case did the fills or clay linings show any evidence for *in situ* burning. The fill matrix of each pit consisted of a single deposit of silty or clayey soil; besides burnt stone, only small quantities of artefactual material were recovered.

The five pits in this category seem to have had a close relationship with roundhouses. Pit 4973 was located within Structure 1, immediately within and to the north of the entrance, while pit 4967 was placed immediately to the rear of the same building (Fig. 2.12). Pit 4565 was located within the vicinity of the entrances to both of the overlapping roundhouses Structure 3 and Structure 4 (Fig. 2.13), while pit 4114 was immediately to the east of the entrance of Structure 6 (Fig. 2.14). The only example not placed in or near a roundhouse was 5006, which was close to the north-western limit of excavation and thus could possibly have been associated with a building beyond this limit.

Clay-lined pits with similar dimensions and profiles (either bowl-shaped or cylindrical) have been found at several early to middle Iron Age settlements in the south Midlands, typically being

found in close association with roundhouses. More specifically, such pits are commonly found within the left hand side of roundhouses (viewed facing out). At Fairfield Park this can be seen with pit 4973 within Structure 1, and possibly also pit 4565 within Structure 3. A clue to the function of clay-lined pits is the fact that they frequently contain concentrations of burnt or heat-cracked stones, as seen at this site in pits 4565, 4967 and 5006. This suggests a use in heating water or in cooking. The role of the clay-lined pits and their parallels from other sites will be considered at greater length below (see Chap. 6).

Other pits (Figs. 2.18–25)

Pits other than cooking pits were largely distributed in a swathe running between the north-west and south-east corners of the excavated area. The densest concentration was to be found immediately to the north-west of Enclosure III, where the pits lay closely spaced together and sometimes intercut. However, none cut or was cut by the ditch of Enclosure III, indicating that this enclosure was 'respected' to some degree. For ease of discussion the pits have been divided into the following categories:

(a) Large *bell-shaped pits* with undercut sides and a flat or slightly concave base
(b) *Flat-based pits* with steep or vertical sides
(c) *Concave pits* with bowl-shaped or irregular profiles

The distributions of these pit categories is shown by Figure 2.25. Each category will be described in turn below.

Bell-shaped pits

Twenty-one large, bell-shaped pits were found at Site A (Table 2.7). The pits ranged from 0.80–1.80 m in diameter and from 0.40–1.24 m in depth. In three cases there is evidence for clay lining around the base or sides of the pit. Bell-shaped pits were concentrated around the north-western enclosure group, and were particularly abundant in the area to the east and south-east of the enclosures. Not all of these need have been contemporary with the enclosures, however: pit 4457 was truncated by Enclosure II and must therefore predate the entire enclosure sequence (Fig. 2.6). Many of the pits in this category produced large finds assemblage, the outstanding example being pit 3285 (Figs 2.20 and 2.21) which contained over 6 kg of pottery, along with fired clay and animal bone.

Bell-shaped pits are usually interpreted as serving a role in grain storage, perhaps for seed corn in particular (Reynolds 1979). The fact that the examples at Fairfield Park retained their undercut profile, despite the relative looseness of the natural across much of the site, suggests that they were used only once and were back-filled fairly soon after they were emptied of their contents. The majority of the fills

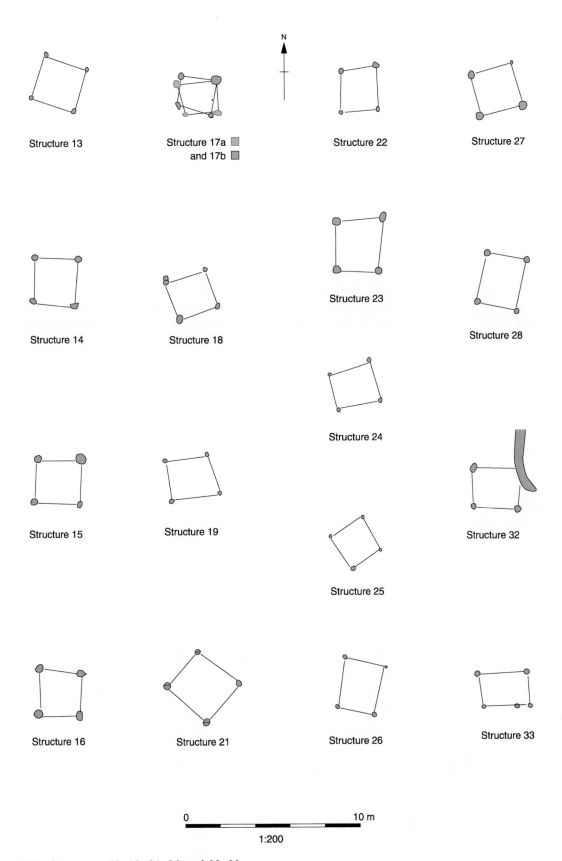

Figure 2.17   Structures 13–19, 21–28 and 32–33.

Table 2.6   Clay-lined 'cooking' pits, Site A.

Pit	Profile	Diameter (m)	Depth (m)	Lining Thickness (m)	Finds
4114	Cylindrical	1.00	0.34	0.05	Pottery, bone, fired clay
4565	Cylindrical	1.26	0.40	0.10	Pottery, bone, quern fragments
4967	Bowl-shaped	1.50 × 1.40	0.27	0.10	Pottery, bone
4973	Cylindrical	0.80 × 0.75	0.20	0.05	Pottery, bone
5006	Bowl-shaped	0.57	0.30	0.03	Pottery, bone

appeared to be deliberate dumps of material, and these included dark organic-rich layers which resembled midden material or hearth waste. However, in several cases there were also one or more episodes of natural erosion interleaved with the dumped deposits. The evidence thus suggests that although the process of back-filling was relatively rapid, it was nonetheless often punctuated by hiatuses. A selection of the pits is described below, to illustrate the range of forms and fill types present.

Pit 153 (Fig. 2.12) had traces of possible clay lining on its sides. On the base of the pit lay a human parietal bone and several fragments of red deer antler. Aside from a single animal rib, the basal fill of silty clay was otherwise 'clean', but all subsequent deposits contained quantities of pottery and animal bone. The uppermost surviving fill also contained an iron object, possibly a knife tang (SF 3; see Fig. 3.19.2).

Pit 292 (Fig. 2.19) had traces of possible clay lining at its base, up to 0.06 m thick. Significant quantities of pottery and animal bone were recovered from the feature, especially from the upper fills. Immediately to the south-east of 292, pit 583 contained a series of dumped fills containing moderate amounts of pottery and animal bone.

Pits 307 and 314 (Fig. 2.19) were close to each other, but any stratigraphic relationship between them had been obliterated by a modern field drain. Pit 307 contained moderate amounts of pottery in its upper fill, while the middle and lower fills were devoid of artefacts. Pit 314 contained substantial quantities of cultural material throughout its fill sequence, and the middle fills were particularly rich in charcoal. Pit 307 cut an earlier bell-shaped pit, 543.

Pit 348 (Fig. 2.19) contained large quantities of pottery and animal bone in its basal fill, while the middle and upper fills were devoid of artefacts. The upper fill did, however, contain a high proportion of charcoal flecks. The feature was subsequently recut as a shallower, bowl-shaped pit, 352, measuring 1.45 m diameter and 0.60 m deep.

Plate 2.3   Clay-lined 'cooking pit' 4565, showing burnt cobbles and quern fragments at base. Scale: 1m.

Plate 2.4   Flat-based pit 4666. Scale: 1m.

Plate 2.5   Pit 5189 and burial 5144, looking north. Scale: 1m.

Table 2.7 Bell-shaped pits, Site A.

Pit	Diameter (m)	Depth (m)	Finds
153	1.60	1.10	Pottery, bone, fired clay, iron object SF 3, human parietal
292	1.60	0.96	Pottery, bone
297	0.80	0.84	Pottery, bone, fired clay
307	1.30	0.80	Pottery, bone
314	1.00	0.56	Pottery, bone, fired clay
348	1.72	1.24	Pottery, bone
364	1.10	0.96	Pottery, bone
484	1.10	0.96	Pottery, bone, fired clay, whetstone
531	1.50	0.95	Pottery, bone
543	0.90	0.46	Pottery, bone
583	1.30	1.04	Pottery, bone
3102	1.30	1.00	Pottery, bone, fired clay
3285	1.56	0.66	Pottery, bone, fired clay
3571	0.85	0.40	Pottery, bone
4457	1.20	0.60	Pottery, bone
4866	2.08	0.52	Pottery, bone
4906	1.08	0.98	Pottery, bone
4964	1.80	0.56	Pottery, bone, fired clay
4982	1.70	0.80	Pottery, bone
5029	1.04	1.20	Pottery, bone
5110	1.20	0.80	Pottery, bone, fired clay, oven plate, human neonate

Pit 484 (Fig. 2.9) had a remarkable lower deposit, 0.25 m thick, containing large fragments of charcoal and 49 burnt, complete or near-complete sheep metapodials. The metapodials bore polishing and striations indicating use in weaving, and this basal fill is thus suggestive of the deposition of a complete burnt loom (see Chap. 3, *Worked bone*). Small quantities of pottery and fired clay were also recovered from this layer. The deposit above contained a large quantity of fired clay (0.5 kg) among other artefactual material. The subsequent fills also yielded many finds, including a whetstone in the uppermost surviving layer.

Pit 3102 (Fig. 2.20–21) showed a sequence of dumped fills containing only modest numbers of finds. After deposition of the final fill, the feature was recut in the form of shallower flat-based pit, 3274 (see below).

Pit 3285 (Fig. 2.20–21) had only slightly undercut sides. It was lined with a layer of dark orange clay (3293), 0.08 m thick, containing numerous rounded cobbles of 0.08–0.10 m length. The lower fills were characterised by a high frequency of charcoal; large quantities of pottery and animal bone were found in all fills.

Outlying pit 3571 (Fig. 2.23) was unusually shallow at only 0.40 m deep. It contained a single backfill deposit that yielded a moderate number of artefacts.

Pit 5029 had an unusually sharply undercut profile (Fig. 2.9). It contained five deposits, the first of which contained significant amounts of charcoal, fire-cracked pebbles, pottery and animal bone (5028).

This was followed by a thin layer of clean orange clay (5027), a second deposit containing fire-cracked stone (5105), a very ashy layer (5106) and a final deposit containing more fire-cracked stone and general occupation debris.

Pit 5110 (Fig. 2.18) contained four layers, all of which produced significant quantities of artefacts including pottery, animal bone, fired clay and charcoal. The second fill also contained articulated neonatal human bone, while the first and third contained articulated sheep/goat remains. The pit was later re-utilised to construct clay-lined pit 5006 (see above).

Flat-based pits

This category encompasses features with a flat base, and fairly straight walls at an angle between 45° and near-vertical. A total of 47 examples were found, almost all of them around the main enclosure group and the area immediately to its north-west (Fig. 2.25). They ranged from 0.75–2.50 m in diameter and from 0.15–0.82 m deep; almost none showed any evidence for recutting. Pits in this category were generally not lined. An exception was pit 5037 (Fig. 2.18), which was 1.40 m in diameter and 0.48 m deep, with a clay lining up to 0.07 m thick across most of its base and sides. The flat-based pits show a similar range of fill sequences to the bell-shaped pits. Again, the majority of the pits seem to have been deliberately back-filled—including some dark, finds-rich layers resembling midden deposits—although some of the deeper pits showed erosion deposits between the dumped layers.

The greatest quantity of finds was recovered from pit 156, located to the east of the main enclosure group (Fig. 2.19). This pit was a cylindrical in form and measured 1.85 m in diameter and 0.75 m deep. After an initial erosion deposit, there was a sequence of seven back-fill layers. The second of these contained an iron poker (SF 2; see Fig. 3.19.3) along with much other artefactual material. The third and fourth fills consisted of redeposited natural, which were followed by three finds-rich layers. Artefacts from the penultimate fill included a human femur and a quantity of structural fired clay, some of which had wattle impressions. A total of 2983 g of pottery and 1230 g of animal bone was recovered from the pit as a whole.

Two further, relatively deep pits in this category contained human remains. Pit 3011 (Fig. 2.8) was 1.35 m in diameter and 0.68 m deep with steep sides. The fill sequence comprised an initial dump of finds-rich material, followed by an episode of natural slumping, then a further artefact-rich dump which contained human juvenile leg bones. This was then followed by redeposited natural and a final finds-rich layer. Pit 4666 (Fig. 2.6 and Pl. 2.4), meanwhile, was 1.76 m in diameter and 0.82 m deep. It contained four back-fill deposits, with finds increasing in quantities towards the top. The uppermost surviving fill contained a human femur.

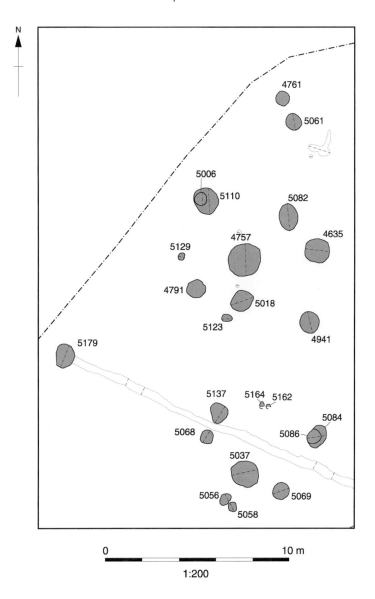

Figure 2.18   Pit group at north-western edge of settlement.

There were also two examples of articulated animal deposits. Pit 4761 (Fig. 2.18) measured 0.87 m diameter and 0.22 m deep, with vertical sides. Traces of burnt material at the base were covered by a layer of orange clay, 0.05 m thick. The main fill of the pit was a dark deposit containing a near-complete sheep/goat skeleton, along with substantial quantities of pottery. Pit 4941 (Fig. 2.18) was 1.16 m in diameter and 0.32 m deep. It contained two dumped fills rich in pottery and animal bone. The lower legs of a sheep/goat and various articulated bones from a dog were found in the upper fill.

Pit 3274 (Figs 2.20–21) was notable for the unusual character of its fills. This feature measured 1.04 m in diameter and 0.62 m deep, and utilised the site of earlier bell-shaped pit 3102. A thin basal layer of pale, chalky silt (3294) was followed by an even layer of brown-orange silt 0.12 m thick along both the sides and base (3275), perhaps representing a mud lining. Above this was a deposit of large flint

nodules (3276), covered by a thin layer of charcoal (4027), although there was no sign of *in situ* burning. The pit was then back-filled with a deposit containing large quantities of pottery and animal bone, a triangular loomweight, and a copper alloy pin terminal (SF 26; see Fig. 3.17.2). The pit was later truncated by posthole 3101 of Structure 30.

Concave pits

A total of 71 pits in this category were recorded. They were widely distributed across the site, although there was a particular concentration in the south-eastern part of the excavated area (Fig. 2.25). They measured up to 2.00 m in diameter, and from 0.06–0.90 m deep, although most were below 0.50 m in depth.

The south-eastern group of pits tended to be particularly shallow, and most contained few or no artefacts. Some could in fact be natural features such

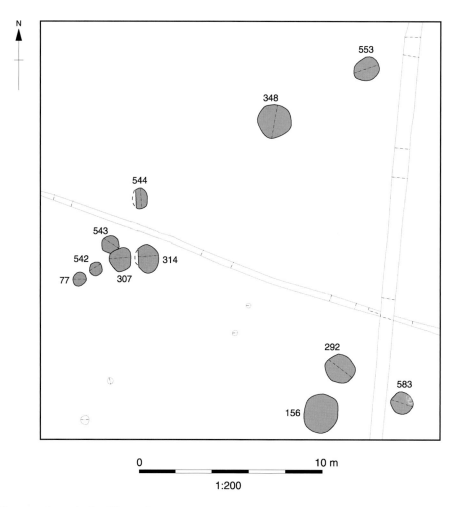

Figure 2.19   Pit group to east of settlement core.

a hollows or tree throw holes. Among the pits that stood out in terms of its contents was 3596 in the far south-east corner of the excavated area (Fig. 2.24). This pit measured 1.32 × 0.95 × 0.23 m in size, and contained much pottery, animal bone and fire-cracked stone. The bone included a significant amount of sawn and chopped red deer antler (730 g), forming the largest deposit of antler on the site.

Another atypical pit for this area was 3195 (Fig. 2.20), measuring 2.32 × 1.58 × 0.50 m. The initial fill of redeposited natural was followed by a dump of material rich in charcoal and artefacts. This was followed by further sterile natural and a final deposit that again had plentiful charcoal and artefactual material, including a copper alloy ring (see Fig. 3.17.1). Notably, a jet ring or pendent (SF 51; see Fig. 3.17.6) was found in the upper fill of another concave pit in this area (3630; Fig. 2.3).

The concave pits from the north-western part of the site were more variable in their dimensions. The deepest was pit 149 (2.00 m diameter and 0.90 m deep), located in the interior of Structure 2 (Fig. 2.12), although it is unclear whether it was contemporary with the building. It had a series of perhaps naturally deposited silty clay fills, which contained only

modest quantities of cultural material. Another atypical feature was pit 4635 (Fig. 2.18), 1.30 m in diameter and 0.54 m deep, with a very irregular profile, perhaps resulting from root action. The lower of the two fills consisted of a green-grey silt which may indicate the presence of cess. Both fills of the pit contained much pottery and animal bone.

Large hollows

Two large hollows were located in the south-eastern part of the excavated area. The more northerly of the two, 3545, measured 5.60 × 4.20 m in size and was 0.90 m deep (Fig. 2.22). It showed a sequence of five fills. The two lower fills consisted of relatively 'clean' redeposited clay (3746–7), and the two middle fills of green-tinged silty clay, possibly a 'cess' deposit (3588–9). The deliberately dumped upper fill of dark grey silty clay contained abundant cultural material including a very large amount of unabraded pottery sherds and animal bone (3587). The second hollow, 4089 (Fig. 2.3), was only partially exposed at the southern limit of excavation. It measured at least 3.40 m wide and 0.70 m deep. The lower fill of orange-brown clay was again overlain by a darker deposit rich in charcoal, pottery and animal bone.

38

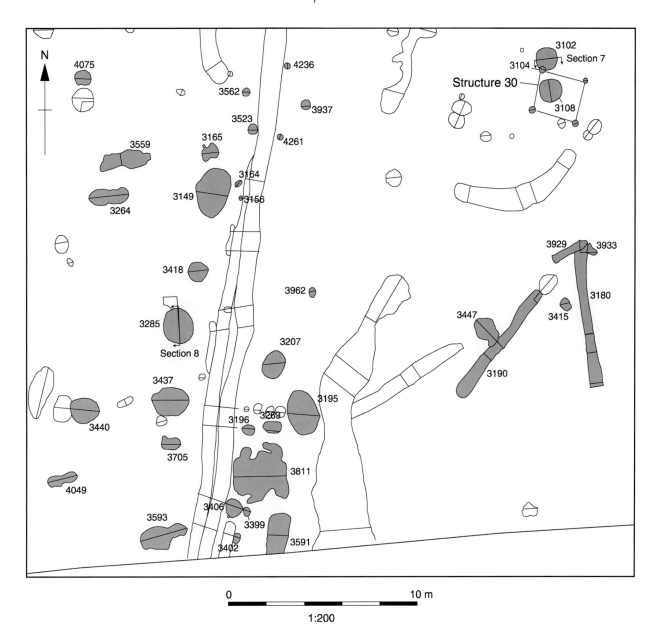

Figure 2.20   Pit group to south-east of settlement core.

It is possible that these features served as ponds or sump-pits, although it should be noted that the palynological evidence from hollow 3545 gave no indications of standing water.

Natural features

Several tree throw holes and root holes penetrating the buried soil in the eastern half of the site contained early Iron Age material. In most cases only a few artefacts were recovered, but atypically large tree-throw hole 3811 (Fig. 2.20) contained substantial quantities of pottery, animal bone and fired clay.

Site B

Phase 2 settlement features were densely distributed across the western half of Site B (Fig. 2.26). They

included part of a substantial enclosure, up to three roundhouses and a series of four-post structures and pits. The density of features and artefacts tailed off towards the east, with the north-eastern corner of the site being essentially empty.

Enclosure VIII (Figs 2.28–29)

Enclosure VIII dominated the north-western part of Site B, being demarcated by a substantial curvilinear ditch that continued beyond the limits of excavation (Pl. 2.6). The exposed area of the enclosure measured 32 m E-W by 30 m N-S; if the enclosure was roughly circular then its diameter may have been in the region of 60 m. An entranceway lay in the south-eastern side.

The enclosure ditch showed two phases, although the initial phase only survived at the butt ends either side of the entranceway; elsewhere it was

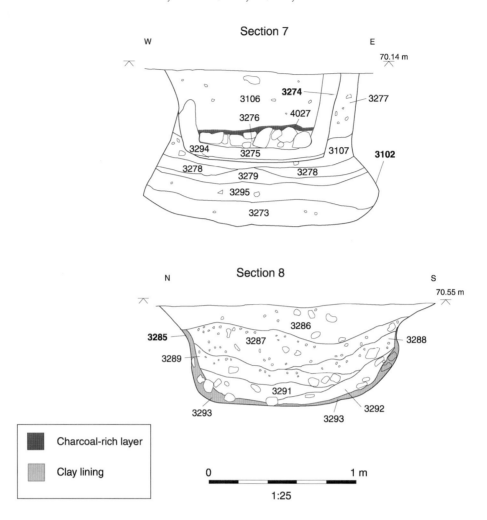

Figure 2.21   Sections from pit group to south-east of settlement core.

presumably completely eradicated by the much deeper second cut. The butt ends of the initial phase (2310) measured 2.60–2.75 m wide and 0.54–0.56 m deep, and both showed a sequence of primary silting overlain by a layer of redeposited 'natural'. This upper layer can be interpreted as a deliberate back-fill associated with the digging of the second ditch cut, an action which increased the width of the entranceway from 3.60 m to 6.35 m. The remodelled enclosure ditch (2210) posed a much more significant barrier than had the earlier ditch, measuring 2.33–3.12 m wide and 1.10–1.40 m deep, with a steep V-shaped cut. Up to six fills of silty clay or silty sand could be observed in the excavated slots. At the butt ends, the lower fills appear to have slumped in from the inner side of the enclosure, suggesting the existence of an internal up-cast bank, although this was not evident elsewhere in the ditch circuit. In all of the excavated slots, artefacts in the form of pottery and animal bone were present in the upper two to three layers but not in the lower fills, indicating that initial episodes of silting and erosion preceded any deliberate deposition. Large quantities of animal bone were found in both terminal ends of the recut ditch, but otherwise finds were relatively modest

compared to many of the pits within and to the south of the enclosure.

It is tempting to suppose that roundhouse Struc-ture 34 was contemporary with Enclosure VIII, given that it was placed squarely within the enclosed area, almost directly opposite the entranceway. Other features present within the enclosed area include three four-post structures (Structures 40, 43 and 44) and fourteen pits of varying forms (see below).

Roundhouses

The roundhouses at Site B were similar to those at Site A, being demarcated by shallow pennanular gullies with silty fills. They had a more limited size range, however, all having internal diameters of between 10.0 and 11.8 m (Table 2.8). None of the gullies showed any evidence of recutting, and there were no certain remains of the buildings themselves or their internal fixtures.

Structure 34 (Fig. 2.29)

Structure 34 was an eaves-gully of 11.5 m diameter, the northernmost part of which continued beyond

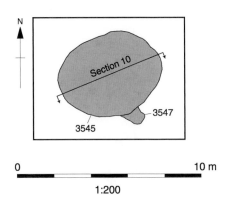

0   10 m

1:200

Section 10

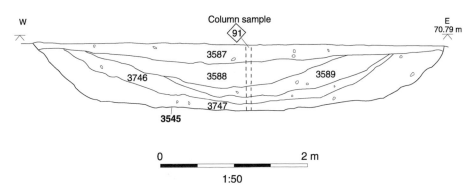

0   2 m

1:50

Figure 2.22   Hollow 3545.

the limit of excavation. The entranceway faced ESE and was 3.60 m wide. Through most of its length the eaves-gully was 0.12–0.35 m deep, but at the southern butt end the depth was reduced to only 0.02 m. This suggests that the width of the entranceway may have been exaggerated by truncation of the gully. Finds were generally modest, although a large quantity of probable structural fired clay (1.1 kg) was found at the northern butt end.

The southern side of the gully circuit cut three flat-based pits (2182, 2246 and 2248), and was in turn cut by a further pair of similar pits (2023 and 2143).

Three postholes lay within the area enclosed by the gully, all on the eastern side, in the vicinity of the entranceway. These ranged from 0.23–0.45 m in diameter and 0.10–0.33 m in depth.

Structure 35 (Fig. 2.30)

Structure 35 was an eaves-gully of 10.75 m diameter, with a 4.00 m wide entrance facing ESE. The gully

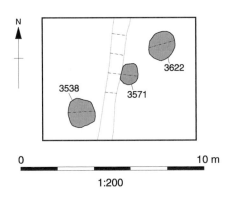

0   10 m

1:200

Figure 2.23   Pit group at south-eastern edge of site.

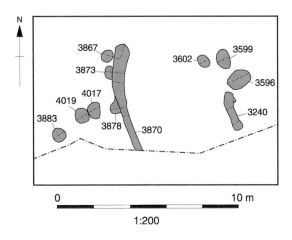

0   10 m

1:200

Figure 2.24   Gullies 3240 and 3870 and associated features.

41

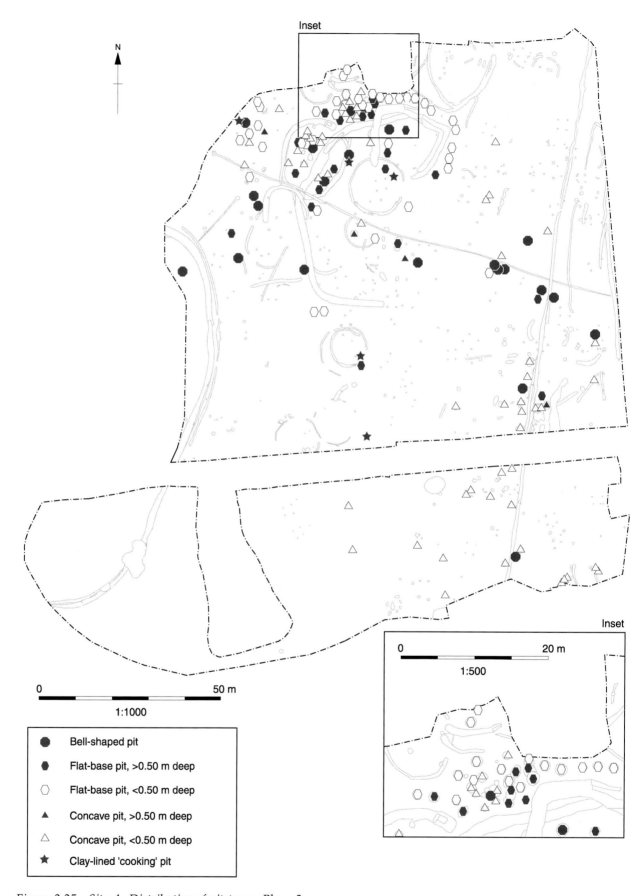

Inset

0   50 m

1:1000

0   20 m

1:500

Inset

●   Bell-shaped pit

⬡   Flat-base pit, >0.50 m deep

⬡   Flat-base pit, <0.50 m deep

▲   Concave pit, >0.50 m deep

△   Concave pit, <0.50 m deep

★   Clay-lined 'cooking' pit

Figure 2.25   Site A. Distribution of pit types, Phase 2.

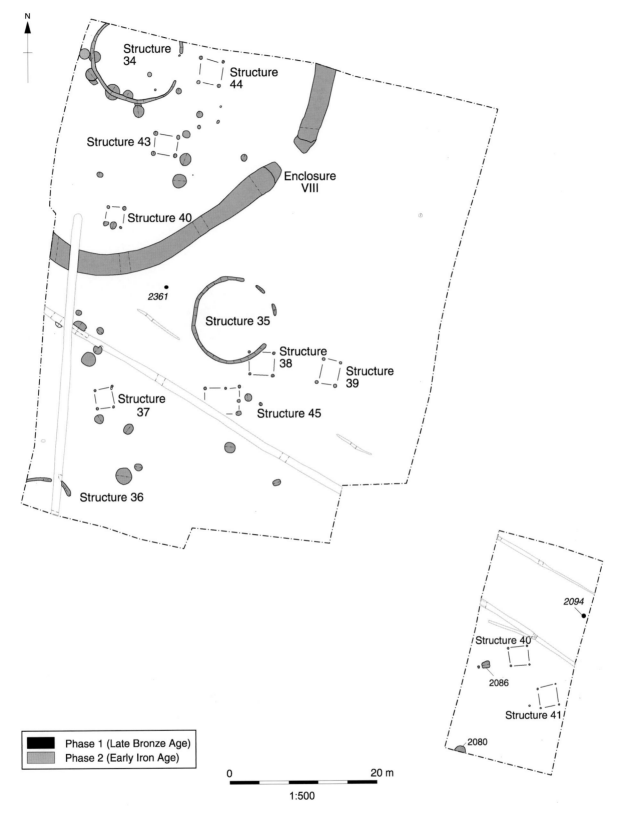

N

Structure
34

Structure
44

Structure 43

Enclosure
VIII

Structure 40

2361

Structure 35

Structure
38

Structure
39

Structure
37

Structure 45

Structure 36

2094

Structure 40

2086

Structure 41

2080

Phase 1 (Late Bronze Age)
Phase 2 (Early Iron Age)

0   20 m

1:500

Figure 2.26   Site B. Phases 1 and 2: Late Bronze Age and early Iron Age. Late Bronze Age features labelled in italics. See Fig. 2.27 for location of detailed plans.

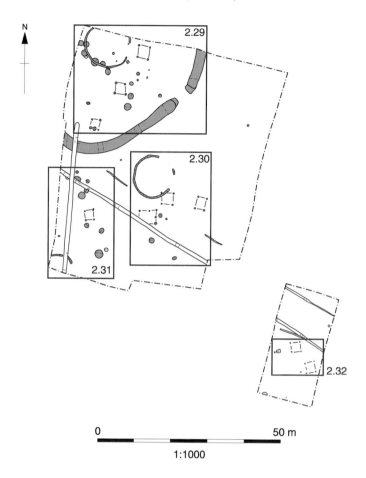

Figure 2.27   Site B. Location of detailed plans of Phase 2 settlement.

circuit was relatively complete, although it had been truncated away at two points on its north-eastern side. Finds were not large in quantity but were markedly concentrated in the front half of the structure. The gully was straddled by Structure 38, which thus cannot have been contemporary.

Structure 36 (Fig. 2.31)

Structure 36 was a possible roundhouse of *c* 10–11 m diameter partially exposed in the SW corner of the excavated area. It took the form of two short curvilinear gullies, perhaps representing part of the northern side of an eaves-gully circuit. The eastern gully continued beyond the limit of excavation, while the western terminated in a butt end that may mark an entranceway. However, the manifest difference in the fills of the two gullies (light brown silty clay for the western gully, light grey silty sand for the eastern) casts doubt on whether they were related to each other.

Four-post structures

A total of eight four-post structures were present at Site B (Structures 37–44; Figs 2.29–32), which were similar in most respects to those at Site A. They had a comparable size range of 2.40–3.25 m long

(Table 2.9), and again had orientations which tended to fall around the cardinal directions. Only one of the four-post structures showed any evidence for re-building or repair, namely Structure 37 (Fig. 2.31), the north-east corner of which was marked by a pair of intercutting postholes. None of the four-post structures showed a direct stratigraphic relationship to any other feature, although Structure 38 cannot have been contemporary with roundhouse Structure 35, with which it overlapped (Fig. 2.30). Structure 44 was awkwardly located in front of the entrance to roundhouse Structure 34 (Fig. 2.29), and thus seems unlikely to have coexisted with it.

The individual postholes averaged 0.37 m in dia-meter and 0.22 m in depth, closely comparable to the values from Site A, and had a maximum depth of 0.38 m. Posthole 2033 from Structure 37 and posthole 1203 from Structure 44 (Fig. 2.29) were lined with stone cobbles which must have served as post-packing. Randomly distributed sandstone and flint cobbles from the fills of various other postholes could perhaps represent disturbed packing. No post-pipes were apparent. Finds other than stones were sparse, although posthole 2353 of Structure 38 was something of an anomaly, containing 900 g of pottery evenly distributed though its fill (Fig. 2.30). This material was perhaps redeposited from the overlapping roundhouse Structure 35.

44

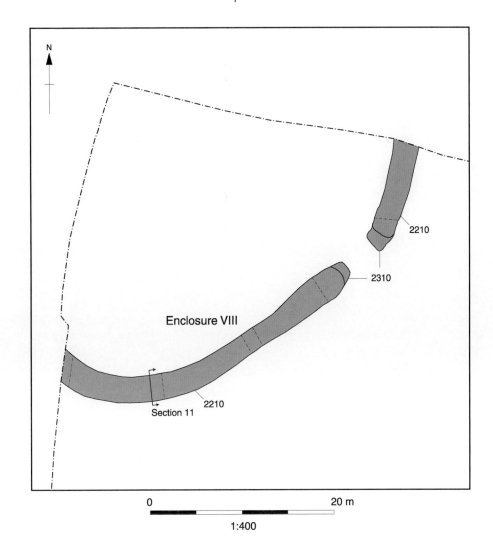

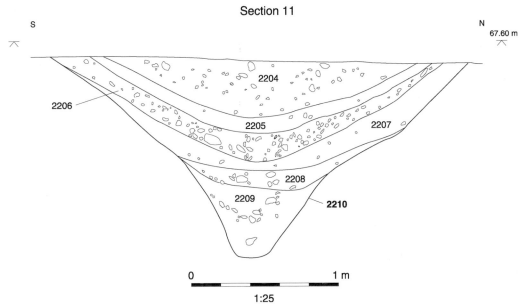

Figure 2.28   Enclosure VIII (other features not shown).

Plate 2.6   Site B under excavation, looking north. The Romano-British trackway can be seen in front of the two excavators; behind them lies the curving ditch of Enclosure VIII. The background shows the view towards Stotfold in the valley of the River Ivel.

Structure 45 (Fig. 2.30)

Structure 45 consisted of five postholes in a right-angled arrangement lying to the south of round-house Structure 35. This could hypothetically represent the northern and eastern sides of a rectangular structure measuring 4.60 m E-W by 3.50 m N-S, the south-west corner of which has been obliterated by Romano-British ditch 2312. The postholes varied between 0.30–0.51 m in diameter and 0.05–0.32 m in depth. Small quantities of pottery and animal bone were recovered.

Pits

Twenty-eight pits were encountered at Site B, mostly concentrated within Enclosure VIII and in the area to its south (Fig. 2.34). As at Site A, bell-shaped, flat-based and concave pits were represented.

The clay-lined 'cooking pits' seen at Site A were not present, however.

Bell-shaped pits

There were twelve bell-shaped pits, of which seven occurred within Enclosure VIII, four to its south, and one in the detached south-eastern area of the excavation. They ranged from 0.84–2.25 m in diameter and 0.45–1.42 m in depth (Table 2.10). As with the examples from Site A, they typically showed a series of finds-rich, deliberate back-fill deposits, sometimes interleaved with episodes of natural slumping.

Pit 2043 was the deepest of the bell-shaped pits, and had a remarkably complex sequence of fills (Figs 2.31 and 2.33 and Pl. 2.7). These fills produced a huge quantity of artefacts, including 10.7 kg of pottery,

Table 2.8   Roundhouses, Site B.

Structure	Internal diameter (m)	Eaves-gully dimensions		Finds from eaves-gullies		
		Width (m)	Depth (m)	Pottery (g)	Animal bone (g)	Other
34	11.8	0.42–0.46	0.02–0.35	197	257	Fired clay
35	10.5	0.32–0.66	0.09–0.23	34	418	Worked pebble
36	c 10–11 m	0.50	0.08–0.13	11	–	

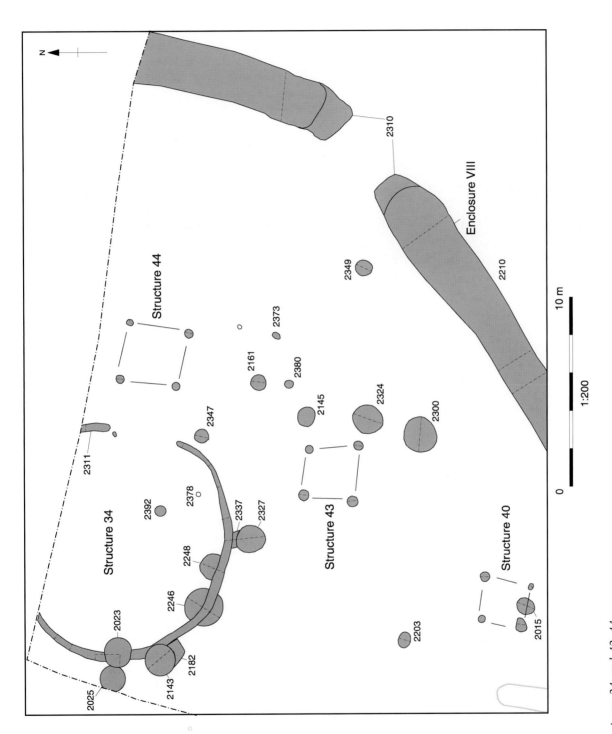

Figure 2.29 Structures 34 and 42–44.

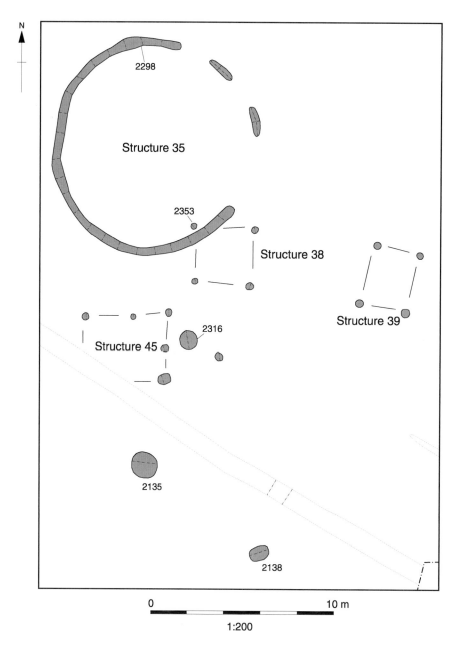

Figure 2.30   Structures 35, 38, 39 and 45.

although in comparison relatively little animal bone was found (just over 1 kg). The lower half of the pit contained a series of finds-rich back-fills (2174, 2171, 2142) interleaved with natural slumping deposits (2173, 2170). The second back-fill deposit, 2171, contained a human rib and an antler ring (see Fig. 3.12.5). The middle fills of the pit consisted of alternating shallow dumps of dark, finds rich material (2118, 2107, 2091, 2056), redeposited or-ange-brown silty clay natural (2058, 2055, 2051), and very pale layers that appeared to contain a high proportion of degraded chalk (2116, 2097, 2059, 2057, 2046). This was followed by a fill with many large sandstone and flint cobbles (2045), before a final deposit rich in cultural material (2044).

Other bell-shaped pits tended to show a simpler depositional sequence, with a limited number of dumped, back-fill deposits. Articulated animal bone deposits occurred in two cases. Pit 2088 (Fig. 2.31) contained a pig skeleton, placed in the eastern half of the feature, *c* 0.10 m above its base. Pit 2300 (Fig. 2.29) meanwhile contained a dog skeleton in its lowest back-fill layer, which directly overlay the primary erosion deposits. This layer also contained general occupation debris. Other notable finds from bell-shaped pits included an iron ring-headed pin (SF 24; see Fig. 3.17.5) from the uppermost surviving fill of pit 2327 (Fig. 2.29).

Pit 2080, lying somewhat isolated at the south-east corner of the site (Fig. 2.26), formed a contrast with

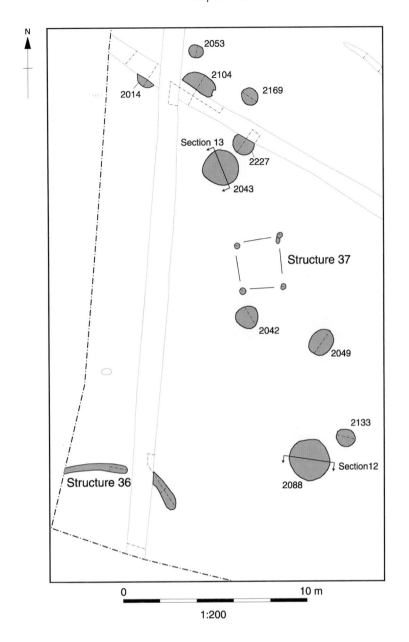

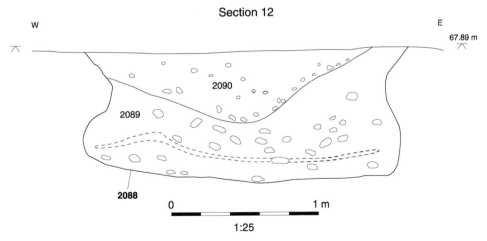

Figure 2.31 Structures 36 and 37 and associated features.

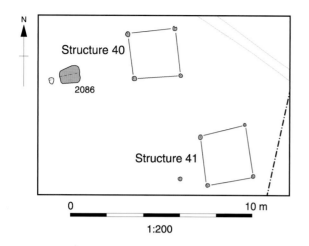

Structure 40

2086

Structure 41

0   10 m

1:200

Figure 2.32   Structures 40 and 41.

Table 2.9   Four-post structures, Site B.

Structure	Dimensions (m)		Posthole diameters (m)	Posthole depths (m)
	Min	Max		
37	2.20	2.40	0.20–0.35	0.03–0.21
38	2.90	3.30	0.30–0.40	0.14–0.27
39	2.45	3.20	0.37–0.46	0.17–0.22
40	2.15	2.60	0.37–0.46	0.16–0.20
41	2.35	2.55	0.24–0.30	0.16–0.24
42	2.50	2.75	0.22–0.26	0.16–0.27
43	2.70	2.95	0.55–0.68	0.27–0.38
44	3.00	3.25	0.42–0.50	0.23–0.34

the finds-rich pits in the vicinity of Enclosure VIII. It contained very few artefacts, despite its large size, suggesting that there was only a low level of contemporary activity in the immediate vicinity.

Flat-based pits

Five pits were recorded in this category, all with straight, near-vertical sides, ranging from 1.10–2.10 m in diameter and 0.20–0.57 m in depth (Table 2.11).

Four of these pits were clustered in a tight row along the line of the eaves-gully to Structure 34, with pits 2182 and 2246 preceding the gully and pits 2023 and 2143 succeeding it (Fig. 2.29). In the middle of this row there was a sequence whereby pit 2182 was cut by the eaves-gully, which was in turn truncated by pit 2143. Pit 2182 contained an articulated pig burial at its base, enclosed in a back-fill of redeposited natural that was then capped by a second deposit of largely sterile material. Pit 2143 meanwhile contained a partial neonate inhumation. The other two pits in the row each contained a single back-fill deposit with large amounts of animal bone and smaller quantities of pottery and other debris.

Section 13

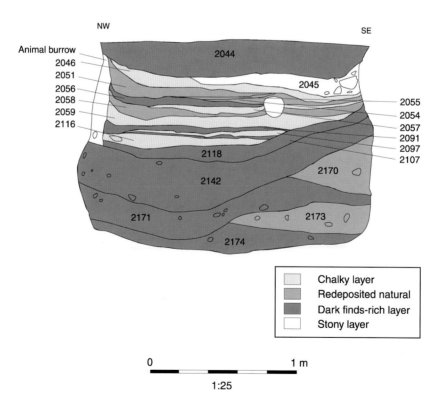

Figure 2.33   Section of pit 2043.

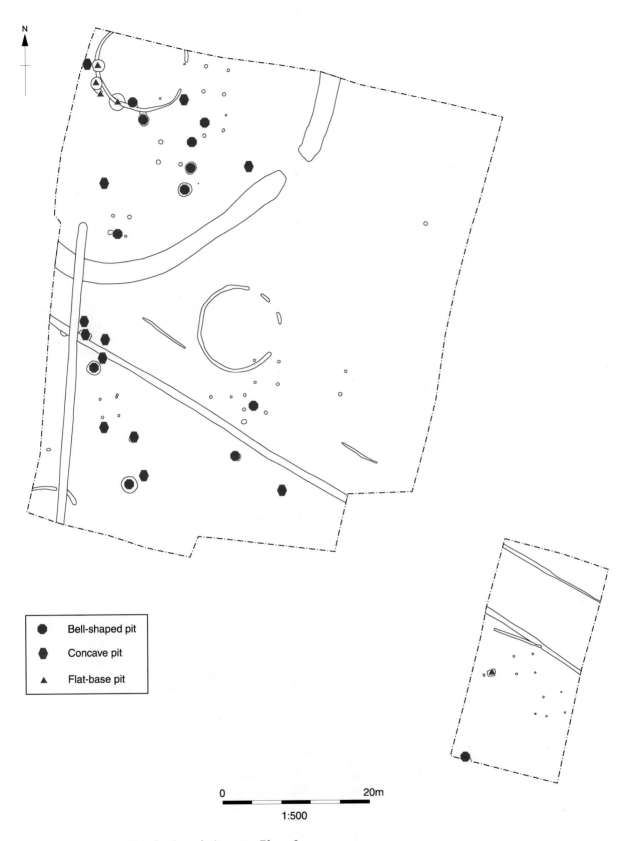

Figure 2.34 Site B. Distribution of pit types, Phase 2.

Concave pits

The eleven pits in this category were all shallow, with depths of 0.07–0.31 m, although they varied widely in diameter with a maximum of 2.00 m. Most contained only moderate numbers of finds, although pit 2025 (Fig. 2.29) yielded a significant amount of animal bone.

Table 2.10 Bell-shaped pits, Site B.

Pit	Diameter (m)	Depth (m)	Finds
2015	1.04	0.89	Pottery, bone
2043	1.90	1.42	Pottery, bone, quern fragment, antler ring, human rib
2080	1.34	0.94	Pottery, bone
2088	2.25	0.86	Pottery, bone
2135	1.20	1.00	Pottery, bone
2145	0.84	0.91	Pottery, bone, fired clay
2161	1.30	0.83	Pottery, bone
2248	1.60	0.45	Pottery, bone
2300	1.85	0.94	Pottery, bone, fired clay, possible stone mould
2316	1.00	0.68	Pottery, bone
2324	1.60	0.86	Pottery, bone
2327	1.55	1.27	Pottery, bone, fired clay, ring-headed pin

PHASE 3: MIDDLE IRON AGE (FIG. 2.35)

While the settlement at Site B had been abandoned by the end of the early Iron Age, a few features at Site A contained pottery datable to the middle Iron Age (c 4th/3rd to 1st centuries BC), indicating some limited continuity of occupation. The final reworking of the main north-western enclosure group took place in this period. Other contemporary features included a roundhouse (Structure 4) and three pits.

In the main enclosure group, part of the western side of Enclosure III seems to have been recut in the form of a shallow gully (4780), up to 1.20 m wide and 0.30 m deep. Middle Iron Age pottery including scored ware was recovered from this feature. The upper fills of the ditch of Enclosure IV also contained middle Iron Age pottery, suggesting that its final in-filling occurred during this phase. Similarly, the upper fill of Enclosure V contained an iron involuted brooch (SF 148; see Fig. 3.17.4) dating to the 3rd–2nd centuries BC.

Structure 4 (Fig. 2.13) was located to the south of the enclosure group, and took the form of an eaves-gully measuring 9.2 m diameter, with a south-east facing entrance. It cut the Phase 2 roundhouse Structure 3 (see above), its centre being shifted 1.5 m to the north-west in relation to the earlier building. Pottery, animal bone and significant quantities of unworked stone were recovered from both the northern and southern eaves-gully terminals, in contrast to the other excavated slots which were devoid of artefacts. Three postholes (4922, 4930 and 4971) fell within the area enclosed by the eaves-gully, but could equally well have been associated with Structure 3. Clay-lined pit 4565 was placed centrally in the entranceway of the eaves-gully, but as argued above this is perhaps more likely to have been an internal feature of Structure 3.

Four pits scattered across the site contained certainly middle Iron Age pottery. In two cases this material came from the uppermost surviving fill only, while the lower fills contained early Iron Age pottery (flat-based pit 3049 and bell-shaped pit 3285; Fig. 2.35). Pits 383 and 4798 were more securely

Plate 2.7 Pit 2043. Scale: 1m.

Table 2.11 Flat-based pits, Site B.

Pit	Diameter (m)	Depth (m)	Finds
2023	1.50	0.20	Pottery, bone
2086	1.12	0.22	Pottery, bone
2143	1.45	0.57	Pottery, bone, fired clay, human neonate
2182	1.10	0.39	Pottery, bone
2246	2.10	0.50	Pottery, bone

datable to this period, containing middle Iron Age pottery in their primary fills (Fig. 2.35). Both were both flat-based features, 0.40 m deep.

PHASE 4: ROMANO-BRITISH PERIOD

Site A (Fig. 2.36)

Very little activity seems to have occurred at Site A during the Romano-British period, with only two

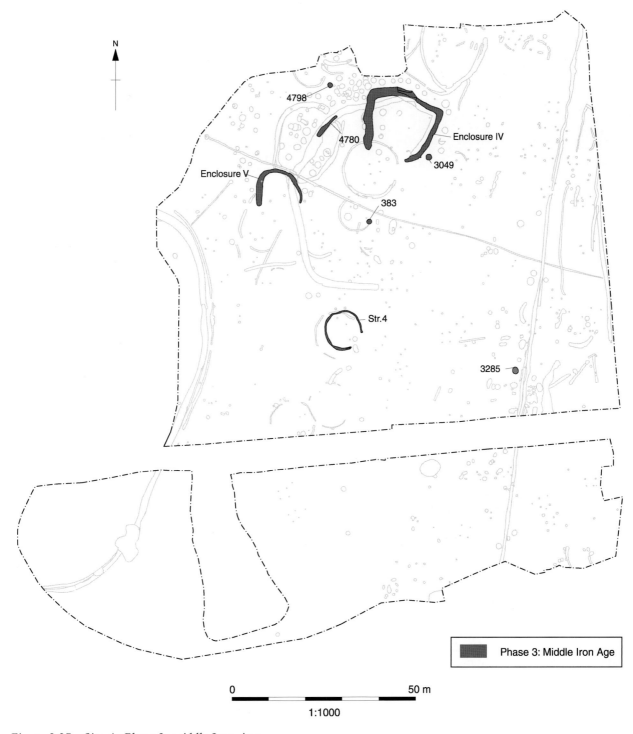

Figure 2.35 Site A. Phase 3: middle Iron Age.

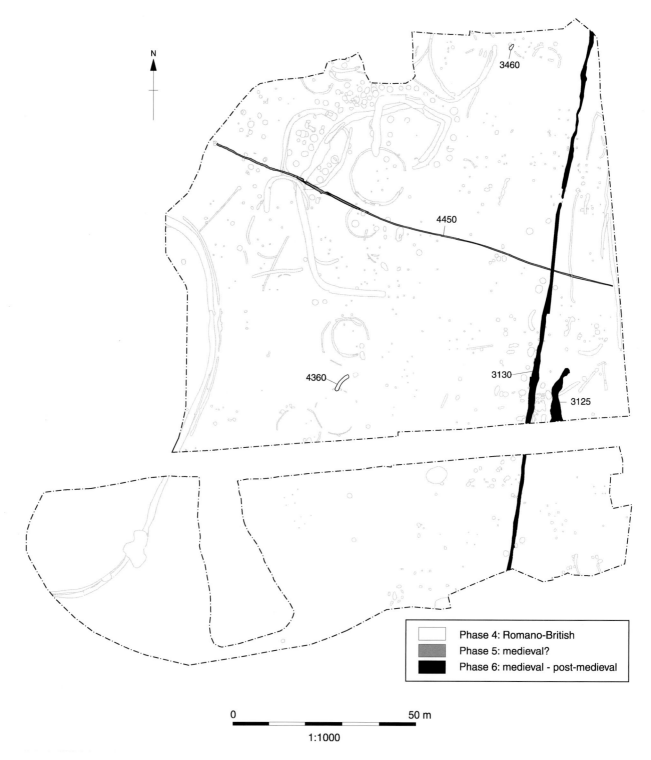

N

3460

4450

4360

3130

3125

	Phase 4: Romano-British
	Phase 5: medieval?
	Phase 6: medieval - post-medieval

0   50 m

1:1000

Figure 2.36   Site A. Phases 4–6: Romano-British to post-medieval.

features present. Short curvilinear gully 4360 cut roundhouse Structure 6 and contained a whetstone of Romano-British type. Elongated pit 3460 meanwhile contained a single sherd of Roman pottery along with residual early Iron Age material. Single Roman sherds were also recovered from Phase 5 ditch 4450 and possible Phase 6 hedge-line 3125.

Site B (Fig. 2.37)

A trackway was laid out across Site B during this period, demarcated by a pair of parallel ditches on a NW-SE alignment. The trackway was 5.3–8.0 m wide, becoming broader to the east. It could be traced for 85 m, continuing beyond the limits of

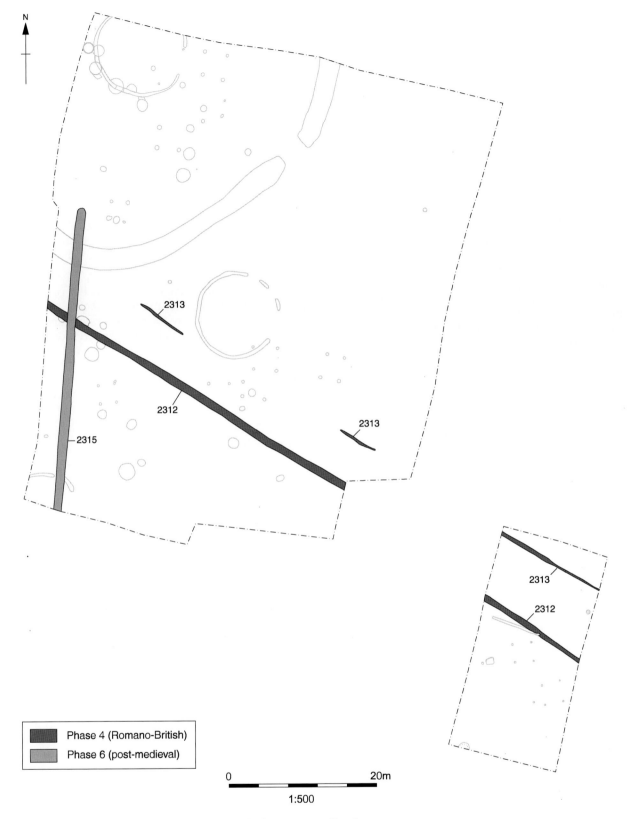

Figure 2.37   Site B. Phases 4–6: Romano-British to post-medieval.

excavation at either end. No traces of metalling were observed. The southern ditch, 2312, had a V-shaped cut and varied between 0.64–1.00 m wide and 0.14–0.50 m deep. Near the western edge of

the excavated area, it was observed that ditch 2312 cut early Iron Age pits 2104 and 2227 and was in turn cut by modern ditch 2315. The northern ditch, 2313, had been more severely truncated and was only sporadically visible, the surviving segments measuring between 0.34–0.51 m wide and 0.04–0.08 m deep. Both ditches had a single fill of grey-brown silty clay. While the majority of the pottery from the ditches dated to the early Iron Age, this must be residual. A few pieces of Roman pottery were also recovered, including a sherd of Central Gaulish samian dating to the 2nd century AD.

PHASE 5: MEDIEVAL PERIOD? (FIG. 2.36)

Ditch 4450 crossed the entire width of Site A on a NW-SE alignment, a length of 115 m being exposed. Whilst the ditch clearly continued beyond the western limit of excavation, it faded out due to truncation immediately before reaching the eastern limit. It clearly post-dated the Iron Age settlement, but pre-dated the post-medieval furrows which followed a quite different alignment across the site (see Fig. 1.7).

The dimensions of ditch 4450 varied from 0.16–0.68 m wide and 0.08–0.40 m deep, being shallowest at its eastern end. The U-shaped cut had a single fill of grey-brown to orange-brown clay silt. Artefactual material recovered from the ditch was scant in quantity, mainly consisting of redeposited Iron Age pottery. Redeposition of earlier material may also account for the radiocarbon date obtained from this feature, which was very similar to those from the Phase 2 settlement (see *Radiocarbon dates* below). A more likely date for the ditch is provided by the pottery from fill 152, which included one probable medieval sherd along with one dating to the Roman period. A hand-made iron nail was also recovered from the ditch.

PHASE 6: MEDIEVAL/POST-MEDIEVAL PERIOD

Site A (Fig. 2.36)

Gully 3130 crossed Site A on a NNE-SSW alignment, cutting Phase 5 ditch 4450. This feature almost certainly represents the boundary between the former open fields of Marshfield and Highfield, depicted on the enclosure award map of 1848 (Doggett 1983). This boundary was swept away by the enclosure and does not appear on the OS first edition 1:10,560 scale map of 1891–92. The gully was 0.29–0.84 m wide and 0.05–0.40 m deep with a U-shaped profile, and had been recut twice in some places. The pale, naturally deposited silty fills contained very few finds, mostly redeposited early Iron Age material. Irregular gully or hedge-line 3125 lay roughly parallel to 3130, and may thus have been contemporary, although finds again consisted of residual Iron Age material along with one tiny Roman sherd.

Site B (Fig. 2.37)

At Site B, a N-S-aligned ditch which ran parallel to the western limit of excavation (2315) was evidently

modern, as it cut through the subsoil which sealed all the archaeology on the site. Small fragments of post-medieval ceramic building material were recovered from the ditch.

RADIOCARBON DATING

Selection of samples

Eleven samples were submitted to the Rafter Laboratory (New Zealand) for Accelerator Mass Spectrometry dating (Table 2.12). At the time when the samples were submitted it was not appreciated that there was a phase of later Bronze Age activity preceding the main Iron Age settlement, and the primary aims in the selection of the samples were to:

1 Provide absolute dates relating to the only good stratigraphic sequence in the Iron Age occupation—namely the north-western enclosure group at Site A—which it was hoped would increase the value of the pottery assemblage as a type series for the region
2 Determine whether or not the Iron Age settlement at Site B was approximately contemporary with that at Site A

The first aim was addressed by samples from contexts 3057, 4491, 4661, 4707 and 4984, and the second by samples from contexts 2095, and 2223 and 2333. The remaining three samples had more specific aims. One sample each was submitted from Enclosure I (context 4342) and from the stratigraphically late ditch 4450, both of which were of uncertain date. The final sample came from pit fill 3631, with the dual purpose of indicating whether the activity in the south-eastern part of Site A was contemporary with that to the north-west, and of providing an associated date for the unusual jet object found in this fill.

There was a lack of articulated bone or hand-recovered charred material from contexts of interest, leading to a reliance on carbonised cereal grain recovered from the flots of the environmental bulk samples. This must be borne in mind when interpreting the results, as the presence of intrusive or residual grains cannot be ruled out. The sample from cremation burial 2094 was taken from charcoal (*Prunus* sp.) presumed to represent pyre material. The sample from context 2333 was taken from the carbonised residue within a ceramic cup, at the request of the pottery specialist. Radiocarbon determinations have been calibrated (Fig. 2.38) using the atmospheric data of Reimer *et al.* (2004), and the calibration program OxCal v.3.10 (Bronk Ramsey 1995; 2001). The calibrated ranges are cited at the 95% confidence level, and have been rounded outwards to the nearest 10 years, all of the errors being greater than or equal to 25 years.

Table 2.12 *Radiocarbon dates.*

Lab no.	Site	Context	Radiocarbon age BP	δ¹³C (‰)	Material	Context type	Calibrated date range (66% confidence)	Calibrated date range (95% confidence)
NZA-21866	A	4661	2127 ± 30	−25	Cereal grain	Lower fill of ditch Enclosure III (Phase 2)	200–100 cal BC	350–310 cal BC 210–50 cal BC
NZA-21867	B	2223	1571 ± 30	−23.5	Cereal grain	Basal fill of ditch, Enclosure VIII (Phase 2)	430–540 cal AD	420–560 cal AD
NZA-21868	A	4491	2186 ± 30	−24.3	Cereal grain	Basal fill of ditch, Enclosure II (Phase 2)	360–280 cal BC 240–190 cal BC	370–160 cal BC
NZA-21952	A	4342	2916 ± 25	−24	Cereal grain	Middle fill of ditch, Enclosure I (Phase 1)	1190–1170 cal BC 1160–1140 cal BC 1130–1040 cal BC	1250–1230 cal BC 1220–1010 cal BC
NZA-21953	A	3057	2263 ± 25	−23.34	Cereal grain	Sole fill of pit 3046 of pit row 3530 (Phase 2)	390–350 cal BC 280–260 cal BC	400–350 cal BC 300–210 cal BC
NZA-21954	A	4707	2126 ± 25	−23.68	Cereal grain	Sole fill of eaves-gully, Structure 1 (Phase 2)	200–150 cal BC 140–110 cal BC	350–320 cal BC 210–50 cal BC
NZA-21955	A	4984	2093 ± 40	−22.63	Cereal grain	Middle fill of pit 4866 of pit row 3530 (Phase 2)	180–40 cal BC	340–320 cal BC 210–0 cal BC
NZA-21956	A	4872	2123 ± 50	−22.26	Cereal grain	Sole fill of ditch 4450 (Phase 5)	340–320 cal BC 210–50 cal BC	360–0 cal BC
NZA-21957	A	3631	2137 ± 25	−23.87	Cereal grain	Upper fill of pit 3630 (Phase 2)	200–160 cal BC 130–120 cal BC	350–310 cal BC 210–90 cal BC
NZA-22005	B	2333	2376 ± 40	−27.36	Charred residue from pot	Middle fill of pit 2327 (Phase 2)	480–460 cal BC 420–390 cal BC	730–690 cal BC 540–380 cal BC
NZA-22062	B	2095	2687 ± 40	−25.46	Charcoal (*Prunus* sp.)	Sole fill of cremation burial 2094 (Phase 1)	900–870 cal BC 850–800 cal BC	920–790 cal BC

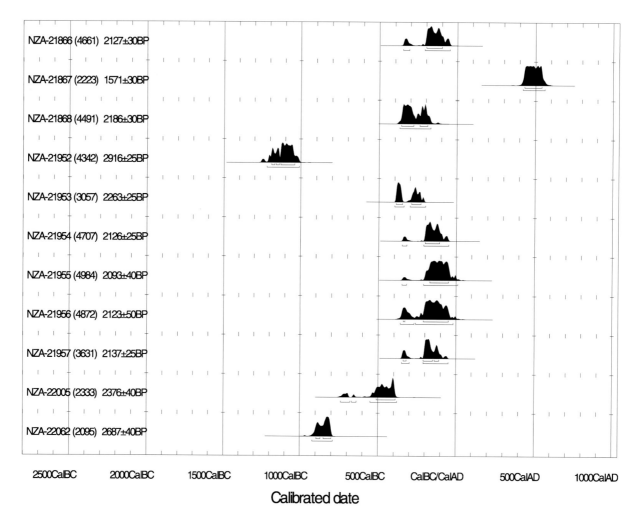

Figure 2.38   Probability distributions of radiocarbon dates.

Discussion

Samples from Phase 1 features

Charcoal from cremation burial 2094 (NZA-22062) produced a date range of 920–790 cal BC. The charcoal is assumed to represent pyre material and hence can be regarded as securely related to the burial. The date range is comparable to determinations obtained on similar burials elsewhere in the region (see Chapter 6).

The sample from Enclosure I (NZA-21952) produced a date range of 1250–1230 cal BC/1220–1010 cal BC. The sample derives from a middle fill of the recut of the ditch, and hence does not demonstrate the date of the construction of the enclosure. Furthermore, it should be noted that probable early Iron Age pottery was recovered from lower fills of the recut of the enclosure ditch elsewhere along the circuit (see above). This raises the possibility that the grain submitted for dating was residual.

Samples from Phase 2 features

Analysis of the pottery from the early Iron Age settlements at Sites A and B has suggested that the main period of activity was during the 5th–4th centuries BC (see Chapter 3). All six of the radiocarbon determinations from Phase 2 features at Site A are compatible with this, although they give no indications that the occupation commenced prior to the 4th century BC. The date range for the sample from pit 3046 lies in the 4th–3rd centuries BC (NZA-21953), that from Enclosure II in the 4th–2nd centuries BC (NZA-21868), and those from Enclosure III (NZA-21866), Structure 1 (NZA-21954), pit 3630 (NZA-21957) and pit 4866 (NZA-21955) in the 4th–1st centuries BC. While there is thus no conflict between the ceramic and radiocarbon dating evidence at the 95% confidence level, the late emphasis of several of the dates when calibrated at the 68% confidence level is notable (Table 2.12).

At Site B, less evidence is available. Cremation burial 2094 (NZA-22-62) proved to be unrelated to the Iron Age occupation. The sample from Enclosure VIII (NZA-21867) surprisingly produced a date in the Anglo-Saxon period, which must be considered the result of intrusive material, given the abundant early Iron Age pottery from the ditch and its clear spatial relationship with roundhouse Structure 34. This left only a single sample, from pit 2327

58

(NZA-22005), which produced a relatively wide date range of 730–690 cal BC/540–380 cal BC. While the later end of this date range just overlaps with two of the date ranges from Phase 2 features at Site A, it falls short of the remaining four. This could suggest a slightly earlier emphasis for the settlement at Site B, although clearly it would be unwise to place too much weight on the evidence of a single sample.

Samples from Phase 5 features

The single sample from Phase 5 ditch 4450 (NZA-21956) produced a determination of 360–1 cal BC, which does not tally with the suggested medieval date of the feature. However, the determination may well derive from redeposited material, given the presence of Iron Age pottery in the ditch.

Chapter 3: Material Culture

FLINT
by Rebecca Devaney

Introduction

A total of 392 pieces of struck flint were recovered (Table 3.1). A further 12 fragments (50 g) of burnt unworked flint were retrieved from 11 contexts. A small proportion of the assemblage is likely to derive from Mesolithic, Neolithic or early Bronze Age industries. This includes debitage and re-touched pieces including a broken arrowhead, which were recognised on the basis of technolo-gical characteristics. No archaeological features were dated to these periods, suggesting that the flint is residual. However, its presence implies human activity at the site prior to the Iron Age occupation. It is suggested that the majority of the flint assemblage is technologically later prehistoric in date. This is based on the recognition of characteristics that are said to be diagnostic of late Bronze Age or Iron Age flint working. For many years the existence of worked flint from these periods was refuted, for example by Saville (1981), but it has gradually become more widely accepted (Ford *et al.* 1984; Young and Humphrey 1999).

Methodology

The flint was catalogued according to broad debit-age, core or tool type. Information about burning and breakage was recorded and where identifiable, raw material type was also noted. Where possible dating was attempted. In addition, cores were weighed and burnt unworked flint was quantified by count and weight. The data was entered into an MS Access database.

A selection of material was subject to metrical analysis and examined for technological character-istics, the purpose of the further analysis being to ascertain the presence of late Bronze Age or Iron Age flint working. The maximum lengths and breadths of selected complete flints were measured using graph paper. Technological analysis involved the recording of a series of diagnostic attributes, including butt type (Inizan *et al.* 1999, fig. 62), termination type (Cotterell and Kamminga 1987, fig. 4), probable hammer mode (eg Onhuma and Bergman 1982) and flake type (Harding 1990). The presence of platform edge abrasion and dorsal blade scars was also recorded. The results of the analysis were compared to the diagnostic charac-teristics of late Bronze Age and Iron Age flint working as suggested by Young and Humphrey (1999, 232–3).

Provenance

The worked flint was spread between 176 contexts (157 from Site A and 19 from Site B). All the features that contained flint are dated to the late Bronze Age or later, with the majority dated to the early-middle Iron Age. The flint forms a fairly low density spread across the site, with most contexts containing less than ten pieces. However, contexts 3074 and 3133 produced 43 and 35 pieces respectively. Both contexts are part of the buried soil at Site A that lay above the natural and was cut by all recorded features.

Raw material

Where identifiable, the predominant raw material is gravel flint. In general this flint has a thin, abraded and often stained cortex and is likely to derive from local sources, such as river gravels. In many cases the material is of a low quality, frequently exhibiting thermal flaws. There is also a small number of possible chalk-derived flints, which are identified by a thick white cortex. As the site is located on chalk bedrock, it is surprising that this type of flint was not utilised more frequently. However, the frequency of use was probably related to the accessibility and quality of the flint deposits.

Condition

In general, the condition of the assemblage is good. The majority of the pieces are in a fresh condition or show slight post-depositional damage. A small number of pieces exhibit moderate post-depositional damage, and only a few are heavily damaged or rolled. Unretouched edges are most frequently damaged, and this implies limited post-depositional disturbance. Surface alteration is minimal with most pieces being uncorticated. Cortication of varying degrees was seen on less than 50 pieces, spread between a number of contexts. Just three pieces are affected by iron staining.

The assemblage

Technologically, the worked flint assemblage is mixed and includes pieces characteristic of both earlier and later prehistoric industries, with the later material being best represented. Due to the low numbers of flints per feature and the possibility that all the flints are residual, the material will be discussed as one group.

Unretouched debitage dominates the assemblage (340 pieces). Of this total, 244 pieces are flakes and 46 are blades, blade-like flakes or bladelets. The latter proportion (14%) is fairly low and implies a minimal

Table 3.1   Summary of worked flint by excavation area.

Excavation area	Site A	Site B	Total
Flake	225	19	244
Blade	17	3	20
Blade-like flake	24		24
Bladelet	2		2
Chip	6		6
Rejuvenation flake core face/edge	1		1
Flake from ground implement		1	1
Janus flake (thinning flake)	1		1
Irregular waste	38	3	41
Single platform flake core		1	1
Multiplatform flake core	3	1	4
Keeled flake core	3		3
Core on a flake	4		4
Tested nodule/bashed lump	4		4
Unclassifiable/fragmentary core	11		11
End and side scraper	2		2
End scraper	1		1
Side scraper	1		1
Scraper on a non-flake blank	1		1
Fragmentary/unclassifiable arrowhead	1		1
Retouched blade	7		7
Retouched flake	5	1	6
Serrated flake	1		1
Fabricator	1		1
Miscellaneous retouch	4		4
Total	363	29	392
No. burnt	15 (4%)	1 (3%)	16 (4%)
No. broken	129 (36%)	7 (24%)	136 (35%)
No. retouched	24 (7%)	1 (3%)	25 (6%)

presence of Mesolithic or earlier Neolithic material (Ford 1987, 79, table 2). A small number of pieces have technological characteristics consistent with an industry of this period, such as platform edge abrasion and bulbs of percussion reminiscent of soft hammer reduction. Many pieces, recognised as being technologically earlier in date, appear to be made on a better quality raw material that is generally darker in colour than the rest of the assemblage. There is a small cluster of technologically earlier pieces in the north-west corner of Site B and many occur in the buried soil at Site A; however, they are also located in other features and suggest that residual pieces are present across the site.

The rest of the debitage is thought to derive from a later prehistoric industry and may be contemporary with the Iron Age occupation of the site. Obtuse striking angles, wide striking platforms and irregular or unrecognisable butts are common. Primary and secondary (trimming) flakes predominate with 58 (of the 77 pieces analysed for technological analysis) exhibiting partial dorsal cortex. Incipient cones of percussion are common on butts and dorsal surfaces and imply a lack of care on the part of the knapper. Finally, many flakes have thermal flaws, which suggest the use of a poor quality raw material.

These characteristics are said to be associated with late Bronze Age or Iron Age flint working (Young and Humphrey 1999, 232–3).

A key characteristic of later prehistoric flint working is the manufacture of short, squat flakes (Young and Humphrey 1999, 233). A total of 75 complete flints from a range of contexts were therefore measured and the ratios between length and breadth calculated (Table 3.2). A significant proportion (59%) of the sample has a length/breadth ratio of less than 1.5. This indicates the presence of short, squat flakes and suggests the presence of later prehistoric flintwork. Ratios of over 1.5 and 2 refer to blade-like flakes and blades respectively. However, many of the blades do not have technological characteristics

Table 3.2   Summary of metrical analysis of worked flint.

Length/breadth ratio	Count	% of total
< 1.5	44	59
≥ 1.5 and < 2	21	28
≥ 2	10	13
Total	75	100

consistent with an earlier industry and therefore appear to be later in date, possibly being unplanned blade removals.

The assemblage also contains one rejuvenation flake, one flake from a ground implement and one janus flake. The rejuvenation flake (ctx 4311, gully 4360) is hard hammer struck, has a plunging termination and use-wear along both lateral edges. The flake from a ground implement (ctx 2183, pit 2182) is a squat removal, possibly taken from a polished axe. It was struck transversely across the grain of the polish and the curvature of the implement. The material is a light grey mottled flint and almost certainly from a chalk flint source. This piece is unlike anything else in the assemblage and indicates the re-use of a Neolithic implement. The janus (thinning) flake (buried soil 3074) is a removal from the ventral surface of another flake and therefore appears to have two ventral surfaces. Although the flake from a ground implement has a *terminus post quem*, the three pieces described here are otherwise undateable.

A total of 27 cores were recovered from the site, although 14 of these are fragmentary or unclassifiable. Typologically distinctive cores include one single platform flake core, four multiplatform flake cores, three keeled flake cores and four cores on flakes. Weight varies from 20 g to 158 g, the cores on flakes generally being the smallest. Most of the cores are irregularly worked with fairly small removals and many incipient cones of percussion. These characteristics are frequently associated with later prehistoric flint working (Young and Humphrey 1999, 233). One of the multi-platform flake cores (ctx 4806, Enclosure IV) has iron-stained previous removals, which suggests it has been re-used. The more recent removals are also smaller in size. More evidence for re-use can be seen on one of the cores on a flake (Fig. 3.1.1). The original flake surfaces (including possible scraper retouch) exhibit moderate cortication compared to the uncorticated later removals. The practice of recycling flint is another suggested characteristic of late Bronze Age and Iron Age flint working (Young and Humphrey 1999, 233).

The fragmentary or unclassifiable cores are generally small in size (4 g to 82 g) and are irregularly worked. Thermal surfaces are often present and some are broken. Three tested nodules were also recovered, one of which has a modern break and is in two halves. The nodules are quite small, weighing between 50 g and 68 g, and have few removals. The irregular and inefficient use of the cores implies the lack of a careful and planned reduction strategy and supports the suggestion of later prehistoric flint working.

The retouched element of the assemblage consists of 25 pieces and is dominated by flints with undiagnostic retouch (18 pieces). The latter include seven retouched blades, six retouched flakes, four pieces with miscellaneous retouch and one serrated flake. Undoubtedly some of the retouched blades are earlier in date, exhibiting technological characteristics such as platform edge abrasion and bulbs of

percussion reminiscent of soft hammer reduction. However, this does not account for the pieces making up the rest of the group, many of which are technologically poor and have more sporadic retouch. The pieces with miscellaneous retouch include two thermal flakes, one with irregular retouch and the other with a scraping edge and a piercing point, and two possible knife fragments. Both of the knife fragments have bifacial retouch, one of which is a possible scale-flaked knife and is made on a thermal flake. There are five scrapers, including two end and side scrapers, one end scraper, one side scraper and one scraper on a non-flake blank. The latter is made on a large, primary, thermal flake and has irregular retouch around one end. One of the end and side scrapers is carefully made on a chalk-derived flint (Fig. 3.1.2) and may be Neolithic in date. The other scrapers are quite small, have direct retouch on one or more edges and are consistent with a later prehistoric date (Fig. 3.1.3). The retouching of thermal flakes and the presence of a limited range of obvious tool types (in this case scrapers) is consistent with a late Bronze Age and Iron Age industry (Young and Humphrey 1999, 232).

The fragmentary arrowhead (Fig. 3.1.4) has bifacial, invasive retouch and is most likely the top half of either an earlier Neolithic leaf arrowhead or an early Bronze Age barbed and tanged arrowhead (Green 1984, 19). It is therefore clearly residual. The fabricator consists of a large side-trimming blade with cortical backing to the length of the left-hand side (Fig. 3.1.5). The tool has been minimally worked, exhibiting an area of direct retouch to the distal right-hand side. A limited area of inverse, semi-invasive retouch has been applied to the proximal right-hand side. The proximal and distal points of the tool exhibit a heavy, rounded use-wear, which is typically present on fabricators. Whilst these tools can date from the Mesolithic period, this example is probably Neolithic or Bronze Age in date.

Discussion

The flint from Fairfield Park represents a long time period, possibly stretching from the Mesolithic to the Iron Age. While the majority of the material can be broadly dated to the later prehistoric period, clearly some of the material is residual from earlier phases (Mesolithic and Neolithic). This includes pieces with technologically earlier characteristics such as platform edge abrasion and bulbs reminiscent of soft hammer reduction. One of the end and side scrapers, the fragmentary arrowhead, the fabricator and various other pieces may also date to this period. The presence of this material suggests human activity at the site long before the Iron Age occupation.

However, it is suggested that the bulk of the assemblage may derive from a late Bronze Age or Iron Age industry and was therefore contemporary with the Iron Age occupation of the site. Young and Humphrey (1999, 232–3) suggest that a flint assemblage from this period will exhibit most of the following characteristics:

- Utilisation of highly localised raw materials – some of which may be of very low quality
- Small assemblage numbers
- Simple core/flake technology, employing hard hammer, direct percussion
- Lack of skill in knapping, evidenced by:
    i. Obtuse striking angles
    ii. A high instance of step or hinge terminations
    iii. Thick, wide striking platforms
    iv. Irregular dorsal flake scar patterns on flakes
    v. Short, squat flakes – length/breadth ratio 1:1
    vi. A high instance of chips and chunks
    vii. Irregular core morphology
    viii. The presence of incipient cones of percussion on core striking platforms
- A restricted range of formal tool types (scrapers, awls etc)
- Crude hammerstones
- A predominance of secondary and inner flakes
- Possible evidence for recycling of lithic material

From this list, the following characteristics can be observed in the assemblage from Fairfield Park. The bulk of the assemblage is made on poor quality, locally derived material that frequently exhibits thermal fractures. The better quality, chalk material derived from the local bedrock appears to have only been utilised for a minority of pieces that are thought to be Mesolithic or Neolithic in date. A simple core/flake technology consisting of hard hammer reduction has been shown to be dominant. Only 14% of the unretouched debitage consist of blades, many of which appear to be unintentional blade removals that do not exhibit the technological characteristics consistent with formal blade production, such as platform edge abrasion and bulbs reminiscent of soft hammer reduction. A lack of knapping care is demonstrated by the presence of five of the eight listed characteristics (obtuse striking angles; wide striking platforms; short, squat flakes with length/breadth ratios close to 1:1; irregular core morphology; incipient cones of percussion). There is clearly a restricted range of formal tool types comprising five scrapers, a fragmentary arrowhead and a fabricator. The predominance of secondary flakes is clearly evident, comprising 58 of the 77 examined. The possibility of recycling flint material has been highlighted, specifically in the cases of one of the multiplatform flake cores and a core on a flake. The relatively good condition of the assemblage supports the suggestion of Iron Age flint working. If the whole of the assemblage were residual from an earlier period, greater levels of post-depositional damage might be expected.

In the past it was assumed that flint tools were immediately superseded by the introduction of iron. However, it is likely that iron tools were rare for some time after their introduction and that where

flint was more easily available it continued to be used for everyday activities, admittedly on a smaller scale than in earlier periods. Therefore, it is suggested that the majority of the Fairfield Park flint assemblage is contemporary with the Iron Age occupation of the site. The flint represents an expedient, flake-oriented, hard-hammer reduction strategy carried out by people with limited knapping expertise to create simple tools.

Catalogue of illustrated flint (Fig. 3.1)

1 **Core on a flake.** Re-used old flake, old surfaces have moderate cortication, small removals on dorsal surface, larger removals on ventral surface. Possible scraper retouch. 20 g. Site A, pit 4844, ctx 4845. Phase 2.
2 **End and side scraper.** Proximal break, direct retouch to distal end, proximal left and medial right. Chalk flint. Possibly Neolithic. Site A, buried soil 3133.
3 **End and side scraper.** Side trimming, direct retouch on left side and distal end. Corticated. Site A, buried soil 3133. SF 98.
4 **Arrowhead.** Top half only, bifacial invasive retouch, possible leaf-shaped or barbed and tanged arrowhead. Early Neolithic or early Bronze Age. Site A, buried soil 3074. SF 41.
5 **Fabricator.** Minimally-retouched fabricator made on large, side-trimming blade. Area of direct retouch to distal right-hand side. Inverse, semi-invasive retouch to proximal right-hand side. Heavy rounded use-wear (typical fabricator wear) to distal and proximal points. Cortical backing left-hand side. Probably Neolithic or early Bronze Age. Site A, pit 364, ctx 365. Phase 2.

POTTERY
based on a report by Emily Edwards

The excavations at Sites A and B yielded a total of 15,206 sherds (130.8 kg) of pottery (Table 3.3). Nearly all the material dates to the late Bronze Age and Iron Age (99.5%). A few sherds of Roman, medieval and post-medieval date were also recovered, but are not considered further in this report. The later prehistoric pottery from Sites A and B is largely similar, with most appearing to belong to one phase of occupation during the latter stages of the early Iron Age (c 5th–4th centuries BC). This represents the largest Iron Age assemblage published to date from Bedfordshire. Of particular note is a very large group of 10.7 kg of pottery from a single pit at Site B (2043), which included a fine bowl with unusual rim-top decoration (Fig. 3.6.103 and Pl. 3.1).

This account of the pottery has been drawn from a longer report held in the site archive. The assemblage will be discussed chronologically by ceramic period, rather than by stratigraphic phase.

Context and condition of assemblage

Most of the assemblage (85% by weight) was recovered from Site A, where 17 features contained more than 100 sherds. By contrast at Site B, only one pit (2043) contained over 100 sherds (1353 sherds). The overall distribution of pottery at Sites A and B is shown by Figures 3.7 and 3.8. Most of the assemblage (62.1%) was recovered from pit fills, with the

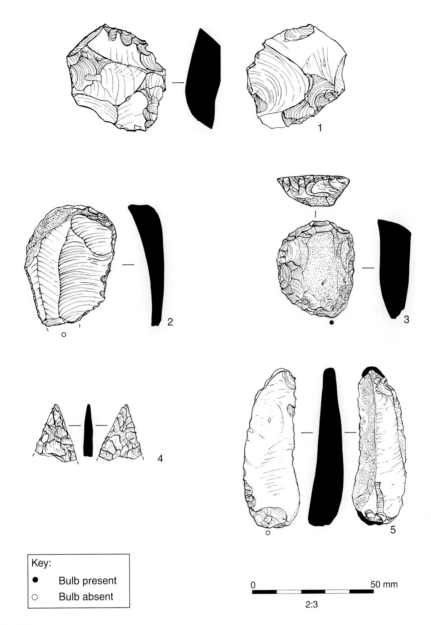

Key:
● Bulb present
○ Bulb absent

0   50 mm

2:3

Figure 3.1   Worked flint.

remainder coming from other features such as dit-ches, gullies and postholes.

With an overall mean sherd weight of 13.5 g, the condition of the assemblage was fairly good. The material from pits tended to be better preserved than that from ditches and gullies (Table 3.4). Individual features containing pottery in an unusually good condition included pit 5026, which only contained three very large sherds (46–86 g), each from a different vessel.

Fabrics

The assemblage was analysed following the guide-lines recommended for the recording of prehisto-ric pottery (PCRG 1997). Fabrics were ascribed macroscopically on the basis of the main inclusions present assisted by the aid of a binocular microscope (×20); small crumbs were not assigned to a fabric type. A total of 25 prehistoric fabrics were identi-fied, and are described in Table 3.5. This table also shows the nearest equivalent to each fabric in the Bedfordshire type series held by Albion Archaeology.

The assemblage is very diverse with a number of different ware groups including those dominated by flint, grog, organic matter, calareous, sandy and various mixed inclusions. Sandy fabrics dominate the assemblage, with fabrics containing fossil shell or other calcareous inclusions forming a significant minority (Table 3.5). It is uncertain whether any of the sand and shell was deliberately added as temper, as opposed to being naturally present in the clay. There are also much smaller amounts of pottery

Table 3.3   Quantification of pottery by ceramic phase.

Ceramic date	Site A			Site B		
	Sherd count	% by sherd count	Weight (g)	Sherd count	% by sherd count	Weight (g)
Late Bronze Age	42	0.3	391	4	0.2	146
Late Bronze Age or early Iron Age	16	0.1	119	0	0	0
Early Iron Age	11,209	86.8	96,437	2229	97.1	19,304
Early or middle Iron Age	1412	10.9	11,414	60	2.6	657
Middle Iron Age	108	0.8	1912	0	0	0
Middle or late Iron Age	2	<0.1	37	0	0	0
Iron Age	52	0.4	265	0	0	0
Roman	3	<0.1	3	2	0.1	7
Medieval?	1	<0.1	3	0	0	0
Post-medieval	7	0.1	19	0	0	0
Indeterminate	59	0.5	90	0	0	0
Totals	12,911	100.0	110,690	2295	100.0	20,114

characterised by deliberately added flint or grog temper.

The area around Fairfield Park is characterised by diverse geology (Fig. 1.2), and it is clear that more than one clay source was used to manufacture the vessels seen in the assemblage. Many of the fabrics (eg F01A, F06C, F14, F15, F16, F18, F19, F20, F21, F19, F28 and F29) contained naturally occurring ironstone, mica and sparse flint, which may suggest a Quaternary clay source, presumably the local Anglian Glacial Till. The presence of relatively large quartzite fragments in some sherds (fabrics F19 and F29) may also indicate the use of clays associated with the Letchworth Gravels, found in the immediate vicinity of the site (Smith and Rose 1997;

Watts *et al.* 2005). A small number of sherds containing glauconitic sand (fabric F38A) may have derived from the Woburn Sands, which outcrop *c* 8 km to the north-west.

Four fabrics (F04, F19, F21 and F22) comprising 24% of the assemblage contained significant amounts of organic material. Much of this organic material is still present within the section at fresh breaks, rather than being merely observable by the presence of voids on the surface. The unusual quantity of organic tempered pottery at Fairfield Park might indicate an exploitation of an organic-rich clay deposit, although it is also possible that plant material was deliberately added as temper.

The assemblage

Late Bronze Age

A total of 46 sherds (537 g) of late Bronze Age pottery were recovered, with a further 16 sherds (119 g) ascribed to either the late Bronze Age or early Iron Age. This material was recovered both from Phase 1 contexts and as residual material from later

0 _____ 100 mm

1:2

Plate 3.1   Decorated bowl from pit 2043.

Table 3.4   Mean sherd weights from different feature types.

Mean sherd weight (g)	All features (%)	Pits (%)	Gullies (%)	Ditches (%)	Pit 2043 (%)
0–5	28	22	31	44	57
6–10	23	24	26	22	17
11–15	14	15	13	12	9
16–20	9	9	9	8	5
21–25	5	7	5	3	3
26–30	4	5	4	2	2
31–35	3	3	3	2	1
Above 35	14	15	9	7	6
Mean weight	13.5	15.9	8.9	11.8	16.4

Table 3.5   Pottery fabrics.

Bedfordshire type series equivalent		% by sherd count	Description
F	Indeterminate	10%	
F01A	Coarse flint	2%	Poorly-sorted flint, 20%, 0.5–6 mm. Well-sorted rounded quartzite sand, 5%. Rare ironstone
F01B	Fine flint	1%	Very well-sorted crushed flint, up to 2 mm. No sand.
F01C	Quartz and flint	<1%	Well-sorted flint 2 mm to poorly sorted 4 mm, 20%. 10–20% well-sorted, rounded quartz sand, 0.5
F03	Grog and sand	<1%	1% angular grog, 1 mm. Common, well-sorted, fine sand 10%.
F04	Organic	<1%	20% <, thin linear voids (grass). No sand. Can be rough, smoothed or burnished
F06C	Coarse grog	<1%	5–10% angular grog, up to 5 mm. 2% flint, 1 mm. Sand 5%, up to 2 mm.
F14	Fine mixed inclusions	1%	5% fine (red, black and clear) quartzitic sand. 5% organic. 1% rounded ironstone 1 mm. 1% calcareous (chalk?) 1 mm. Flint, angular, 1 mm. 5% mica. 2% shell. 1% argillaceous fragments (some with fossil adhering to surface)
F15	Coarse mixed inclusions	2%	10–15% poorly sorted, rounded to subangular quartzite sand (red, black, clear). 5–10% organic. 2% calcined flint, up to 5 mm. 2% quartz, 6 mm. 2% fossil shell. 1% chalk. Rare (less than 1%) ironstone
F16A	Calcareous	4%	10–30% crushed fossil (Bryozoa and echinoids), less than 3 mm. Rare quartz sand
F16B	Fine shelly (soapy)	<1%	20–30% crushed, thin-walled alluvial shell, up to 4 mm. 5% organics. No sand, 1% mica. Soapy feeling fabric
F17	Grog	<1%	2% subangular grog
F18	Fine sand and shell	6%	10–30% crushed fossil shell (bryozoa and echinoids), less than 3 mm with fine 5% quartzite sand
F19	Sand/organic	21%	10% subrounded quartzite sand, up to 6 mm. 5–20% organic, often preserved within the clay. 1% ironstone. Sometimes rare calcined flint, 0.5 mm
F20	Calcareous	6%	Chalk/limestone 10% up to 4 mm, sand 10–20% up to 1 mm, 1% flint and ironstone with a laminated structure containing ellipsoid voids.
F21	Shell/organic	3%	10–20% crushed fossil shell (including Bryozoa). 10–20% carbonised organic material or voids. Often leached. 1% ironstone, 2% sub rounded sand
F22	Grog and organic	<1%	2% subangular grog. 10–15% carbonised organic matter or voids.
F23	Grog/shell/ sand	<1%	2% subangular grog. 2% finely crushed fossilised shell. 2% sub-angular quartz sand
F27	Shell/grog	<1%	2% subangular grog. 2% finely crushed fossilised shell
F28	Fine sand	18%	10% quartzite and glauconitic sand, up to 2 mm. 5% rounded ironstone inclusions up to 5 mm. Rare, tiny fragments of crushed calcareous, possibly shell
F29	Coarse sand	27%	Poorly sorted round to subangular quartzite sand, up to 7 mm. 5% ironstone
F30	Sand/calcareous	<1%	20% limestone up to 3 mm. 2% sand
F32	Sand and flint	<1%	Fine common quartzite sand and 5% flint, 4 mm. Organic 5%.
F35	Micaceous	<1%	10% mica and 10–20% fine glauconitic sand
F38A	Glauconitic (Fairfield Park variant)	1%	5–10% rounded glauconitic sand, up to 0.5 mm. Other inclusions may include quartz sand, mica, organics, flint or shell
R01A	Central Gaulish samian	<1%	
R06B	Romano-British coarse grey ware	<1%	
R06C	Romano-British fine grey ware	<1%	

features. The material has been dated largely on the grounds of fabric.

Table 3.6 gives a breakdown of fabrics, showing that flint or flint and sand are the dominant inclusions. Flint temper was used within the region throughout the late Bronze Age and earliest Iron Age. Locally, at Blackhorse Road, Letchworth, almost 50% of the late Bronze Age to early Iron Age assemblage was flint and sand tempered (Birley 1988, 79). Other material ascribed to the late Bronze Age includes a number of sherds in fabrics F19 and F29 containing relatively large, angular fragments of

Table 3.6 Late Bronze Age and late Bronze Age/early Iron Age pottery fabrics.

Fabric		LBA			LBA/EIA		
		Sherd Count	Weight (g)	% by sherd count	Sherd Count	Weight (g)	% by sherd count
F01A	Coarse flint	25	199	54.3	8	40	50
F14	Fine mixed	–	–	–	3	22	18.8
F19	Sand/organic	–	–	–	2	13	12.5
F28	Fine sand	–	–	–	2	28	12.5
F29	Coarse sand	2	11	4.3	–	–	–
F32	Sand and flint	19	327	41.3	1	15	6.3

crushed quartzite. On the gravel terraces of the Upper Thames Valley, quartzite fabrics are strongly indicative of a late Bronze Age date (Barclay 2001, 130), although this has yet to be demonstrated within Bedfordshire. It should be noted that this material was absent from Phase 1 contexts, and derived solely from early Iron Age features.

The only feature sherd within the late Bronze Age assemblage was the rim from an open bowl, ornamented with fingernail impressions on the rim top. Vessels ascribed to the late Bronze Age/early Iron Age included a small open bowl (Fig. 3.2.1) and a straight-sided bowl or jar (Fig. 3.6.95).

Early Iron Age

The bulk of the assemblage, a total of 13,438 sherds (115.7 kg), has been dated to the early Iron Age. In addition, it is likely that much of the material given a broad 'early or middle Iron Age' date also in fact belongs to this period. Key groups within the assemblage include pit 2043 (1339 sherds; Fig. 3.6.100–4) and hollow 3545 (953 sherds; Fig. 3.4.37–57).

Table 3.7 summarises the early Iron Age fabrics. This shows a dominance of coarse sandy wares (F29), followed by sand and organic (F19) and fine sand (F28) fabrics respectively. The large amounts of F28 and F29 are not unusual for early to middle Iron Age settlements in southern and central Bedfordshire, being paralleled at Salford (Slowikowski 2005), Flitwick (McSloy 1999), and Bunyan Centre, Bedford (La Niece and Slowikowski 1999). It is unusual, however, for F19 to be so well represented, although this fabric was noted in small quantities at Flitwick, Willington (McSloy 1996) and Topler's Hill (Wells 2004), where it formed 14% of the assemblage by

Table 3.7 Early Iron Age and early or middle Iron Age pottery fabrics.

Fabric		EIA			EIA or MIA		
		Sherd Count	Weight (g)	% by sherd count	Sherd Count	Weight (g)	% by sherd count
F	Indeterminate	1426	1831	10.6	2	20	0.1
F01A	Coarse flint	173	1003	1.3	4	86	0.3
F03	Grog and sand	7	93	0.1	1	30	0.1
F04	Organic	2	97	<0.1	1	5	0.1
F06C	Coarse grog	4	20	<0.1	1	4	0.1
F14	Fine mixed	79	803	0.6	–	–	–
F15	Coarse mixed	235	2613	1.7	1	11	0.1
F16A	Calcareous	523	7753	3.9	66	635	4.5
F16B	Fine shelly	6	174	<0.1	–	–	–
F17	Grog	2	10	<0.1	–	–	–
F18	Fine sand and shell	784	8603	5.8	106	778	7.2
F19	Sand/organic	2539	25,378	18.9	573	4787	39.1
F20	Calcareous	836	9051	6.2	33	280	2.3
F21	Shell/organic	332	4986	2.5	71	928	4.8
F22	Grog and organic	2	15	<0.1	–	–	–
F23	Grog/shell/ sand	11	86	0.1	–	–	–
F27	Shell/grog	4	4	<0.1	–	–	–
F28	Fine sand	2379	18,545	17.7	270	1982	18.4
F29	Coarse sand	3700	30,939	27.5	286	2012	19.5
F30	Sand/calcareous	1	6	<0.1	–	–	–
F32	Sand and flint	300	2377	2.2	35	421	2.4
F35	Micaceous	13	176	0.1	–	–	–
F38A	Glauconitic	80	1178	0.6	16	92	1.1

sherd count. Notably, sand and calcareous fabric F30 was rare at Fairfield Park (<1%), yet formed the largest single component (49%) of the early to middle Iron Age assemblage at Groveland Way, Stotfold (Wells forthcoming), just 2 km away. Meanwhile, micaceous fabric F35, again representing less than 1% at Fairfield Park, formed the largest single component (41%) at the early to middle Iron Age site at Topler's Hill, 5 km to the north. This suggests that a considerable degree of variability in fabric types could occur in this period on a very local level.

The basic typology of early Iron Age vessels from southern England has been outlined by Barrett (1980). Coarse jars (Class I) are the most common type, augmented by smaller numbers of fine jars (Class II), coarse bowls (Class III), fine bowls (Class IV) and cups (Class V). The fine/coarse distinction is based mainly on inclusion size, but also relates to surface treatment and decoration. Fine vessels often have burnished surfaces and complex decoration of incised lines and/or punched dots, while for coarse vessels decoration is restricted to rows of fingertip or fingernail impressions. These traits can be seen in the Fairfield Park assemblage, which was dominated by coarse jars, with fine bowls also well represented. Fine jars, coarse bowls and cups were less common.

A more detailed form typology can been applied to the assemblage, based on Hill's (2004) scheme for the contemporary site at Wandlebury, Cambs, with additions. The main forms present were as follows:

A. *Tripartite jars with slightly flared necks and a distinct rounded shoulder* (Figs 3.2.18, 3.5.65, 3.5.75. 3.5.81, 3.6.84 and 3.6.100). A common form. Coarse examples may be decorated with a row of fingertip impressions around the shoulder (Fig. 3.2.18). Fine examples may be burnished and decorated with incised lines and/or punched dots (Fig. 3.5.65).
B. *Bipartite jars with a distinct rounded shoulder* (Fig. 3.2.11). Generally coarse and undecorated.
C. *'Flower pot' jars with slightly flared profiles* (Figs 3.2.3, 3.3.36 and 3.4.48). Generally undecorated.
D. *High-shouldered jars* (Figs 3.2.9, 3.2.23, 3.3.29, 3.4.42, 3.4.47, 3.5.67, 3.5.74, 3.5.77, 3.5.80 and 3.6.112). A common form. Coarse examples can be decorated with fingernail impressions on the rim and/or fingertip impressions on the shoulder (Figs 3.2.23 and 3.5.77). Finer burnished examples are also present (Figs 3.2.9 and 3.4.42).
E. *Barrel-shaped jars* (Figs 3.2.14, 3.3.27, 3.3.30, 3.4.40 and 3.6.82). Generally coarse. Sometimes decorated with a row of fingertip impressions around the body (Fig. 3.2.14).
F. *Jars with slightly S-shaped profiles, often with T-shaped or internally expanded rims* (Fig. 3.3.25). Generally coarse and undecorated.
G. *Tripartite jars with flared necks and T-shaped or internally expanded rims* (Figs 3.2.13, 3.2.15, 3.2.22, 3.4.45, 3.5.69, 3.6.101 and 3.6.108). Always large, coarse vessels. Often decorated with fingernail impressions on the front and/or inner face of the rim (Figs 3.5.69, 3.6.101 and 3.6.108).
H. *Tripartite bowls with a marked shoulder and a flared neck* (Figs 3.2.10, 3.3.35, 3.4.50, 3.4.58, 3.5.73, 3.6.99, 3.6.104 and 3.6.106). Often have foot-ring or pedestal bases (Figs 3.4.58, 3.5.73 and 3.6.106). Typically fine and burnished. Often decorated with bands of incised chevrons on the shoulder or neck, which can be infilled with white calcareous paste (Figs 3.2.10, 3.4.50, 3.6.99 and 3.6.104).
I. *Rounded bowls with slightly everted or triangular rims*. Typically fine and burnished. Two examples have a very unusual motif of incised hatched triangles on the rim top (Fig. 3.5.70 and 3.6.103); one of these is also decorated with incised chevrons on the body and has been fired to a deep red colour (Fig. 3.6.103 and Pl. 3.1).
J. *Cups*. Nine examples found, varying widely in form. Profiles include simple open (Fig. 3.5.71), open tapering to a very narrow base (Fig. 3.5.66), ovoid (Fig. 3.4.39) and slack-shouldered with a narrow mouth (Fig. 3.2.7). Rim diameters range from 50–90 mm. Never decorated.

Applied bosses (Fig. 3.4.46 and Fig. 3.5.64) or pierced lugs (Fig. 3.6.85) were present on a few sherds, although in no case was the overall vessel form certain. One base sherd from pit 153 had three holes drilled after firing (Fig. 3.2.4), perhaps intended for a function such as draining liquids or as a steamer.

Few clear patterns can be seen in the fabrics used to manufacture particular vessel forms. Unsurprisingly, given the overall fabric composition of the assemblage, most vessel forms were mainly made from sandy wares. An exception was the large jars with T-shaped or internally expanded rims (forms F and G), which were frequently made from calcareous or shelly fabrics (F16A, F18, F20 and F21).

The assemblage shows an overall rim diameter range of 50 mm to 450 mm, with clusters at 140–50 mm, 180–200 mm and 270–80 mm. The vessel forms found at Sites A and B were very similar, although eight of the nine cups came from Site A.

Middle Iron Age

A total of 108 sherds (1912 g) of pottery has been ascribed to the middle Iron Age, all of which came from Site A. The fabrics are similar to those seen in the early Iron Age assemblage, although sand and organic fabrics (F19) now form the largest component (Table 3.8).

Vessel forms consisted of ovoid (Fig. 3.6.92) and slack- or round-shouldered (Fig. 3.6.86-7) jars/bowls. Decoration of middle Iron Age vessels was restricted to a few examples of fingernail or fingertip impressions on the rim top. Few sherds were burnished, although a number bore rough scoring on the outer surface (Fig. 3.6.88–91). 'Scored ware' is a recurring feature of middle Iron Age assemblages in Bedfordshire and further afield in the East Midlands (Elsdon 1992). It has been recovered locally at

Table 3.8   Middle Iron Age pottery fabrics.

Fabric		Sherd Count	Weight (g)	% by sherd count
F14	Fine mixed inclusions	1	4	0.9
F18	Fine sand and shell	3	44	2.8
F19	Sand/organic	70	1126	64.8
F20	Calcareous	3	26	2.8
F21	Shell/organic	4	174	3.7
F28	Fine sand	10	167	9.3
F29	Coarse sand	17	371	15.7

Blackhorse Road, Letchworth (Birley 1988) and at the Groveland Way (Wells forthcoming) and Queen Street (Wessex Archaeology 2006) sites in Stotfold.

Charred residues

Charred residues were found on 213 sherds. Where these could be ascribed to a form category, most appeared to be from jars. This suggests that jars were mainly relied upon for the preparation of starchy foods. Charred residue was also found in a cup with a diameter of 60 mm, however.

Pottery from the BCAS evaluation

A total of 351 sherds (2925 g) of later prehistoric pottery was recovered during the earlier BCAS evaluation at Fairfield Park (BCAS 1997). The material came from three areas: Trenches 9 and 43 within Site A, Trench 10 within Site C, and Trench 22, which had been placed to investigate the ditches on the eastern edge of the hilltop identified during the geophysical survey (see Fig. 1.4). The pottery has been scanned for the purposes of comparison with the main assemblage; no detailed recording or analysis has been carried out.

Most of the material from Trenches 9 and 43 was similar to that recovered during the subsequent open area excavation of Site A, and requires no further comment. However, one vessel of different character was recovered from Trench 43 in the southern part of the site. This was an angular flint-tempered bowl decorated with furrows above the shoulder and fingertip impressions and grooved nested chevrons on and below the shoulder (Fig. 3.2.2). It can be ascribed to the 'Darmsden-Linton' style of decorated pottery (Cunliffe 1991, 76), possibly dating to the earliest part of the Iron Age, *c* 800–500 BC (Martin 1999), and has particularly close affinities to a vessel from the type-site of Darmsden, Suffolk (Cunliffe 1991, fig. A.12, 7). As vessels in this style are normally restricted to East Anglia, a non-local origin is possible.

The pottery from Trench 10 (Site C) divides into two groups. The material from the early pits was predominantly in flint-tempered and calcareous fabrics rather than the sand or organic fabrics which dominate at Sites A and B. Forms were few as the pottery was so abraded and broken; T-shaped and

externally expanded rims and one shouldered vessel were noted. The material can be broadly ascribed to the late Bronze Age/early Iron Age, but more precise dating is difficult. It seems likely to be earlier than the Phase 2 occupation at Sites A and B, although whether it is contemporary with Phase 1 is unclear. The remainder of the material from Trench 10, largely from ditch contexts, comprises late Iron Age/early Roman sherds in grog- and sand-tempered fabrics. The pottery from the Roman cremation burial was not examined.

The pottery from ditch 497 in Trench 22 included a quartzite and organic tempered, round-shouldered vessel probably dating to the earlier Anglo-Saxon period (mid 5th to 7th centuries AD). This is notable as the only Anglo-Saxon pottery identified from any of the investigations at Fairfield Park. Residual later prehistoric sherds were also recovered from the same context.

Discussion

The early Iron Age assemblage broadly belongs to the so-called 'Chinnor-Wandlebury' style of the Chilterns and neighbouring areas (Cunliffe 1991), conventionally dated to the latter stages of the early Iron Age. The association of coarse jars of forms A–F (see above) with fine, tripartite bowls often decorated with incised chevrons can be paralleled at a number of sites along the Chiltern ridge. These include Holwell, Herts (Applebaum 1934; Shepherd *et al.* forthcoming), Jack's Hill, Great Wymondley, Herts (Tebbutt 1931; Cunliffe 1991, fig. A:11), Puddlehill, Beds (Matthews 1976), Wandlebury, Cambs (Hartley 1957; Hill 2004; Webley 2005), Bledlow, Bucks (Saunders 1972), Ellesborough, Bucks (*ibid.*) and Chinnor, Oxon (Richardson and Young 1951). The same basic combination of forms can also be seen at Stansted, Essex (Brown 2004), although here the bowls appear to lack the incised linear decoration.

The large, tripartite jars with flaring T-shaped rims are rather more unusual for the Chilterns area. Jars of this type are more commonly found at early Iron Age sites further north in the East Midlands, such as Gretton, Northants (Jackson and Knight 1985) and Fiskerton, Lincs (Elsdon and Knight 2003).

Most difficult to parallel are the two fine rounded bowls decorated on the rim with incised hatched triangles. No other examples of this form of decoration are known to the author, and it may perhaps have been a very local trait.

The later early Iron Age date suggested for the assemblage is compatible with the radiocarbon dating evidence, which indicates that the main occupation of Site A occurred no earlier than the 4th century BC (see Chapter 2). At Site B, a radiocarbon determination was obtained from charred residue adhering to a sherd from an ovoid cup in fabric F29 (pit 2327, ctx 2333; not illustrated), unfortunately producing a relatively broad date range of 730–690 cal BC/540–380 cal BC (NZA-22005; 2376 ± 40 BP).

Other sites in southern Britain with similar assemblages have also produced absolute dates in the latter stages of the early Iron Age. At Stansted, pit group 2187 has produced a radiocarbon date of 518–384 cal BC. This group included high-shouldered and bipartite jars along with flared tripartite bowls with footring or pedestal bases, although as noted above bowls with linear incised decoration were absent (Brown 2004). Evidence from sites in the East Midlands indicates that tripartite jars with flared T-shaped rims were also current around the close of the early Iron Age. The best example is at Fiskerton, where a group of tripartite flared-rim jars have a dendrochronological *terminus post quem* of 375–4 BC (Elsdon and Knight 2003). All the evidence therefore points to a 5th to 4th century BC date for the early Iron Age assemblage from Fairfield Park.

Catalogue of illustrated pottery (Figs 3.2–6)

Site A

1. Pit 3111, ctx 3112. Fabric F28. Open bowl. LBA/EIA.
2. BCAS evaluation, Trench 43, ctx 1003. Angular, flint-tempered bowl decorated with furrows above the shoulder with fingertips and grooved nested triangles on and below the shoulder. EIA.
3. Ditch 104, ctx 102. Fabric F29. Form C. EIA.
4. Pit 153, ctx 193. Fabric F28. Base sherd with three post-firing drilled holes. EIA.
5. Pit 153, ctx 193. Fabric F28. Burnished sherd with incised decoration. EIA.
6. Pit 156, ctx 157. Fabric F19. Burnished rim. EIA.
7. Pit 156, ctx 157. Fabric F29. Form J. EIA.
8. Pit 156, ctx 158. Fabric F28. Combed body sherd. EIA.
9. Pit 156, ctx 161. Fabric F28. Form D, black fabric, burnished. EIA.
10. Pit 156, ctx 161. Fabric F28. Form H, decorated with incised chevrons filled with white paste. Black fabric, burnished. EIA
11. Pit 194, ctx 196. Fabric F28. Form B. EIA.
12. Ditch segment 236 (Enclosure III), ctx 255. Fabric F21. Form A or I. EIA.
13. Pit 307, ctx 308. Fabric F16A. Form G. EIA
14. Pit 351, ctx 533. Fabric F19. Form E, fingertip impressions on shoulder. EIA.
15. Pit 364, ctx 365. Fabric F21. Form G. EIA.
16. Pit 364, ctx 366. Fabric F38A. Part of a pedestal base, incised post-firing decoration in form of triangle. EIA.
17. Eaves-gully segment 405 (Structure 2), ctx 406. Fabric F29. Burnished body sherd, decorated with small circular punches. EIA.
18. Ditch segment 489 (Enclosure V), ctx 490. Fabric F29. Form A? Decorated with fingertip impressions on the shoulder. EIA.
19. Pit 3011, ctx 3010. Fabric F28. Sherd decorated with rows of small circular punches. EIA.
20. Pit 3020, ctx 3021. Fabric F19. Shoulder decorated with a pair of fingertip impressions. EIA.
21. Pit 3049, ctx 3051. Fabric F28. Rim decorated with deeply incised diagonal lines. EIA.
22. Pit 3131, ctx 3132. Fabric F19. Form G. EIA.
23. Pit 3108, ctx 3166 and 3109. Fabric F14. Form D, decorated with fingertip impressions on shoulder and fingernail impressions on rim top. EIA.
24. Pit 3195, ctx 3249. Fabric F28. Form A? EIA.
25. Pit 3195, ctx 3253. Fabric F20. Form F. EIA.
26. Pit 3285, ctx 3286. Fabric F19. Form D or H. EIA.
27. Pit 3285, ctx 3288. Fabric F29. Form E. EIA.
28. Pit 3285, ctx 3291. Fabric F28. Form D or H. EIA.
29. Pit 3285, ctx 3292. Fabric F29. Form D. EIA.
30. Pit 3285, ctx 3292. Fabric F29. Form E. EIA.
31. Pit 3285, ctx 3293. Fabric F18. Form A? EIA.
32. Posthole 3321, ctx 3322. Fabric F16A. Internally-expanded rim with fingertip impression on neck. EIA.
33. Ditch segment 3395 (post-medieval ditch 3130), ctx 3394. Fabric F29. Body sherd decorated with rows of small circular punches. EIA.
34. Ditch segment 3462 (post-medieval ditch 3130), ctx 3461. Fabric F38A. Rim sherd decorated with incised triangles, filled with white paste. EIA.
35. Ditch segment 3471 (Enclosure IV), ctx 3472. Fabric F28. Form H. EIA.
36. Posthole 3527, ctx 3528. Fabric F29. Form C. EIA.
37. Pit 3545, ctx 3587. Fabric F20. Body sherd decorated with fine combing. EIA.
38. Pit 3545, ctx 3587. Fabric F19. Shoulder sherd decorated with fingernail impressions. EIA.
39. Pit 3545, ctx 3587. Fabric F20. Form J. EIA.
40. Pit 3545, ctx 3587. Fabric F29. Form E. EIA.
41. Pit 3545, ctx 3587. Fabric F14. Burnished shoulder sherd decorated with incised lines. EIA.
42. Pit 3545, ctx 3587. Fabric F29. Form D, burnished. EIA.
43. Pit 3545, ctx 3587. Fabric F20. Burnished. Shoulder sherd decorated with a fingertip impression. EIA.
44. Pit 3545, ctx 3587. Fabric F28. Everted rim. EIA.
45. Pit 3545, ctx 3587. Fabric F16A. Form G. EIA.
46. Pit 3545, ctx 3587. Fabric F28. Boss on shoulder. EIA.
47. Pit 3545, ctx 3587. Fabric F28. Form D. EIA.
48. Pit 3545, ctx 3587. Fabric F28. Form C. EIA.
49. Pit 3545, ctx 3587. Fabric F28. T-shaped rim. EIA.
50. Pit 3545, ctx 3588. Fabric F38A. Form H, decorated with incised triangles and small circular punches. EIA.
51. Pit 3545, ctx 3588. Fabric F38A. Form B? EIA.
52. Pit 3545, ctx 3588. Body sherd decorated with circular punches. EIA.
53. Pit 3545, ctx 3588. Fabric F28. Fingertip-decorated shoulder. EIA.
54. Pit 3545, ctx 3588. Fabric F18. Fingernail-decorated shoulder. EIA.
55. Pit 3545, ctx 3589. Fabric F18. Body sherd decorated with incised chevrons and small circular punches. EIA.
56. Pit 3545, ctx 3589. Fabric F28. Combed body sherd. EIA.
57. Pit 3545, ctx 3589. Fabric 28. Burnished pedestal base. EIA.
58. Posthole 3634, ctx 3635. Fabric F29. Form H. EIA.
59. Tree-throw hole 3811, ctx 3813. Fabric F28. Burnished body sherd decorated with incised chevrons. EIA.
60. Tree-throw hole 3811, ctx 3813. Fabric F28. Burnished body sherd with 'tramline' decoration of parallel incised lines and small circular punches. EIA.
61. Tree-throw hole 3811, ctx 3813. Fabric F18. Fingertip-decorated shoulder. EIA.
62. Posthole 3937, ctx 3938. Fabric F29. Rim decorated with incised triangles. EIA.
63. Hollow 4089, ctx 4095. Fabric F28. Burnished rim decorated with incised chevrons. EIA.
64. Hollow 4089, ctx 4095. Fabric 28. Body sherd with applied boss. EIA.
65. Pit 4114, ctx 4115. Fabric F28. Form A? Burnished. Decorated with incised triangles and small circular punches. EIA.
66. Ditch segment 4468 (Enclosure IV), ctx 4469. Fabric F28. Form J. EIA.
67. Ditch 4538, ctx 4537. Fabric F19. Form D. EIA.
68. Eaves-gully segment 4600 (Structure I), ctx 4599. Fabric F29. Fingertip-decorated shoulder. EIA.
69. Pit 4635, ctx 4669. Fabric F18. Form G. Fingernail impressions on front and inner face of rim. EIA.
70. Pit 4757, ctx 4756. Fabric F19. Form I. Decorated with hatched, incised triangles on rim top. Cf. no. 103. EIA.
71. Pit 4844, ctx 4845. Fabric F19. Form J. EIA.
72. Pit 4905, ctx 4904. Fabric F19. Form A or H. Decorated with fingertip impressions on shoulder. EIA.
73. Pit 4905, ctx 4904. Fabric F28. Form H. EIA.
74. Pit 4941, ctx 4942. Fabric F19. Form D. EIA.
75. Pit 4941, ctx 4948. Fabric F19. Form A. EIA.
76. Pit 4964, ctx 4965. Fabric F29. Vertical incisions on inner face of rim. EIA.
77. Pit 4866, ctx 4983. Fabric F29. Form D. Fingernail impressions on rim top. EIA.
78. Pit 4999, ctx 5001. Fabric F19. Form J. EIA.

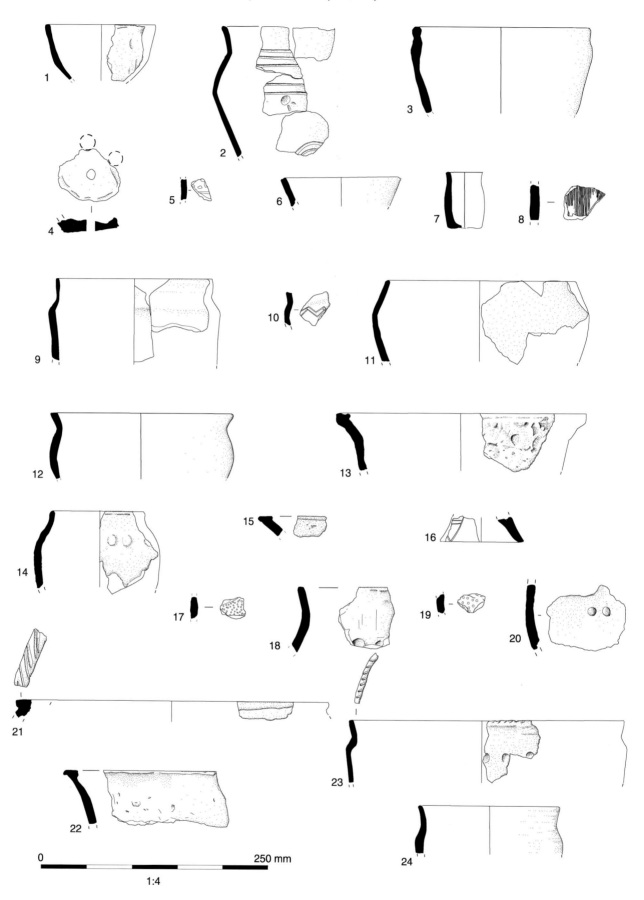

Figure 3.2   Pottery, nos 1–24.

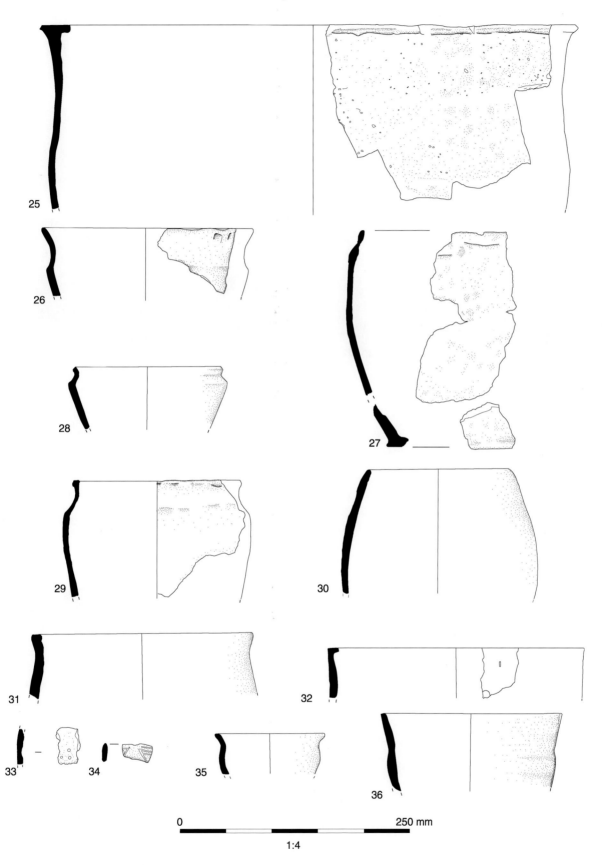

Figure 3.3   Pottery, nos 25–36.

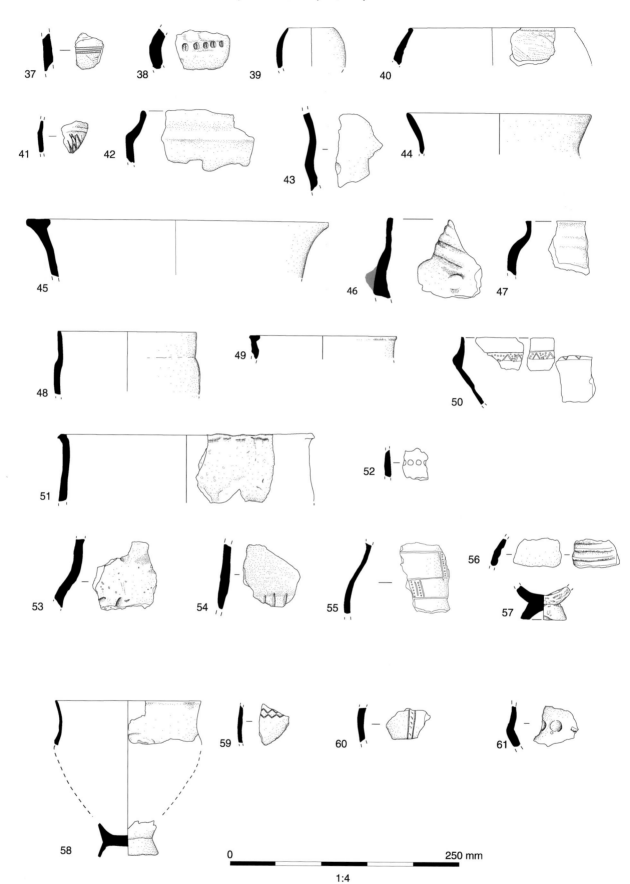

Figure 3.4   Pottery, nos 37–61.

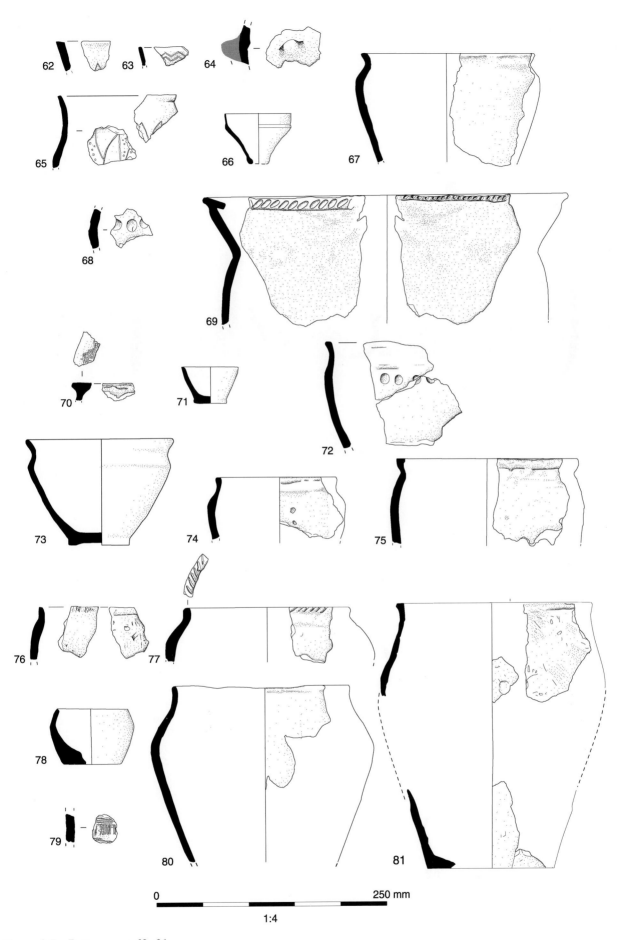

Figure 3.5   Pottery, nos 62–81.

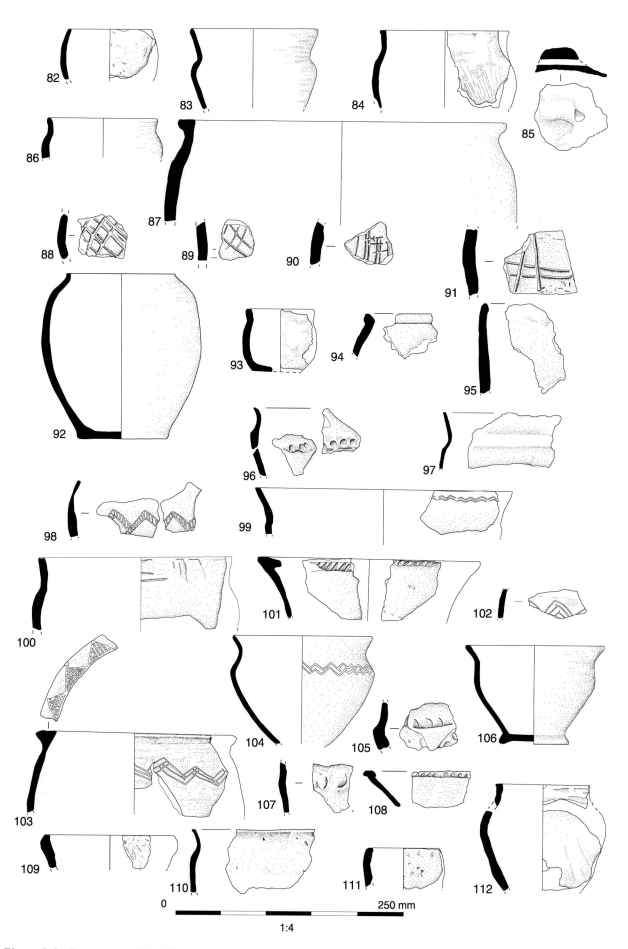

Figure 3.6   Pottery, nos 82–112.

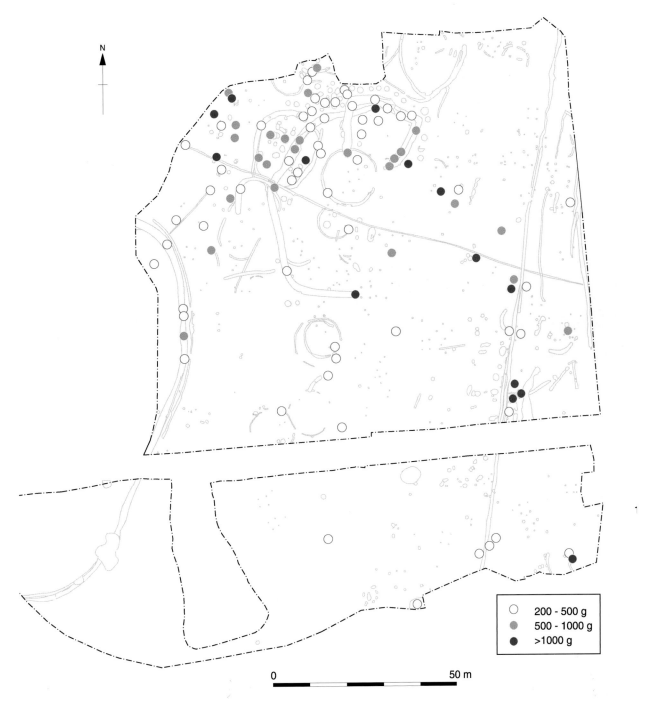

Figure 3.7   Site A. Distribution of pottery by excavated slot.

79. Pit 5068, ctx 5065. Fabric F29. Body sherd decorated with fine combing. EIA.
80. Pit 5137, ctx 5136. Fabric F18. Form D. EIA.
81. Pit 5137, ctx 5136. Fabric F19. Form A. EIA.
82. Pit 5137, ctx 5136. Fabric F19. Form E. EIA.
83. Pit 5137, ctx 5136. Fabric F28. Form H? EIA.
84. Pit 5061, ctx 5161. Fabric F29. Form A. Scratching on body. Charred residue on exterior. EIA.
85. Pit 3285, ctx 3287. Fabric F29. Body sherd with pierced lug. EIA or MIA.
86. Ditch segment 401 (Enclosure I), ctx 404. Fabric F29. EIA or MIA.
87. Ditch segment 431 (Enclosure III), ctx 432. Fabric F20. EIA or MIA

88. Pit 3049, ctx 3053. Fabric F20. Scored body sherd. MIA.
89. Ditch segment 3393 (post-medieval ditch 3130), ctx 3392. Fabric F28. Scored body sherd. MIA.
90. Ditch segment 3905 (Enclosure IV), ctx 3906. Fabric F20. Scored body sherd. MIA.
91. Ditch segment 4683 (Enclosure V), ctx 4710. Fabric F29. Scored body sherd. MIA.
92. Pit 4798, ctx 4800. Fabric F19. MIA.
93. Pit 4997, ctx 4998. Fabric F19. EIA or MIA.
94. Ditch 4695, ctx 4699. Fabric F01B. Burnished. MIA or LIA.

Site B

95. Ditch segment 2186 (Enclosure VIII), ctx 2187. Fabric F32. Straight-walled jar or bowl. LBA?.

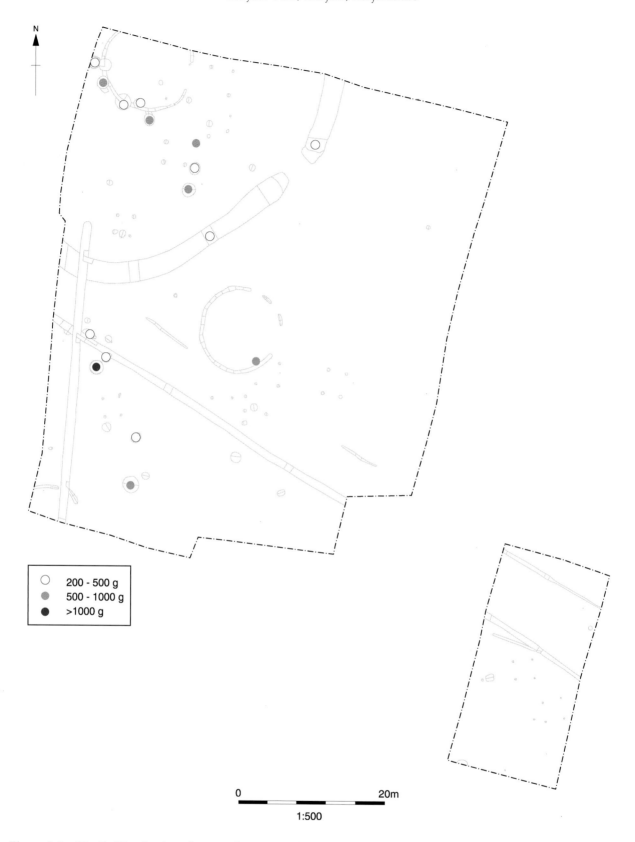

Figure 3.8   Site B. Distribution of pottery by excavated slot.

96. Pit 2043, ctx 2043. Fabric F19. Form D? Fingertip-decorated shoulder. Charred residue on exterior. EIA.
97. Pit 2043, ctx 2043. Fabric F28. Form A or H. Burnished. EIA.
98. Pit 2088, ctx 2090. Fabric F28. Burnished. Decorated with incised triangles. EIA.

99. Posthole 2122, ctx 2121. Fabric F29. Form H. Decorated with incised chevrons. EIA.
100. Pit 2043, ctx 2142. Fabric F29. Form A. EIA.
101. Pit 2043, ctx 2142. Fabric F29. Form G. Decorated with finger-nail impressions on the front and inner face of the rim. EIA.

102. Pit 2043, ctx 2142. Fabric F29. Burnished body sherd decorated with incised chevrons. EIA.
103. Pit 2043, ctx 2142. Fabric F29. Form I. Decorated on rim top with hatched incised triangles, and with incised chevrons on shoulder. Fired to a bright red colour (see Pl. 3.1). EIA.
104. Pit 2043, ctx 2174. Fabric F29. Form H. Black fabric, burnished. Decorated with incised chevrons containing traces of white paste. EIA.
105. Pit 2145, ctx 2153. Fabric F29. Fingernail-decorated shoulder. EIA.
106. Pit 2145, ctx 2158. Fabric F18. Form H. Burnished. EIA.
107. Pit 2227, ctx 2225. Fabric F29. Body sherd with fingertip decoration. EIA.
108. Pit 2227, ctx 2225. Fabric F21. Form G. Decorated with fingernail impressions on the rim front. EIA.
109. Eaves-gully segment 2254 (Structure 34), ctx 2256. Fabric F19. Rounded rim sherd. EIA.
110. Pit 2300, ctx 2306. Fabric F19. Form D? EIA.
111. Pit 2248, ctx 2253. Fabric F29. Form J. Burnished. Charred residue on interior. EIA.
112. Ditch segment 2245 (Enclosure VIII), ctx 2242. Fabric F21. Form D. EIA.

FIRED CLAY
by Emily Edwards

A total of 802 fragments of fired clay (14,934 g) was recovered, nearly all from early Iron Age contexts (Figs 3.9–11). Artefacts include 'loomweights', a partially perforated clay ball and a large, crudely formed 'block'. The remainder of the assemblage comprised structural fired clay and amorphous pieces. The overall quantity and range of fired clay appears fairly typical for a settlement of this period. Notably, however, the fired clay recovered from Site B was dominated by structural clay, while most of the 'loomweights' came from Site A.

Fabrics

The assemblage has been divided into fabrics through the identification of inclusion types, under × 20 magnification. Where applicable, the fabric codes are those explained in the pottery report (Table 3.5).

1. F29. Sandy
2. F20. Calcareous
3. F15. Mixed inclusion, large calcined flint, limestone, chalk, shell, sand
4. F00. Indeterminate
5. Rare inclusions with some voids
6. F19. Sandy organic
7. No inclusions

None of the fabrics appeared to have undergone any process of paste preparation, with many of the inclusions representing naturally occurring materials rather than deliberately added temper. There may have been some association between fabric and object type, as the majority of 'loomweights' were manufactured using Fabric 4 (mixed inclusions), whilst the majority of structural clay was manufactured using Fabric 1 (sandy). All of the fabrics could be of local origin.

'Loomweights'

A total of 107 fragments (4888 g) of a minimum of 13 'loomweights' were recovered from 12 contexts (Table 3.9 and Figs 3.9.1–2 and 3.11). All, apart from one example, came from Site A. Seven were recognisably of triangular form. While objects of this kind have traditionally been interpreted as weights used with vertical looms, it has been argued that they were in fact associated with ovens, perhaps serving as firebricks (Poole 1991, 380).

Most 'loomweights', with the exception of SF 27 from posthole 3101, are represented by small fragments which give little clue as to dimension. It is likely that fragments from posthole 3101 represent two examples, one of which is very large (Fig. 3.9.1) whilst the other has, unusually, two piercings sitting side by side on one face (Fig. 3.9.2). The larger object (SF 27) is not complete, but measures 170 mm long by 68 mm thick. It is a Danebury Type 1 'loomweight', as determined by its weight (main range between 1200–2080 g) and the presence of diagonal piercings through each of the three corners (Poole 1991, 375). The smaller fragment

Table 3.9 'Loomweights' or oven bricks.

Site	Phase	Feature	Context	SF no.	Type	Count	Weight	Fabric
A	2	Pit 156	157	–	LW?	6	194	1
A	2	Pit 411	412	–	LW?	1	606	4
A	2	Posthole 3101	3105	27	TLW	5	2285	4
A	2	Posthole 3101	3105	–	TLW	18	405	4
A	2	Pit 3102	3107	–	TLW?	7	149	2
A	2	Pit 3545	3587	–	LW?	1	21	1
A	2	Tree-throw 3811	3812	–	TLW?	39	645	4
A	2	Pit 4114	4115	–	TLW?	5	166	4
A	2	Pit 4761	4762	–	LW?	13	144	4
A	2	Posthole 5156	5157	–	LW?	9	92	1
A	6	Hedgerow 3125	3516	42	LW	1	11	1
A	–	Buried soil	3074	–	TLW?	1	41	1
B	2	Pit 2138	2139	–	TLW?	1	129	4
Total						107	4888	

LW: 'loomweight', TLW: triangular 'loomweight'

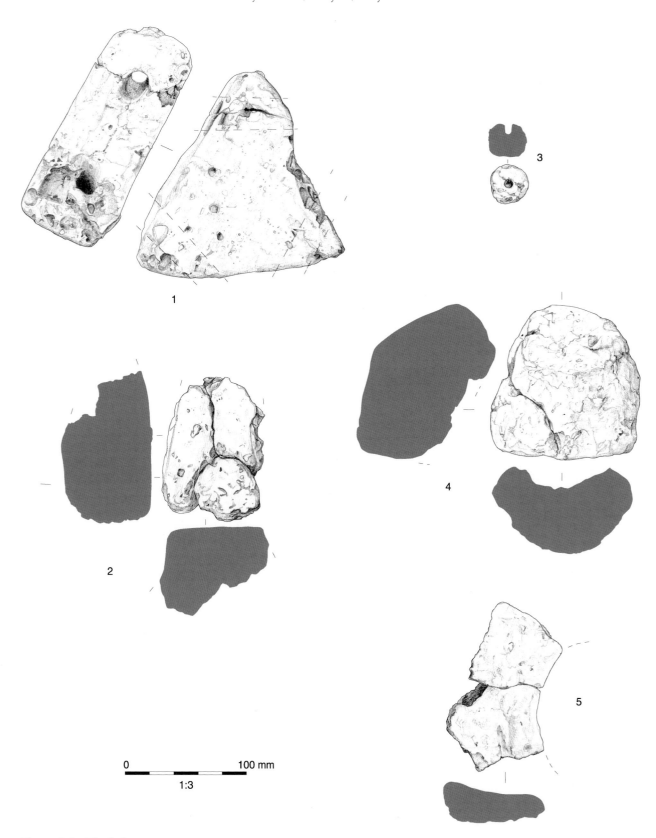

Figure 3.9   Fired clay.

from posthole 3101 could not be paralleled; although there are examples of weights with two piercings on one side, none have two piercings made alongside each other.

Other artefacts

Two further artefacts were identified. The first was a small ball with a partial piercing in Fabric 5

(Fig. 3.9.3), recovered from pit 156 (ctx 157). Similar objects have been found at sites of this period across southern England. Their purpose is unknown, although they are (in appearance) very small ceramic versions of the stone weights from Danebury (Brown 1984, 410–11, figs 7.51–2) with knobs and holes at the top. Poole (1984, 398) suggests that they might be weights for bow drills, or pinheads or pommels.

The second artefact was a large, irregularly cylindrical object with a flat base and rounded top, also in Fabric 5, from pit 314 (Fig. 3.9.4). It is possible that this object is also partially diagonally pierced to a depth of 50 mm; it is difficult to determine whether the original surface still remains, and the hole could equally be the result of damage. The object could perhaps have been a weight of some sort.

Structural fired clay and oven furniture

Some 295 small fragments (5099 g) of structural clay were recovered from 35 contexts, largely pits, of which 118 (1971 g) were from Site A and 177 (3128 g) from Site B (Table 3.10). This notable difference can be accounted for by the large assemblage of 133 fragments (1739 g) from pit 2043 at Site B. The largest assemblage from Site A came from pit 156 (56 pieces, 896 g). The overall distribution of structural fired clay at Site A is shown by Figure 3.10.

Traces of vertical rods were present on many of the fragments, all of which had been fired to a white colour. There were no wiped or convex surfaces, although many flat surfaces were noted. Rather than originating from burnt daub walls, these pieces probably mostly derive from clay ovens.

In addition, some fragments of a possible oven plate were recovered from pit 5110 (Fig. 3.9.5). This had a central perforation of c 150 mm diameter, and can be compared to an example from Harrold, Beds. (Eagles and Evison 1970, fig. 4). Some thick fragments from hollow 3545 may have performed similar functions.

Amorphous fired clay

A total 343 (3352 g) fragments of amorphous fired clay was recovered (Table 3.10). These had no

Table 3.10 Summary of structural and amorphous fired clay.

Fabric	Site A		Site B	
	Structural	Amorphous	Structural	Amorphous
1	57 (1236 g)	74 (779 g)	113 (1792 g)	5 (28 g)
2	22 (507 g)	135 (947 g)	11 (89 g)	–
3	3 (86 g)	112 (1092 g)	53 (1247 g)	–
4	–	10 (43 g)	–	1 (2 g)
5	30 (76 g)	44 (434 g)	–	–
6	6 (66 g)	–	–	–
7	–	1 (27 g)	–	–
Total	118 (1971 g)	377 (3322 g)	177 (3128 g)	6 (30 g)

discernible form or function, but many undoubtedly derive from ovens and hearths used for domestic and craft activities. Most of this material is fired to a reddish-brown colour.

Catalogue of illustrated fired clay (Fig. 3.9)

1 **Triangular 'loomweight'.** 185 mm long. Single piercing at each corner. Fabric 4. Site A, Structure 30, posthole 3101, ctx 3105 (see plan Fig. 2.20). Phase 2. SF 27.
2 **Triangular 'loomweight' fragment.** Two piercings made side by side. Fabric 4. Site A, Structure 30, posthole 3101, ctx 3105 (see plan Fig. 2.20). Phase 2.
3 **Partially pierced ball.** Evenly made 10 mm deep hole, 6 mm diameter. Fabric 8. Site A, pit 156, ctx 157 (see plan Fig. 2.19). Phase 2.
4 **Roughly cylindrical object.** The object has one flat end and one rounded end. Possible 50 mm deep piercing. Fabric 8. Site A, pit 314, ctx 318 (see plan Fig. 2.19). Phase 2.
5 **Possible oven plate fragment.** Circular perforation c 150 mm in diameter. Fabric 2. Site A, pit 5110, ctx 5113 (see plan Fig. 2.18). Phase 2.

WORKED BONE
by Leigh Allen and Leo Webley

A number of worked bone objects were recovered from Phase 2 (early Iron Age) settlement features (Figs 3.12–13). The most notable find was an assemblage of 49 complete or near-complete grooved and polished sheep metapodials, retrieved from a single pit fill at Site A. Other artefacts consisted of a spindle whorl, a 'gouge', a possible tool handle and a possible fastener from Site A, and an antler ring from Site B.

Grooved and polished sheep metapodials

The sheep metapodials were recovered from context 488, a deliberate back-fill deposit midway down pit 484 (see plan Fig. 2.9), containing much charcoal. They consist of 13 metacarpals (8 complete) and 36 metatarsals (15 complete). Two of the complete metacarpals and seven of the complete metatarsals were unfused. The length of the complete examples ranged from 82–129 mm, with a mean of 113 mm. The bones appear to have been scorched before they were deposited.

All of these objects have areas of polish on the shaft, which often also show transverse wear striations (Pls 3.2–3). This wear most frequently occurs on the sides of the shaft, and exclusively so in the case of the metacarpals. As noted on examples from other Iron Age sites, the wear is often concentrated in bands 10–20 mm across and up to 70 mm apart on opposite sides of the bone (Britnell 2000a). In some cases the high degree of wear on either side of the bone has caused a slight narrowing of the shaft at the distal and proximal ends, although this is not as marked as examples recovered from Danebury and Meare Village East where relatively deep V-shaped grooves are present (Sellwood 1984, fig. 7.37.3.188; Coles 1987, fig. 361). One metatarsal

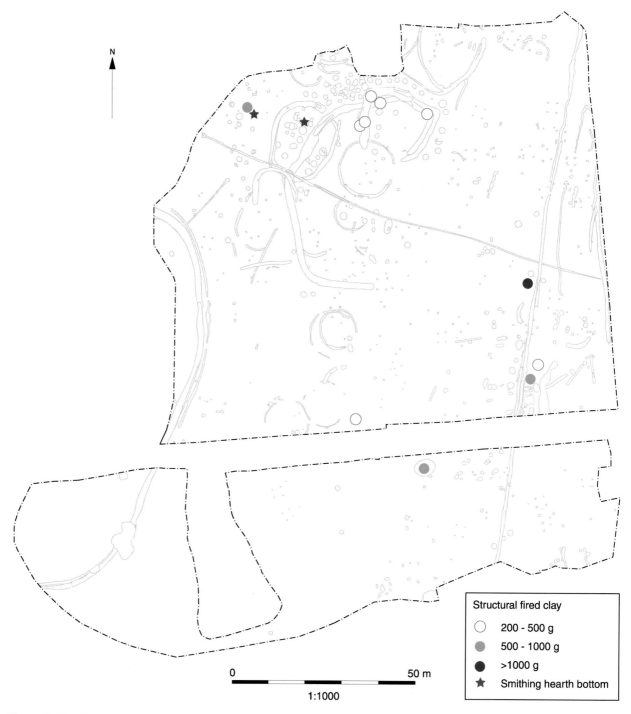

Figure 3.10   Site A. Distribution of structural fired clay and smithing hearth bottoms.

has an area on the upper face of the shaft with very definite fine cuts or grooves rather than striations. Under a microscope the polish can be seen to extend all the way to the base of the groove.

It has been suggested elsewhere that objects of this kind were either bobbins for yarn (Sellwood 1984, 392) or were used with a loom (Britnell 2000a, 186). The marks on the Fairfield Park examples could have been made by a very fine thread being pulled across a fairly fresh bone with some considerable force or under a great deal of tension. However, it is difficult

to imagine this being done repeatedly in the same spot by the same thread in order to cause the amount of wear that exists on these bones. Is it possible that fine grooves were initially cut with a knife and subsequently worn smooth by the action of the thread.

These objects are regularly found in small numbers on Iron Age sites across the country but an assemblage of this size from a single context is unparalleled. The deposition of a large number in a single pit fill suggests that they derive from a single event such as the disposal of a complete loom.

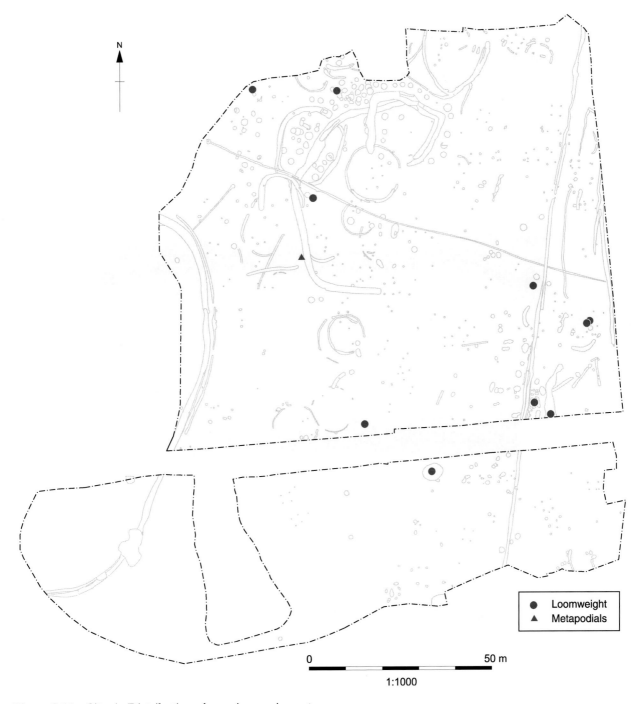

Figure 3.11   Site A. Distribution of weaving equipment.

Other objects (Fig. 3.12)

1   **Possible tool handle.** Object with an oval section, carved with a raised band at either end. Made from a large mammal rib. Possibly a handle from a knife or similar tool; although the narrower end of the object is damaged, it shows hints of a slot to receive the tang. Site A, pit 3111, ctx 3113. Phase 2.

2   **'Gouge'.** Implement made from a horse tibia that has been chopped obliquely at the distal end, and shaped to a flattened point at the tip. Both the upper and lower faces of the tip are worn smooth through use. The tool has broken at the proximal end. Objects of similar form are common on Iron Age sites, being typically referred to as 'gouges' or as pin-beaters for use with a loom (Sellwood 1984; Britnell 2000b). However, they are usually made from sheep or goat long bones, and are

hence smaller than this example. Site A, Enclosure ditch V, ctx 4679. Phase 2.

3   **Spindle whorl.** A flattened sphere with a drilled perforation, made from the pelvis of a large mammal. Site A, Enclosure ditch III, ctx 4951. Phase 2.

4   **Possible toggle/fastener.** Object made from a large mammal rib. The bone has been cut at each end to form a rectangle (one end is rather roughly cut) and has then been polished all over. There are two circular 'hourglass' perforations, drilled from both sides. One face carries shallow, transverse incisions at either end and between the two perforations, which could be a crude attempt at ornamentation. Similar objects have been found at a number of Iron Age sites, including Chinnor, Oxon (early Iron Age; Richardson and Young 1951, pl. 19b.7), East Stagsden, Beds (middle Iron Age; Dawson 2000b,

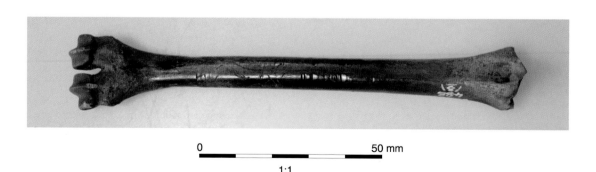

0 ──────── 50 mm

1:1

Plate 3.2   Sheep/goat metatarsal weaving tools from pit 484.

Plate 3.3 Sheep/goat metacarpal weaving tools from pit 484.

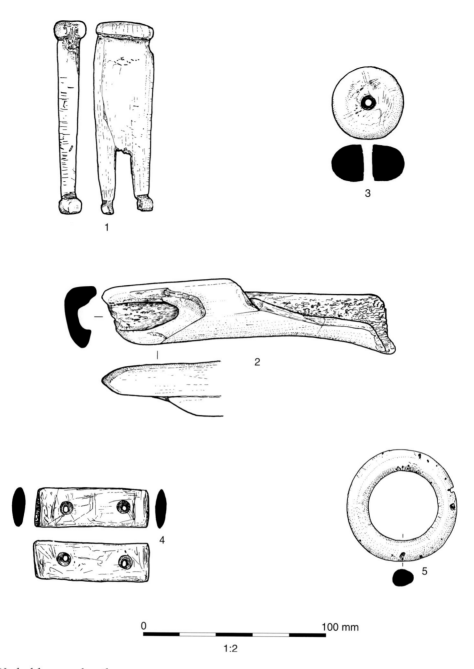

0   100 mm

1:2

Figure 3.12   Worked bone and antler.

fig. 60.138), Barley, Herts (middle Iron Age; Cra'ster 1960, pl. 9, p and q), Weekley, Northants (Jackson and Dix 1987, fig. 27.66), Meare, Somerset (Gray 1966, pl. 55, B41) and Danebury, Hants (Sellwood 1984, fig. 7.39.3.210). Site A, ctx 5049, pit 5041. Phase 2.

5   **Ring.** Oval-sectioned ring made from the burr of an antler, probably from a red deer. The object is very well finished and smoothed all over; no use-wear is apparent. This artefact cannot be closely paralleled and its function is obscure. Site B, ctx 2171, pit 2043. Phase 2.

WORKED STONE
by Ruth Shaffrey

An extensive assemblage of 200 stone items was recovered, including 25 worked objects consisting of 13 probable saddle querns, 4 rotary querns,

4 whetstones, 2 processors, 1 possible mould and 1 probable floor stone. In addition, some lava fragments possibly from a quern came from Site B. The remainder of the assemblage comprised burnt or heat-cracked stones and pebbles, which occurred widely across the site. They are likely to have been collected from the Letchworth Gravel, a deposit that occurs around the site (Hopson *et al.* 1996, 77).

Querns

Saddle querns

As typical for a site of this period, a number of saddle querns were found: four definite examples

86

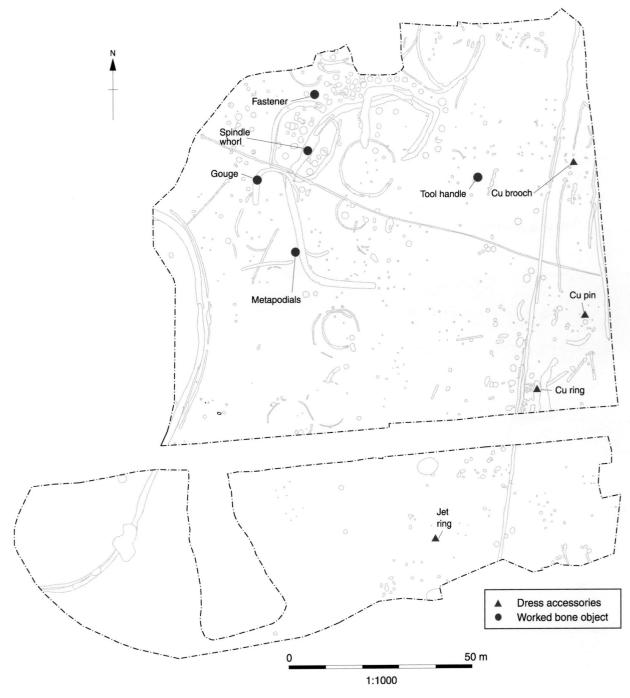

Figure 3.13   Site A. Distribution of worked bone objects and dress accessories.

and nine probable fragments. All but one of these were from Site A. Saddle querns can occur as either formed examples, shaped and dressed on all surfaces, or unformed examples, utilising large chunks of unshaped stones or boulders. Both types of saddle quern were found at Fairfield Park although most of the unformed specimens, made from boulders, show some attempt to dress their rough surfaces (eg SF 1). One example (SF 22: Fig. 3.14.4) has been extremely well used on both faces and one example is complete (SF 4: Fig. 3.14.1).

Most of the saddle querns were recovered from pits or postholes and were contemporary with the main phase of settlement.

The saddle querns were made from sandstone and Greensand, along with a single example (SF 22) probably made from sarsen. None of the Greensand querns can be attributed to the well-known sources at Lodsworth in Sussex (Peacock 1986) and Folkestone in Kent (Keller 1988), and their origin is unclear. The nearest local source of Greensand lies *c* 8 km to the north-west.

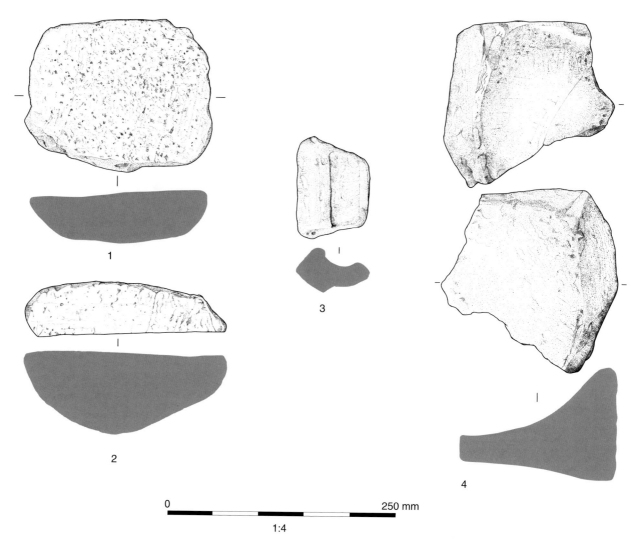

Figure 3.14   Worked stone.

Catalogue

1   **Saddle quern fragment, unformed.** Fine-grained, slightly micaceous, well-sorted, pink sandstone. The grinding surface has been finely pecked but is worn smooth and is quite flat. Made from a boulder but dressed all over. Base is slightly thicker on one side. Well-worn on all the edges including the burnt and broken ones. Measures 170 mm wide × 220 mm remaining length × 40–77 mm max thickness. Site A, Structure 1, eaves-gully fill 29 (see plan Fig. 2.12). Phase 2. SF 1.

2   **Complete saddle quern, formed (Fig. 3.14.1).** Probable Greensand. Worked round the edges to form shape. Finely pecked all over with slightly concave grinding surface. Measures 222 mm long × 160 mm wide × 48 mm max thickness. Site A, pit 194 (see plan Fig. 2.12). Phase 2. SF 4.

3   **Saddle quern fragment, formed.** Fine to medium-grained well-sorted Greensand. Slightly concave grinding surface has been worked but has worn smooth in patches and is scratched. Base is roughly worked. Measures 230 mm wide × 155 mm length remaining × 88 mm max thickness. Site A, Structure 29, posthole 223, ctx 225 (see plan 2.12). Phase 2. SF 5.

4   **Probable saddle quern fragment.** Orange feldspathic sandstone. One curved edge which is pecked. Site A, pit 352 (recut of pit 348), ctx 355 (see plan Fig. 2.19). Phase 2.

5   **Probable saddle quern fragment.** Medium-grained well-sorted slightly pink sandstone. Grinding surface is flat and pecked. Burnt. Measures 160 × 130 × 95 mm. Site A, pit 3111, ctx 3112 (see plan Fig. 2.3). Phase 2. SF 29.

6   **Crude grinding stone or unformed saddle quern.** Cream/pink red banded medium-grained quartz sandstone. Boulder, not shaped but with flat worked surface. Heavily burnt and blackened on exposed surfaces. Measures 210 ×>120 × 60 mm. Site A, Structure 16, posthole 3121, ctx 3122. Phase 2. SF 30.

7   **Probable saddle quern fragments.** Medium-grained reddish well-sorted quartz sandstone. One pecked and slightly concave surface. Burnt. Site A, hollow 3545, ctx 3587 (see plan Fig. 2.22). Phase 2. SF 48.

8   **Probable saddle quern fragment, unformed.** Fine- to medium-grained, well-rounded and well-sorted pink quartz sandstone, slightly micaceous. One worked, flat and smoothed surface on a cobble. Measures 75 mm thick. Site A, posthole 4012, ctx 4011. Phase 2? (no associated datable finds). SF 99.

9   **Slab-shaped, unformed saddle quern.** Cream to pink medium-grained well-sorted sandstone. Large chunk of stone with one slightly concave worked and smoothed surface. Burnt. Site A, pit 4565, ctx 4573 (see plan Fig. 2.13). Phase 2. SF 144.

10   **Probable saddle quern fragment, unformed.** Medium-grained well-sorted Greensand. One curved face which is pecked and worn and one shaped edge. Measures 53 mm thick. Site A, unstratified. SF 153.

11   **Quarter of unformed saddle quern (Fig. 3.14.4).** Probable sarsen. Utilises a natural boulder but is well worked. Very well used with extremely concave faces on both sides. Both grinding surfaces pecked but worn very smooth. Edge is

almost vertical and indicates it was made from a boulder or large cobble. Blackened from burning on one side. Measures at least 210 mm wide and varies from 30 to 120 mm thick. Site B, pit 2043, ctx 2045 (see plan Fig. 2.31). Phase 2. SF 22.

Rotary querns

Five rotary quern fragments, of which two are adjoining, were recovered from a single pit fill (fill 4573, pit 4565; see plan Fig. 2.13 and Pl. 2.3). Three upper stones and one lower probably represent three querns in total, as SF 143 and 141 appear to be matching upper and lower stones. None of the querns are complete, although nearly 80% of the lower stone survives, and all appear to have been utilised prior to deposition. At least three of the querns had been burnt prior to deposition, and had probably been reused as 'pot-boilers' in the clay-lined pit in which they were found. One of them also showed evidence of reuse as a rubbing stone across its rim.

All the rotary querns are examples of the earliest type in this region—the pierced (Hunsbury) beehive quern—and although not particularly thick they are comparable to querns from Hunsbury itself (Ingle 1994). The querns vary tremendously in their quality of workmanship. One specimen (SF 141: Fig. 3.15.2) is particularly well worked and appears to have been deliberately broken in half. It is precisely in the style of Hunsbury querns (Ingle 1994, 23, fig. 1.5) with rounded pecked edges, flat top and grinding surface, large hopper and circular handle slot. Upper stone SF 145/147 is much more crudely made and appears to have had an oval-shaped handle slot as would be expected for the type of stone it is made from (see below; Ingle 1994, 30). The lower stone (SF 143: Fig. 3.15.1) retains the original shape of the boulder from which it was made, but is typical of beehive querns being thick with a narrow spindle socket.

Two of the rotary querns (SF 142 and SF 145/147) are made from a yellowish grey Greensand, consisting almost entirely of quartz grains in a calcite cement but dotted with small black grains of glauconite. This is probably Spilsby Sandstone from Lincolnshire, a rock type which was not commonly used but which is known to occur in the surrounding counties of Northamptonshire, Cambridgeshire and Hertfordshire (Ingle 1994, 30). The remaining rotary querns are made of cream to pink coloured, fine- to medium-grained quartz sandstones containing varying levels of mica and haematite. The sample chosen for thin section (SF 143) revealed a densely compacted rock with little porosity, some quartz cement and the occasional rock fragment. A source for this rock is unknown, but given that a number of the items are clearly made from boulders (eg SF 1, SF 22, SF 30) a nearby source in the form of glacial erratics is possible.

Catalogue

12 **Incomplete lower beehive rotary quern (Fig. 3.15.1).** Medium-grained cream and pink quartz sandstone containing plentiful haematite and muscovite mica. Made from a boulder or knobbly outcrop. 80% survives but only 20% of circumference.

Flat, pecked grinding surface and circular socket. Might be a pair with upper stone 141. Measures *c* 326 mm diameter × 145 mm thick. Site A, pit 4565, ctx 4573. Phase 2. SF 143.

13 **Half an upper beehive rotary quern of pierced (Hunsbury) type (Fig. 3.15.2).** Medium-grained well-sorted slightly mottled sandstone containing some shells and mica. Well-made beehive quern with hopper taking up most of upper surface, circular handle slot piercing the feed pipe, and flat upper and grinding surfaces. Deliberately broken in half and not along the handle slot. Might be a pair with lower stone 143. Measures 280 mm diameter (220 mm diameter on top) × 160 mm thick. Site A, pit 4565, ctx 4573. Phase 2. SF 141.

14 **Upper beehive rotary quern fragment.** Spilsby Sandstone. Grinding surface is very slightly concave. Conical hopper narrows into cylindrical eye. Sides are mostly straight and lead into a flat top. Site A, pit 4565, ctx 4573. Phase 2. SF 142.

15 **Upper beehive rotary quern of pierced (Hunsbury) type (Fig. 3.15.3).** Spilsby Sandstone. Crudely made with probable flat grinding surface. Handle slot is wide and oval and pierces the feed pipe. In two fragments. Measures >250 mm diameter × >120 mm thick. Site A, pit 4565, ctx 4573. Phase 2. SF 145/147.

Undiagnostic quern fragments

Possible quern fragments of uncertain form were recovered from two contexts. The lava fragments from early Iron Age posthole 2353 might be assumed to be intrusive, but lava has now been recorded from Iron Age contexts at a few sites in the region, most locally at Blackhorse Road, Letchworth (Moss-Eccardt 1988, 100). The possible quern fragment from gully 3130 is in a medieval/post-medieval context and is hence presumably residual.

Catalogue

16 **Possible quern fragment.** Has one worked surface. Site A, gully 3130, ctx 3242. Phase 6. SF 31.
17 **Probable quern fragments.** Lava. Very weathered and small fragments of lava. Probably from querns but no worked surfaces survive. Site B, Structure 38, posthole 2353, ctx 2354 (see plan Fig. 2.30). Phase 2.

Discussion of quern assemblage

The quern assemblage from Fairfield Park is of broad ranging interest because it includes good examples of both saddle and rotary querns of different qualities and lithologies in well-dated contexts. The rotary querns are of particular interest because it is fairly unusual to recover them from closely dated early Iron Age contexts. The rotary quern is generally believed to have been introduced in Britain during the middle Iron Age but the transition was lengthy, the changeover varied regionally and the rotary quern did not become ubiquitous until the early Roman period.

The Fairfield Park rotary querns were all found in a single pit dated by pottery to around the 5th–4th centuries BC (Fig. 3.16). This is in line with the evidence from Danebury which suggests a 4th century BC date for the introduction of the rotary quern (Brown 1984, 418) and that from Gussage All Saints which suggested a 5th century BC date (Buckley 1979, 91). One of the querns had been reutilised as a rubbing stone, suggesting that it had

Figure 3.15   Rotary querns.

Table 3.11 Querns from early to middle Iron Age sites in the region around Fairfield Park.

Site	County	Distance from Fairfield Park (km)	Rotary querns	Saddle querns
Fairfield Park	Beds.	–	4	13
Puddlehill	Beds.	20	3	16
Barley	Herts.	21	2 (M-LIA)	11
Biddenham Loop	Beds.	24	0	>1
Pennyland	Bucks.	35	0	3 (IA)
Bancroft	Bucks.	38	1	1

been used for its original function some reasonable length of time prior to deposition. The early date of the Fairfield Park rotary querns, whilst being in line with evidence nationally, makes them the earliest dated examples in the region (Table 3.11). Excavations at Groveland Way/Norton Road, Stotfold, have produced rotary querns only from late Iron Age and Romano-British contexts (Holly Duncan pers. comm.). Rotary querns were found at Puddlehill (20 km south-west) in pits dated to the middle Iron Age onwards, but all earlier pits contained only saddle querns (Matthews 1976). At Aldwick, Barley, (21 km north-east) rotary querns were found in middle to late Iron Age pits (Cra'ster 1960, 35, fig. 6.7 and 6.12) and at Bancroft (38 km west) a single rotary quern was excavated from a middle Iron Age context (Tyrell 1994, 370, fig. 194).

The two Spilsby sandstone rotary querns are of added interest because very few dated examples appear to be known, the nearest being two middle to late Iron Age examples from Barley (Ingle 1994; Cra'ster 1960, 35). These examples suggest not only that the stone was exploited from the very introduction of the rotary quern, but that it was distributed over some distance.

Despite the early date of the rotary querns, and their single deposition event, they represent more than just a single, possibly accidental, acquisition. Whilst all being of the pierced beehive quern type, they originated in at least two different source areas and are of very different qualities of workmanship. Their presence on the site at such an early date may suggest an element of high status to those who were able to acquire rotary querns so early, from more than one source (at least one from some distance), and also to discard so many in one deposit. There was generally little remarkable about the way most saddle querns were deposited. An exception to this is a single complete unburnt saddle quern (SF 4) that was found in the upper fill of pit 194, a cylindrical feature containing abundant charcoal and burnt stone. The quern appeared to have been added as a separate disposal, which may imply a 'special' treatment of the pit.

Whetstones

Several stones demonstrate signs of wear indicative of use as whetstones. Three are 'natural' whetstones,

utilising naturally occurring pieces of stone, although one of them also makes use of a discarded rubber (SF 132: Fig. 3.14.2). A fourth example is a classic cigar-shaped whetstone (SF 136) of Roman date. The source of the ferruginous sandstone used for this object is not clear, although bands of ferruginous sandstone are sometimes associated with Greensand.

Catalogue

18 **Whetstone, natural.** Fine-grained slightly micaceous sandstone. Elongate and flat, wide whetstone, worn on all surfaces but with diagonal wear on one face from use as a whetstone. Very burnt and blackened on two faces. Measures 103 × 62 × 17 mm. Site A, pit 484, ctx 485 (see plan Fig. 2.9). Phase 2. SF 7.

19 **Secondary whetstone and possible rubber (Fig. 3.14.2).** Fine- to medium-grained slightly micaceous pink sandstone. Half a large rubber, broken almost exactly in half with broken edge flattened out and used as a whetstone. Measures 215 × 85 × 53 mm. Site A, Structure 14, posthole fill 4164 (see plan Fig. 2.3). Phase 2. SF 132.

20 **Primary whetstone.** Coarse-grained, poorly-sorted ferruginous sandstone. Cigar-shaped whetstone with clear grooves running across the broken end. Datable to the Roman period. Measures 55 (remaining) × 25 × 15 mm. Gully 4360, ctx 4324 (see plan Fig. 2.36). Phase 4. SF 136.

21 **Secondary slab whetstone.** Medium-grained well-sorted cream and pink quartz sandstone. Slab of stone used as a whetstone on one side, which is worn smooth and has some grooves. Otherwise, not shaped. Also heavily burnt. Measures 180 × 130 × 45 mm. Enclosure I, ditch 4490, ctx 4355. Phase 1 or 2. SF 138.

Other utilised stone

Other artefacts include two processors, one a probable flint knapper (2270) and one a muller (4902), and a small unworked ironstone sphere (2089) ideal for use as a sling shot. One final object worthy of note is a very unusual worked piece of ferruginous sandstone (SF 21). This is a very hard stone that would have been difficult to work but which resembles nothing naturally occurring. The item appears to be incomplete but consists of curved inner and outer edges with straight rim (Fig. 3.14.3). The inside of the object demonstrates some scratch marks and unusual deposits, and although the function of the item is unclear it may have formed part of a mould.

Catalogue

22 **Possible flint knapper.** Medium-grained red sandstone. Large pebble with wear at both ends. Site B, Structure 35, eaves-gully fill 2270 (see plan Fig. 2.30). Phase 2

23 **Possible floor stone.** Greensand. Naturally flat but worked on one face. Measures 236 × 135 × 25 mm. Site A, pit 3049, ctx 3052 (see plan Fig. 2.8). Phase 2.

24 **Muller.** Possible Greensand. Hand-sized cobble with wear marks. Heavily worn and weathered through burning. Site A, pit 4886, ctx 4902 (see plan Fig. 2.8). Phase 2

25 **Sphere.** Ironstone. Small ironstone sphere; unworked. Measures 24 mm diameter. Site B, pit 2088, ctx 2089 (see plan Fig. 2.31). Phase 2

26 **Possible mould (Fig. 3.14.3).** Ferruginous sandstone. Curved piece of arch with curved inner and outer edges of uniform thickness. Curve leading into straight side at the bottom and

Figure 3.16   Site A. Distribution of querns.

flat base. Measures 24 mm thick. SF 21. Site B, pit 2300, ctx 2307 (see plan Fig. 2.29). Phase 2

JET
by Leo Webley

A single fragment from a jet artefact (SF 51) was recovered from the upper fill (3631) of early Iron Age pit 3630 (see plan Fig. 2.3). The object takes the form of an oval-sectioned ring (internal diameter *c* 20 mm) with a domed expansion on the outer side (Fig. 3.17.6). It resembles a finger ring, although it seems rather too bulky to have been worn in this way. While the function of the object is thus uncertain, it may perhaps have been some form of pendant. Although no close parallels can be cited, annular jet objects identified as finger rings, earrings or pendants have occasionally been recovered from Iron Age sites, including settlements and the East Yorkshire inhumation cemeteries (Field and Parker Pearson 2003, 111). A radiocarbon determination of 350–310 cal BC/210–90 cal BC has been obtained on charred grain from the fill from which the artefact was recovered (NZA-21957: 2137 ± 25 BP).

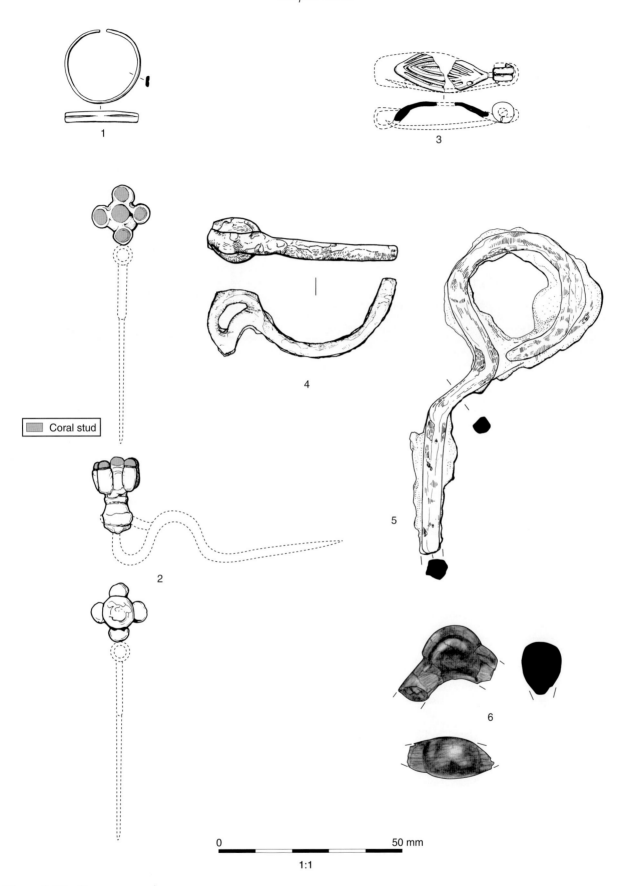

Coral stud

Figure 3.17   Dress accessories.

METALWORK
by Leigh Allen and Leo Webley
with additional information from Valery Rigby
and Ian Stead

Nine metal objects were recovered from later prehistoric contexts. The earliest was a copper alloy awl from a late Bronze Age pit. Early Iron Age settlement features produced six objects; most of these were dress accessories, including a brooch, a finger/toe ring, a ring-headed pin and the terminal from an involuted pin with coral studs. An iron 'poker' was also found, which had been deliberately bent prior to deposition. The latest object was a La Tène involuted brooch, from a stratigraphically late ditch fill ascribed to the middle Iron Age.

Dress accessories (Fig. 3.17)

1   **Ring**. Simple penannular copper alloy ring with a rectangular section and an incised groove running around the outside. The ring is very worn and smooth. One terminal is rounded; the other appears broken across. Site A, ctx 3249, upper fill of pit 3195 (see plan Fig. 2.20). Phase 2.
    Associated dating evidence: a large quantity of early Iron Age pottery was recovered from the pit fill (eg Fig. 3.2.24).

2   **Pin terminal**. Broken terminal from an involuted copper alloy pin, with five settings containing hemispherical coral studs. The settings are symmetrically arranged as a square with a central stud. The coral is now a pale pinkish white but there are traces of colour/adhesive at the junction of the studs and copper alloy, which may reflect the means by which they were secured in place. Probably made as a single casting. Below the head is a collared bead and a trace of the pin shaft just surviving, which would have had a U-shaped bend. Originally the pin would have had a bracing angle which probably also contained a stud. Site A, ctx 3106, upper fill of pit 3274 (see plan Fig. 2.20 and section Fig. 2.21). Phase 2. SF 26.
    Associated dating evidence: 19 sherds of early Iron Age pottery were recovered from the same pit fill.
    Parallels: A direct parallel for this pin has been found at Ludford Camp, Lincs, by a metal detectorist (Fig. 3.18; British Museum acc. 1998.6–2, no. 1). This pin is complete but has lost the coral studs. The dimensions of the pin match exactly with the head from Fairfield to the extent that it seems likely that they originate from the same workshop. Such pins are relatively rare, but another broadly parallel type with coral studs was recovered from the Thames at Hammersmith (British Museum 1925, fig. 108).

3   **Brooch**. Broken and corroded fragments from the leaf-shaped bow of a copper alloy La Tène I brooch (Hull type IBc: Hull and Hawkes 1987). Decorated with a central pointed oval groove and a narrow groove to each side (vesica-shaped ornament). There is also a small fragment of the spring surviving. Datable to the 4th–3rd century BC. Site A, ctx 3575, posthole 3574 (south-east posthole of Structure 17b). Phase 2. SF 44.
    Associated dating evidence: six sherds of Iron Age pottery were recovered from the posthole.
    Parallels: Hull and Hawkes 1987, nos 2931 (Barrington, Cambs) and 3899 (Saham Toney, Norfolk); British Museum 1925, fig. 98 (stray find recovered from Thames); Hattatt 1989, 14, fig. 4, no 1447 (Belton, Norfolk); Harding 1972, 171, pl. 74E (Woodeaton, Oxon); Parrington 1978, 78–80, fig. 59.11 (Abingdon, Oxon).

4   **Brooch**. Catch plate and bow of an iron La Tène involuted brooch (Hull and Hawkes 1987, type 2Ca British type), introduced in the late 3rd century BC. It is unclear whether there was decoration on the catch plate. Site A, ctx 4677, upper fill of ditch 4460 (Enclosure V). Phase 3. SF 148.
    Associated dating evidence: eight sherds of early Iron Age pottery and five sherds of early to middle Iron Age pottery were recovered from the ditch fill.

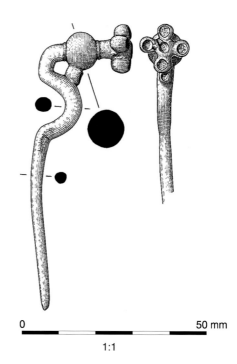

0   50 mm
1:1

Figure 3.18   Copper alloy involuted pin from Ludford, Lincolnshire. Drawn by Stephen Crummy. Reproduced courtesy of the British Museum.

Parallels: Iron examples similar to this are common in the East Yorkshire inhumation cemeteries (Stead 1991); see also Hattatt 2000, 289, fig. 148.229 (Maiden Bradley, Wilts); Harding 1972, 171, pl. 74, M, N and P (Beckley and Woodeaton, Oxon).

5   **Ring-headed pin**. Iron pin with a square section and a penannular head; the tip of the pin is missing. Ring-headed pins are fairly rare finds from Iron Age settlement contexts, and are more often made of copper alloy than iron. Most seem to date to the early Iron Age, although there was some continuity into the middle Iron Age (Dunning 1935; Rigby 2004, 49–50). Site B, ctx 2360, upper fill of bell-shaped pit 2327 (see plan Fig. 2.29). Phase 2. SF 24.
    Associated dating evidence: The pit fill contained significant amounts of early Iron Age pottery. It lay stratigraphically above fill 2333, which produced a radiocarbon determination of 730–690 cal BC/540–380 cal BC (NZA-22005: 237640 BP).
    Parallels: Locally, an iron ring-headed pin has been found at Wilbury hillfort (Applebaum 1949, fig. 15.7). Within the wider Chiltern region, three similar iron ring-headed pins were recovered from the settlement at Chinnor, Oxon, in association with early Iron Age pottery akin to that from Fairfield Park (Richardson and Young 1951, fig. 10.1–3).

Tools and other objects (Fig. 3.19)

1   **Awl**. Small copper alloy awl with a rectangular section, tapering to a point at either end. One of the points is damaged. Typical of the middle to late Bronze Age, although examples from closely dated contexts are rare (see Needham 1986 for a full discussion of the type). Site A, ctx 4251, pit 4250 (see plan Fig. 2.1). Phase 1. SF 135.

2   **Tapering strip**. Rectangular-sectioned tapering iron strip, broken at wider end. Probably the tang of a knife or similar tool. Site A, ctx 154, upper fill of bell-shaped pit 153 (see plan Fig. 2.12). Phase 2. SF 3.

3   **'Poker'**. Iron implement with a spatulate head and a long rectangular-sectioned tang or handle. The tang has been deliberately bent over itself prior to deposition, and now lies

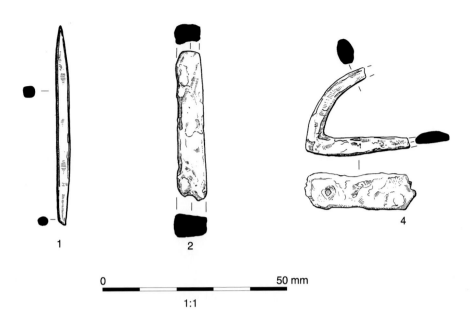

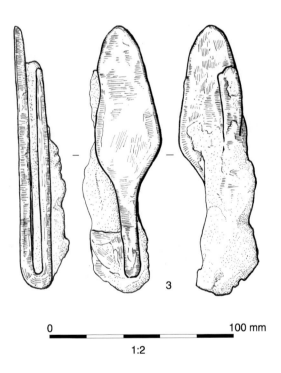

Figure 3.19   Metal tools.

across the back of the head. Artefacts of this type are traditionally described as 'pokers', and may perhaps have served as smith's rakes (Rodwell 1976; MacDonald 2005). Work by Vanessa Fell (cited by MacDonald 2005) has shown that they date from around the 4th century BC through to the Romano-British period. Two main form categories can be distinguished: those with looped ends to the tang, and those without. The Fairfield Park example appears to fall into the latter category, although at *c* 170 mm long, the tang is rather shorter than normal and could thus be broken. Site A, ctx 161, middle fill of flat-based pit 156 (see plan Fig. 2.19). Phase 2. SF 2.

Associated dating evidence: substantial amounts of early Iron Age pottery came from this fill and others within the pit (eg Fig. 3.2.9–10).

Parallels: Within the region, six pokers of similar form were found at Hunsbury hillfort, Northants, though no contextual information is available (George 1917, pl. 14.3–4; Fell 1936, 67, pl. IVb.3).

4   **Fitting?** Fragment from a D-shaped iron object. The straight edge has a flat back designed to be fixed to a flat surface, and the remains of a copper alloy rivet can be discerned at one end. Site A, ctx 3053, pit 3049, pit row 3530 (see plan Fig. 2.8). Phase 2 or 3. SF 101.

Table 3.12   Smithing hearth bottoms.

Site	Feature	Context	Weight (g)	Length (mm)	Breadth (mm)	Depth (mm)	Comment
A	Pit 4635	4634	124	75	60	25	
A	Pit 4996	4994	240	90	70	35	Part missing
B	Ditch 2310	2187	258	80	65	35	

SLAG
by Lynne Keys

A small quantity (just over 1 kg) of iron slag and other high temperature debris was recovered, mostly from Site A and virtually all from Phase 2 contexts. The material was visually examined and categorised on the basis of morphology. Each slag type in each context was weighed but smithing hearth bottoms were weighed individually and measured to obtain their dimensions. Additionally a magnet was run through the soil in bags to detect micro-slags such as hammerscale.

Much of the assemblage consisted of either small fragments of undiagnostic iron slag or material such as vitrified hearth lining, cinder (the more highly fired portion of vitrified hearth lining) and fuel ash slag. The latter materials may be the result of a variety of high temperature activities—including domestic fires—and cannot be taken on their own to indicate that iron-working was taking place. The fuel ash slag could even have originated from the accidental burning down of buildings.

The diagnostic iron slag represented smithing activity. Three plano-convex smithing hearth bottoms were recovered from early Iron Age features, two from Site A and one from Site B. It may be

Table 3.13   Summary of slag (other than smithing hearth bottoms) from Phase 2 features.

	Weight (g)	
	Site A	Site B
Vitrified hearth lining	45	–
Fuel ash slag	28	–
Cinder	29	–
Undiagnostic	236	72
Total	338	72

significant that the two hearth bottoms from Site A were found in pits located close together in the north-western corner of the excavated area (Fig. 3.10), while a third pit in the same area (5110) contains charcoal suggested by Thompson and Francis (Chapter 5) to be consistent with iron working waste. However, no hammerscale (a smithing micro-slag which remains mainly in the immediate area of smithing) was recovered from the site.

The slag from early Iron Age features is summarised by Tables 3.12 and 3.13. A complete listing of the slag can be found in the site archive.

Chapter 4: Osteological Evidence

HUMAN BONE
by Annsofie Witkin

The human skeletal remains from Site A consist of one cremation, two articulated skeletons, two partial but disarticulated skeletons, and four individual disarticulated bones (Fig. 4.1). At Site B, there were two cremations, one partial disarticulated skeleton and a single disarticulated bone. The cremations are believed to date to the late Bronze Age (Phase 1), on the grounds of a radiocarbon determination obtained for burial 2094. The remaining human material is thought to belong to the early Iron Age (Phase 2).

Methodology

The human skeletal and cremated remains were analysed according to the recording standards set out by Brickley and McKinley (2004). Completeness of skeletal remains was scored using four categories, namely poor (0–25%), fair (26–50%) good (51–75%) and excellent (76–100%). Skeletal preservation was scored using a scale ranging from poor (near complete destruction of the cortical surface) to excellent (cortical surfaces of the bones preserved). The skeletal inventory of the articulated remains was recorded pictorially as well as in tables. The disarticulated remains were recorded as to which side and part of the bone was present. Dental inventory was recorded following the Zsigmondy system. Dental notations were recorded by using the universally accepted recording standards and terminology (after Brothwell 1981). The adult remains were sexed by using metric data (Chamberlain 1994). The age of the subadult remains was estimated by using the following methods: perinatal age from limb bones (Scheuer et al. 1980), epiphyseal fusion (Chamberlain 1994) dental development (Moorees et al. 1963), and long bone length (Hoppa 1992). The remains were examined for abnormalities of shape and surface texture. When observed, pathological conditions were recorded. Due to the small size of the assemblages, prevalence was not calculated.

The cremated bone from each context was passed through a sieve stack of 10, 5 and 2 mm mesh size. The bone from each sieve was weighed and calculated as a percentage of the total weight of the cremation. This allowed the degree of fragmentation to be calculated. The degree of fragmentation may indicate if the cremated bones were further processed after the body was burnt. In each of the sieved groups, the bones were examined in detail and sorted into identifiable bone groups, which were defined as skull (including mandible and dentition), axial (clavicle, scapula, ribs, vertebra and pelvic elements), upper limb and lower limb. This may elucidate any deliberate bias in the skeletal elements collected for burial. Each sample was weighed on digital scales and details of colour and largest fragment and, where possible, the presence of individual bones within the defined bone groups was recorded.

In any cremation, the majority of the bones are unidentifiable fragments of long bone shafts and spongy bones. The quantity of the unidentified bone is dependent upon the degree of fragmentation. It is of course easier to identify larger fragments than smaller. Some areas of the skeleton, for example the skull, are also easier to identify than other bones. These are factors which need to be considered when analysing cremation burials.

The estimation of age of a cremated individual is dependent upon the survival of particular skeletal elements indicative of age. In cremations of adult individuals, cranial suture closure (Meindl and Lovejoy 1985), degenerative changes to the auricular surface (Lovejoy et al. 1985) and pubic symphysis (Brooks and Suchey 1990) may be used as a general guide.

Late Bronze Age cremations

One cremated bone deposit occurred at Site A (407) and two at Site B (2094 and 2361). All were un-urned and contained within small pits measuring 0.30–0.50 m in diameter and 0.06–0.28 m deep. The bone from 2361 and from the lower spits of 407 was in good condition. However, abraded and slightly chalky bone fragments were present within the upper spits of 407 and also within 2094. This may be due to erosion from acid solution passing through the burial medium. All of the deposits had been truncated by post-medieval ploughing. This disturbance would also have contributed to the abrasion of bone fragments. It is also likely to have contributed to the very low weight of the bone deposits, the largest of which weighed 61 g (Table 4.1).

The cremation burials comprised three individuals. All were unsexed, two were possibly adults (407 and 2094) and one was a subadult, younger than 18 years (2361).

One cranial vault fragment from burial 2094 had moderate porosity present on the outer surface. This is indicative of porotic hyperostosis caused by anaemia. The lesions were healed and therefore not active at the time of death.

Full details of the cremations are presented below:

Cremation 407 (Adult?)
Skull: 5 cranial vault fragments; 1 occipital fragment
Axial: 1 spinous process fragment; articular facet for the dens; atlas

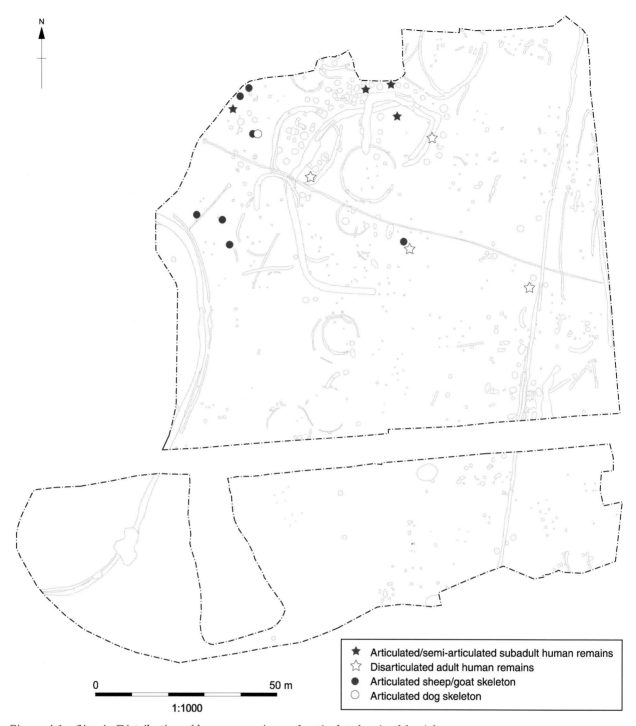

Figure 4.1   Site A. Distribution of human remains and articulated animal burials.

Table 4.1   Summary of cremated bone.

Burial	Total weight (g)	10 mm weight (g)	5 mm weight (g)	2 mm weight (g)	Max. frag. size (mm)	Id. weight (g)	Skull weight (g)	Axial weight (g)	Upper limb weight (g)	Lower limb weight (g)
407	35	3	24	8	25.88	9	4	2	2	1
2094	61	3	30	28	29.18	6	3	0	2	1
2361	52	0	18	34	19.22	6	4	0	1	1

Upper limb: 1 clavicle shaft fragment; 1 ulna shaft fragment
Lower limb: 1 femur shaft fragment
Cremation summary: Colour is white. Some fragments are chalky and abraded.

Cremation 2361 (Subadult)
Skull: 25 cranial vault fragments; teeth: 3 crown fragments, 1 root fragment
Upper limb: 1 radius shaft fragment
Lower limb: 1 fibula shaft fragment
Cremation summary: Colour is white with few light grey fragments. Some fragments are chalky and abraded.

Cremation 2094 (Adult?)
Skull: 13 cranial vault fragments
Upper limb: Left lateral end of clavicle shaft; 2 radius shaft fragments
Lower limb: 1 fibula shaft fragment
Cremation summary: All fragments are white. The fragments are chalky and eroded. The majority of the fragments are very small and no spongy bone is present.

Early Iron Age articulated remains

Two articulated skeletons occurred at Site A, both in features forming part of pit row 3530. Skeleton 4885 was found in the upper part of the sole fill of pit 4867, and skeleton 5144 in a middle fill of pit 5189 (see Pl. 2.5).

Preservation and completeness

The preservation of all the articulated skeletons was good. However, many of the long bones of skeleton 5144 were extensively fragmented with multiple recent post-mortem breaks.

Skeleton 4885 was very incomplete, with only the feet and the distal left tibia and fibula shaft present. Skeleton 5144 was nearly complete. The missing elements comprised distal left humerus, ischium, most of the ilium, right foot and the phalanges of the left foot. Most of the bones from the left side of the skeleton were also fragmented.

Age

Skeleton 4885 could not be aged any closer than between 6 and 10 years. The age estimate was made on the basis of a comparison with the size of the foot bones of skeleton 5144. Since the bones of skeleton 4885 were slightly smaller, it is unlikely that this individual was older than 10 years of age.

Skeleton 5144 was aged between 8 and 16 years. The age estimate from epiphyseal fusion was 12–16 years, while that from long bone length was 8–13 years and that from dental development was 10–12 years. The age range provided for this individual is quite broad, though it is most likely that the individual was aged between 10 and 13 years. Though this individual was too young to be sexed, since sexually diamorphic traits do not appear until after the onset of puberty, the cranium did display some strikingly male traits. These included a square mental region on the mandible and prominent brow ridges. The size and angle of the mastoid also suggested a male individual. It is therefore probable that this was a male, although considering the age of the individual this is tentative.

Skeletal and dental pathology

The only pathological lesions present were on skeleton 5144. The surviving right orbital roof had type 4 cribra orbitalia (Stuart-Macadam 1991). The lesions consisted of foramina which had linked into a trabecular structure. The lesions are caused by iron deficiency. A deficiency of iron may be caused by a poor diet, major blood loss through trauma, or chronic disease such as cancer and parasitic infection of the gut. The porosity results from the skeletal response to anaemia which involves an increase in the production of red blood cells in the marrow (Roberts and Manchester 1995, 167). The lesions were active which indicates the individual was anaemic at the time of death.

The base of the left maxillary sinus was moderately pitted. This type of lesion is indicative of sinusitis. The lesions observed may result from many causes such as allergies, smoke, upper respiratory tract infections and dental abscesses (Roberts and Manchester 1995, 131). The likely cause of this chronic condition in this individual would be smoke inhalation from domestic hearths.

Supra-gingival moderate to heavy calculus deposits were present on the buccal and lingual aspects of all the teeth. Calculus is formed by mineralised plaque and is linked to poor oral hygiene (Hillson 1996, 255).

The biting edge of the right maxillary central incisor was severely chipped which had resulted in the crown being notched shaped. In contrast, the left incisor only had one small chip removed from the mesial edge of the biting surface. This pattern of enamel exfoliation is caused by extramasticatory use. It is not possible to say what type of activity this involved, but ethnographic evidence suggests tasks such as nut cracking, bone crushing or tool making (Larsen 1997, 268).

Early Iron Age disarticulated remains

Disarticulated remains consisted of two partial child skeletons and four individual adult bones from Site A, and one partial child skeleton and one individual adult bone from Site B. The adult bones include three femora, one parietal and one rib. Notably, all of the disarticulated bone from both sites derives from the left side of the body, suggesting deliberate selection. The preservation of the remains was good, with the bone showing no evidence for repeated deposition. The results are summarised in Table 4.2.

Age and sex

A total of 20 skeletal elements were recovered from 8 features. The minimum number of individuals represented by these is six (three children and three adults). This is based on the number of left femora present.

Table 4.2 Summary of disarticulated human remains.

Site	Context	Location	Skeletal element	Preservation and completeness	Side	Age	Sex
A	158	Mid fill of pit 156	Femur	Complete but with fresh post-mortem breaks at midshaft and the proximal end	Left	Adult	Male
A	480	Base of bell-shaped pit 153	Parietal	Near complete with part of the bone towards the temporal region missing	Left	Adult	Female
A	3013	Mid fill of bell-shaped pit 3011	Femur, tibia, fibula, 1st sacral element, metatarsal	Proximal 2/3 of femur; tibia, fibula and metatarsal shafts. The post-mortem damage to the bones is recent	Left	Older child	Unknown
A	3068	Mid fill of ditch, Enclosure IV	Femur	Proximal half of the shaft, the breaks are old but slight recent post-mortem damage to the proximal end	Left	Adult	Female??
A	4877	Upper fill of pit 4666	Femur	Proximal half of the shaft. The post-mortem damage to the distal end is recent	Left	Adult	Male??
A	5112	Mid fill of pit 5110	Ulna, radius, ilium, femur, tibia and fibula	Only slight recent post-mortem damage to the distal end of the tibia	Left	Neonate	Unknown
B	2171	Mid fill of pit 2043	Rib	Neck, angle and body. The breaks present are old	Left	Adult	Unknown
B	2144	Sole fill of pit 2143	Humerus, radius, femur, proximal tibia fragment	Slight post-depositional erosion on the proximal humerus and femur	Left	Neonate	Unknown

The children consist of two neonates aged around 38 weeks *in utero* and one older child aged between 6 and 12 years. The adults could only be aged as over 18 years. One of the adults was definitely male, and the size of the two femoral shafts strongly suggests one female and one male individual.

Skeletal pathology

The parietal bone (context 480) exhibited moderate porosity on the superior part. This type of lesion is known as porotic hyperostisis and is caused by anaemia. The lesion was healed and no longer active at the time of death.

A circular, very slightly depressed fracture was also present on the superior part of this parietal bone (Pl. 4.1). On the endo-cranial surface of the bone, a v-shaped fracture line was present and the bone was protruding slightly from the normal surface. When examined microscopically it was evident that the edges of the lesion were crisp and sharp indicating that no healing had occurred. The traumatic lesion is therefore perimortem. It may well have been the cause of death since the sharp edges on the inner surface of the bone could have pierced the dura mater causing a fatal infection. Alternatively, the blow would have caused a subdural haematoma which could have lead to the subsequent death of the individual.

Striated lamellar bone was present on the medio-distal side of the subadult tibia (context 3013) and the anterio-lateral aspect of the adult female femur shaft (context 3068). The lesions are healed and would have been caused by a nonspecific infection involving the periosteum.

A few cut marks were also present on the distal end of the femur shaft (context 3068), on the anterior and the medial aspect. These were sharp and appear to have been made by a metal implement. The cut marks are ancient, and though it is not possible to ascertain if these were inflicted peri- or post-mortem, they may have been caused by the process of defleshing the bone or possibly when the bone was used as a tool (see below).

Post-mortem modification

The femur shaft from context 3068 was highly polished at the distal end (Pl. 4.2). The bone itself is not deliberately modified. It appears to have broken naturally to a point which has then been used as a tool, causing the bone end to become rounded and polished.

Burial ritual in the early Iron Age

The human remains from the early Iron Age occupation at Fairfield Park represent two different burial rituals: inhumations within the 'pit burial tradition' and the deposition of disarticulated remains. Both rites are commonly attested in Iron Age settlement contexts in southern England (Cunliffe 1992; Hill 1995a; Wait 1985; Wilson 1981). Locally,

Plate 4.1   Left parietal (480) endocranial surface, showing a depressed circular peri-mortem fracture.

examples of human remains deposited in pits at early to middle Iron Age settlements include a series of inhumations from Blackhorse Road, Letchworth (Moss-Eccardt 1988), a disarticulated femur from Broom (Cooper and Edmonds forthcoming) and a humerus fragment from Topler's Hill (Luke 2004).

Articulated inhumations

Though little survived from skeleton 4855, it appears that the inhumation burials from Fairfield Park were crouched and orientated north-south. Skeleton 4855

was lying on its left side and skeleton 5112 was on its right. Neither of the burials were associated with any grave goods. Such characteristics are common within the 'pit burial tradition': approximately 80% of the burials listed by Whimster (1981) were crouched and the prevailing orientation was north-south.

Disarticulated remains

Disarticulated remains from Iron Age sites are generally believed to be the end result of excarnation by exposure away from settlements. Selected bones

0 _____ 100 mm

1:2

Plate 4.2   Left femur (3068) posterior surface, polished distal end of the shaft.

(commonly long bones and crania) or articulating limbs were subsequently retrieved and placed in pits and other settlement contexts (Carr and Knüsel 1997). Ethnographic evidence suggests that not all of the bones from each person were retrieved for secondary burial. Secondary burial is often accompanied by ceremonies involving conspicuous consumption entailing an outlay of wealth which would have taken time to amass. Most of the ancestors may not have received secondary burial because they lacked the necessary accumulated wealth or status (Miles 1965).

The disarticulated remains from Fairfield Park were all from the left side of the body (Table 4.2). Parallels for this are hard to come by since the skeletal elements are often incomplete and therefore unsided. The selection of left elements might mirror the apparent general preference for the body being buried on the left side in inhumation graves. This is contrary to the findings of Wilson (1981, 346–7), who states that disarticulated elements from Iron Age sites are often from the right side of the body. However, the selection of the left side could reflect Iron Age spatial and temporal divisions. Iron Age roundhouses generally had doorways facing east, towards the rising sun, which might have symbolised birth. Left could thus have been equated with west (when facing north), and might therefore have symbolised death (Parker Pearson 1999, 49–53).

ANIMAL BONE
by Matilda Holmes

A total of 14,877 fragments of animal bone were recorded, of which 34% were identified to species (Table 4.3). This is the largest Iron Age faunal assemblage recovered from Bedfordshire, and one of the largest from eastern England as a whole. Most of the dated material (98%) came from early to middle Iron Age deposits (Phases 2–3), while the rest was designated late Bronze Age (Phase 1), Romano-British (Phase 4), medieval (Phase 5) and post-medieval (Phase 6). For the purposes of this report the bones from Phases 2–3 will be considered in detail, and the smaller assemblages from other phases will be examined in terms of species representation only.

The faunal remains from Site A were catalogued by the author, and those from Site B by Emma-Jayne Evans. The catalogues were integrated and used as the basis for this report. Bones were identified using the specialist's reference collection and further guidelines from Cohen and Serjeantson (1996), Prummel (1988) and Schmid (1972). Due to anatomical similarities between sheep and goat, bones of this type were assigned to the category 'sheep/goat', unless a definite identification using guidelines from Prummel and Frisch (1986) or Payne (1985) could be made. Bones that could not be identified to species were, where possible, categorised according to the relative size of the

Table 4.3   Faunal species representation (fragment count).

Species	Phase 1 LBA	Phase 2–3 E–MIA	%	Phase 4 Roman	Phase 5 Medieval?	Phase 6 Med/Pmed	Unphased
Cattle	3	1646	33.8	10	12	1	33
Goat		4	0.1				
Sheep	1	170	3.5	1		1	
Sheep/goat	8	~1835	37.7	15	26	3	36
Pig	4	~401	8.2		5		10
Horse		196	4.0	1	3	2	5
Dog		~48	1.0				3
Wild Bird		1	–				
Deer		41	0.8				1
Rodent*		6	0.1		2		
Fox		1	–				
Cat	1						
Amphibian		2	–				
Articulated remains~		514	10.6				
Total Identified	17	4867		27	48	7	88
Unidentified mammal	22	2906		2	96	9	157
Unidentified large	7	2586		18	35	2	96
unidentified large/medium		4					
Unidentified medium	25	3646		14	62	11	104
Unidentified medium/small		12					
Unidentified small		9					
Unidentified bird		2					
Total	71	14030		61	241	29	445

* = mouse, vole, water vole. ~ = articulated near-complete and partial skeletons: 333 fragments of sheep and sheep/goat, 144 fragments of pig and 37 fragments of dog.

animal represented (small, medium or large). Tooth wear data were included, using guidelines from Grant (1982), as were metrical data (von den Driesch 1976), anatomy, side, zone (Serjeantson 1996), pathology, butchery, bone working and condition (Lyman 1994).

The group of burnt and modified sheep and goat metapodia from Phase 2 pit 484 are included in the fragment count, but not in further counts, as they form part of a single deposit discussed in the worked bone report. Bones from articulated groups are excluded from calculations.

Taphonomy and the nature of the assemblage

The bones were generally in good condition (Serjeantson 1996), yet highly fragmentary, which is common on Iron Age sites (eg Coy 1982). Approximately 3% of the bones showed signs of burning and another 3% had been gnawed, mostly by dogs, but also by rodents. Signs of fresh breakage, which probably occurred during recovery, were seen on 6% of bones, and 1664 fragments were conjoined to make a total of 604 reassembled bones. Many of the conjoined bones had been broken in antiquity. It is therefore possible that these bones were dumped as secondary deposits, rather than as a result of primary refuse disposal.

Figure 4.2 shows the relative proportions of bone from different parts of the body in order of expected preservation (Grant 1984). This is based on the

number of bones which may be expected to be recovered from a complete buried carcass, taking into account the size of bones (eg those which are more likely to be missed during excavation) and density of bone (which affects preservation and therefore ease of identification).

The bones from the major domestic species generally follow a curve that may be expected if whole carcasses were present on the site, where small phalanges are poorly represented and dense mandibles and proximal metapodia are abundant. There are a few notable exceptions, however. In the cattle assemblage there seems to be an over-representation of distal scapulae and tibiae, and fewer proximal femora and distal metapodia (metapodials and metatarsals) than expected. In the sheep assemblage proximal tibiae and metapodia appear to be under-represented. The pig assemblage includes fewer metapodia and rather more radii, distal tibiae and distal scapulae than expected if it originated from complete carcasses.

In general, the bones found more frequently than expected are from meat-bearing parts of the carcass. The apparent under-representation of metapodia could suggest that they were removed to be used for bone working and were deposited elsewhere. From the group deposited in context 488 it is known that sheep/goat metapodia were used for particular purposes, and this may explain their absence from other contexts.

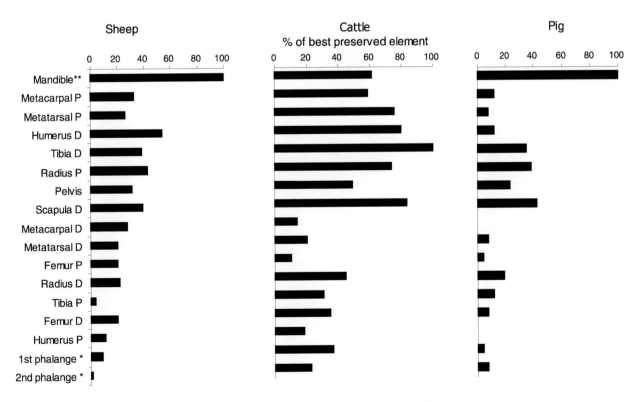

* bone count adjusted to compensate for relative frequencies in relation to other anatomical elements

** mandibles with molars

Figure 4.2   Animal bone. Fragment representation in order of expected preservation (restricted count).

Butchery and carcass utilisation

Evidence for butchery was found on 2% of the bones examined, and was present on all parts of cattle and sheep carcasses in Phase 2, as well as a number of pig and horse bones. Butchery marks were typical of those resulting from skinning and dismemberment, similar to those seen at Abingdon, Oxon (Wilson 1978) and Old Down Farm, Hants (Maltby 1981).

Physical butchery marks were present as knife, chop or saw marks. Knife marks were often seen on the areas of bones where skinning and dismemberment of the joints took place, such as atlas and axis vertebrae, distal tibiae, astragali, calcanei, mandibles, scapulae, distal humeri and proximal radii. Chop marks were more commonly used to break the larger cattle and sheep bones up into manageable sized joints of meat. Transverse chopping of the shaft was commonly found on tibiae, metapodia, pelves, femora, humeri, radii and distal scapulae. Occasionally longitudinal chop marks were also present. Saw marks were relatively uncommon and only seen consistently on antler and cattle and horse metapodials, suggesting that these elements were used in the manufacture of bone objects.

Parts of the skeleton were grouped according to those anatomical elements which may be expected to be associated together (head, vertebrae, upper and lower fore and hind limbs, shins and feet; Fig. 4.3). Sheep and pig vertebrae, phalanges and skull bones (not including mandibles) were rarely found, which is unsurprising, as these are subject to poor preservation, and are often removed as a result of primary butchery (Dobney *et al*. 1996). The presence of significant numbers of cattle, sheep/goat and pig mandibles suggest that these were removed from the skull, probably to aid in the removal of cheek meat and the tongue. Pig lower limb bones (metapodials) are as uncommon as their phalanges, and it may have been the practice to remove these as part of the primary butchery of the carcass. The proximal ends and shafts of cattle metapodials are far more common than the distal ends which may imply that the lower ends of these bones were removed with the feet. Bones from the upperlimbs (scapula, humerus, radius, pelvis, femur and tibia) are well represented for all species, which traditionally hold the most meat and are indicative of domestic waste (Dobney *et al.* 1996).

Articulated remains

'Ritual' deposits are commonplace on Iron Age sites, particularly in the form of complete or partial skeletons (Noddle 1989; Hill 1995a; 1996), although there are obvious problems when judging whether an animal was deliberately placed *in situ* as part of a symbolic act, or as a pragmatic means of disposal for animals which died from illness or natural causes (Grant 1984). Many of the articulated skeletons listed below were found in contexts mixed in with other bones.

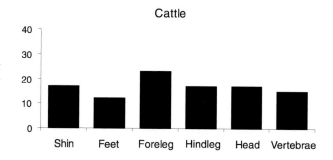

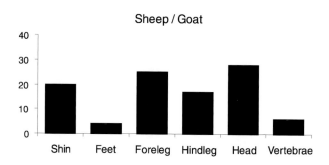

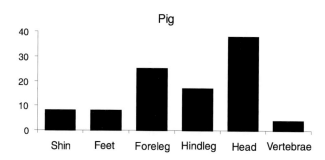

Figure 4.3   Animal bone. Fragment representation by carcass part (restricted count), Phase 2.

A total of ten articulated sheep/goat skeletons were found, comprising nine from Site A and two from Site B (Table 4.4). Five of these skeletons were nearly complete, the others have some elements missing. Three pig skeletons and one young dog skeleton were also found at Site B. All of the articulated deposits came from Phase 2 pit fills.

Three other unusual deposits from pits can be noted. Pit 4941 contained various articulated bones from a dog, and the lower legs of a sheep/goat. Pit 3596 contained 21 sawn and chopped antler fragments in its upper fill, and pit 484 contained 49 burnt and worked sheep/goat metapodials (see *Worked bone*).

Intrasite variation

The analysis of spatial patterning from prehistoric sites is not straightforward. As noted above, many of the deposits at Fairfield Park are likely to be the result of secondary deposition. It is thus probable that the refuse of primary and secondary butchery,

Table 4.4   Articulated animal skeletons from Phase 2 pits.

Site	Feature	Layer	Species	Comments
A	89	Upper fill	Sheep/goat	Lamb less than eight months old
A	194	Middle fill	Sheep	Pre-term
A	322	Primary fill	Sheep	Partial skeleton, less than ten months old
A	531	Middle and top fills	Sheep	Two skeletons, one 18–20 months old (context 535), the other less than 24 months old (context 533)
A	4761	Top fill	Sheep/goat	Two skeletons, both less than ten months old
A	5110	Primary and third fills	Sheep/goat	One new-born skeleton deposited in contexts 5111 and 5113
B	2142	Middle fill	Sheep/goat	Partial skeleton aged approximately ten months
B	2203	Sole fill	Sheep/goat	Less than eight months old
B	2088	Primary fill	Pig	Complete skeleton, between 4 and 8 months old
B	2143	Sole fill	Pig	Partial skeleton from a young animal
B	2182	Primary fill	Pig	Complete skeleton, between 7 and 12 months old
B	2300	Middle fills	Dog	The left side of the skeleton was recovered from context 2188, and the right from 2189. Between three and six months old

bone working and domestic activities were mixed together from different areas of the site before being deposited. The presence of dogs on the site has been confirmed by canid bones in the assemblage, as well as gnaw marks on bones. Dogs and other scavengers will have affected the assemblage by destruction of bones as well as their removal from the site or place of deposition. Such problems have been investigated in detail by Maltby (1985) and Wilson (1996). Despite these caveats, a number of trends in the Fairfield Park assemblage can be noted.

Species representation

Figure 4.4 illustrates a comparison between the relative proportions of species found at Sites A and B. Cattle, pig and horse remains are present in greater numbers at Site B (46%, 13% and 9% respectively, compared to 38%, 9% and 4% at Site A). Conversely, sheep/goat and dog remains are more common at Site A (46% and 1% compared to 31% and 0.5% from Site B). Wild species are found in similar numbers at both sites. All articulated pig

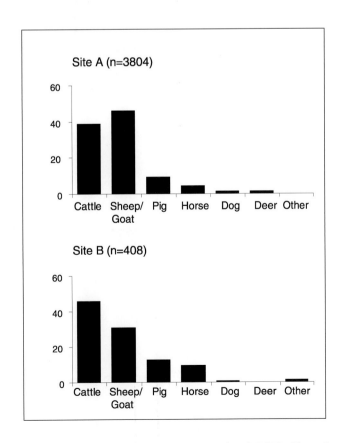

Figure 4.4   Animal bone. Species representation at Sites A and B (NISP), Phase 2.

skeletons came from Site B, yet most of the articulated sheep skeletons were found at Site A.

Figure 4.5 shows the relative proportions of species found in the main feature types on the site (ditch, gully, posthole and pit). Cattle and horse remains were found in similar proportions in ditch and pit deposits, but sheep/goat, pig and dog were found in greater proportions in pit contexts. This trend is similar to those recorded at Old Down Farm and Barton Court Farm (Wilson 1996). Maltby (1985) has suggested that such differences in species representation between feature types can be due to taphonomic factors. Weathering of material in open ditch deposits can lead to bones from smaller mammals being less well preserved than those deposited in pits, which are less exposed. To investigate this possibility, the proportions of loose teeth from different species was quantified by feature type (Fig. 4.6). As teeth are the most robust part of the skeleton, their numbers should be a better reflection of the 'true' proportions of bones deposited. This analysis confirms that the pattern of differential deposition is real. A greater proportion of loose cattle teeth are found in ditch deposits, while those from smaller mammals (sheep/goat and pig) are more common in pits and gullies.

Anatomical grouping of carcass parts

The overall distribution of animal bone from Sites A and B is shown by Figures 4.15 and 4.17. In an attempt to see if any distinct butchery or bone working areas existed a sample of bones were chosen that may be representative of waste products from primary butchery (mandibles and phalanges), bone working (horn and antler) or domestic activities (femora and humeri). Contexts containing more than one fragment of these anatomical elements were plotted onto the plan of Site A (Figure 4.16). This analysis showed that the area to the west of Enclosure II and within Enclosure II to the west of Enclosure III contained a preponderance of mandibles and phalanges (primary butchery waste). The area to the north of Enclosure I, however, seems to contain more humeri, femora, antler and horncores (domestic and boneworking waste) than other areas of the site.

Figure 4.7 compares the proportion of anatomical elements found at Sites A and B. All anatomical elements were found at both sites, although there appear to be more horn core, antler, skull, mandible and metacarpal fragments from Site A, whereas Site B contained more limb bones.

Work on other Iron Age sites by Grant (1984) and Wilson (1993; 1996) has suggested that primary butchery waste was deposited in distinct areas, and that that those bones more likely to have been attached to meat at the time of cooking are more commonly found near hearths and houses. While some patterning in carcass part distribution can be seen at Fairfield Park, overall it can be said that there are no very marked or clear-cut patterns. Deposits are very often mixed, with the majority of features containing both butchery and domestic waste.

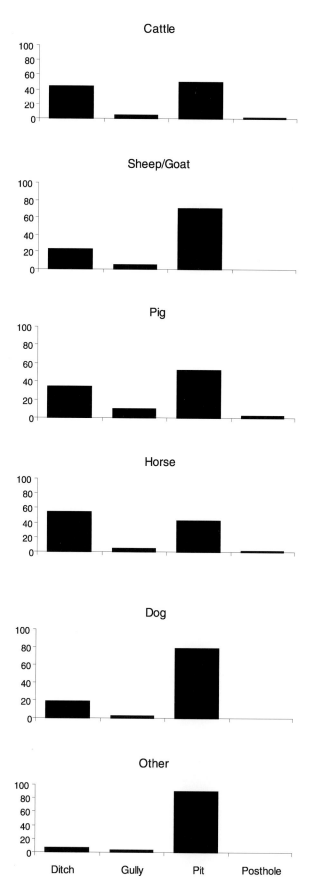

Figure 4.5 Animal bone. % of species recovered by feature (NISP), Phase 2.

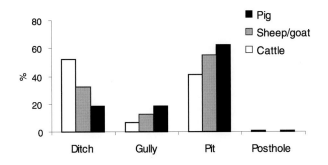

Figure 4.6 Animal bone. Proportion of loose teeth by feature type.

Species representation and diet

As Table 4.3 shows, the majority of the bones found at Fairfield Park came from the major domestic species (cattle, sheep/goat, pig, horse and dog). Wild species were found in very small numbers and included red deer, fox, cat, rodents (mouse, vole and water vole), bird and amphibian.

Phase 1: late Bronze Age

Of the 17 bones identified to species 9 were from sheep, 4 from pig and 3 from cattle. A cat radius from an animal less than nine months old was also recorded. Although rare, wild cat bones have been

found at Bronze Age sites elsewhere in southern England at Runnymede, Surrey (Serjeantson 1996), West Row Fen, Suffolk (Olsen 1994) and Windmill Hill, Wilts (Jope 1965).

Phases 2–3: early-middle Iron Age

Over 40% of the early to middle Iron Age assemblage consists of sheep and goats. Although evidence for goats was found, sheep were positively identified on many more occasions, so the sheep/goat assemblage will be referred to as sheep throughout the report. Goats are common in small numbers on other Iron Ages sites such as Stansted, Essex (Hutton 2004). Cattle are the next most common species, being found in 34% of the assemblage. Pigs are also found in significant numbers (8%). Horses, dogs and deer were present, though in a smaller proportion.

Table 4.5 presents comparative species proportions from early Iron Age assemblages elsewhere in southern England. Similar proportions of cattle and sheep were recorded at Stansted. At Abingdon (Wilson 1978), Dragonby (Harman 1996), Danebury (Grant 1984), Groundwell Farm (Coy 1982) and Old Down Farm (Maltby 1981), numbers of sheep are higher, and cattle lower than the proportions seen at Fairfield Park. The reverse is true at Salford (Roberts 2005) and Wandlebury (Miracle *et al.* 2004), where

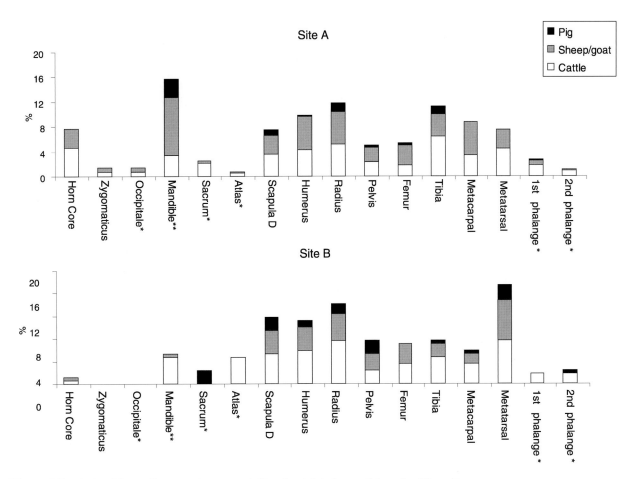

Figure 4.7 Animal bone. Fragment representation (restricted count) by site, Phase 2.

Table 4.5   Faunal species representation from selected Iron Age assemblages in southern England (fragment counts).

Species	Fairfield Park (EIA)		Abingdon, Oxon (E-MIA)		Danebury, Hants (EIA)		Dragonby, Lincs (E-MIA)		Groundwell Farm, Wilts (E-MIA)	
	n	%	n	%	n	%	n	%	n	%
Sheep/Goat	2009	46	727	58	2620	59	1207	56	478	54
Cattle	1646	38	366	29	955	22	649	30	111	13
Pig	401	9	112	9	479	11	276	13	268	30
Horse	196	5	47	4	137	3	32	1	20	2
Dog	48	1	7	1	152	3	3	0	3	0
Other	53	1	4	0	72	2	1	0	2	0
Total	4353		1263		4415		2168		882	

Species	Old Down Farm, Hants (EIA)		Salford, Beds (EIA)		Stansted, Essex (LBA-EIA)		Wandlebury, Cambs (EIA)	
	n	%	n	%	n	%	n	%
Sheep/Goat	1164	51	109	29	904	44	82	18
Cattle	590	26	163	43	734	36	185	40
Pig	279	12	24	6	367	18	75	16
Horse	208	9	77	20	17	1	34	7
Dog	37	2	6	2	6	–	75	16
Other			2	1	14	1	11	2
Total	2278		381		2042		462	

sheep numbers are considerably lower and, at the latter three sites, cattle present in greater numbers. Proportions of pig at Fairfield are similar to those found on many sites, where numbers fluctuate between 6 and 13%, although they were present in greater numbers at Groundwell Farm, Stansted and Wandlebury. Proportions of horse and dog vary significantly between sites.

The most common wild species is red deer, whose presence in the area is represented by antler only. Fox, rodents (vole and mouse), and amphibian make up the rest of the minor species present. Wild species are found in similarly low numbers at most Iron Age sites.

A number of methods have been employed to help understand any bias in the quantitative analysis of the three main domestic species present in Phase 2 (Table 4.6). The Number of Individual Species Present (NISP) is a straightforward count of all fragments identified to species. The epiphysis only method is a restricted count based on the presence of a specific part of the bone (in this case the epiphyses, or growing ends of the bone) which attempts to even out discrepancies between fragment counts of larger animals, whose bones are likely to break into more fragments than those of smaller species. The Minimum Number of Individuals (MNI) is based on the most frequently occurring bone for each species, and the live weight count gives more of an indication of the relative importance of animals in the diet (Vigne 1991; Grant 1984).

The NISP and restricted counts show similar species proportions, where sheep comprise approximately half the assemblage, cattle 41% and pig approximately a tenth. The MNI count implies an increase in the proportion of pig in the assemblage, relative to a decrease in cattle numbers, sheep being found in the same proportion as the former counts.

The most obvious difference in species proportions comes from looking at the live carcass weight of

Table 4.6   Faunal species representation using other methods (Phase 2).

	NISP		Restricted count		Minimum numbers		Meat weight	
	n	%	n	%	n	%	Weight (kg)	%
Cattle	1646	41	386	41	21	31	6300	72
Sheep/goat	2009	50	491	52	35	52	1050	12
Pig	401	10	69	7	11	16	1430	16
Horse	196		62		–	–	–	–
Dog	48		20		–	–	–	–
Total	4300		1028		67		8780	

animals, and their relative importance in the diet. If the bones represent animals used for meat, then beef predominates and comprises around 72% of the meat consumed. Pork and lamb would have been available in similar amounts, although it must be emphasized that the live weights are based on adult animals, and the majority of the pigs at Fairfield Park were subadult, so would possibly be of less importance in the diet. Lamb would have been less significant than the volume of bones suggest.

There are very few wild species present on the site, and it is unlikely they would have featured significantly in the diet of the inhabitants of Fairfield Park. Red deer are represented by antler fragments only, and as such, there is no evidence that they were eaten or even hunted, as shed antlers could be retrieved from the surrounding area. This low representation of wild species is typical of Iron Age settlements.

Phase 4: Roman

Sheep are again the most common species, although cattle are also found, as was one fragment of horse bone.

Phase 5: medieval

Of the 48 fragments representing this phase sheep predominate. Cattle, pig, horse and rodent are also present. However, associated artefacts suggest that residuality is a significant issue with the material from this phase.

Phase 6: medieval to post-medieval

Only seven fragments from this phase were identified to species and include cattle, sheep and horse. Again, residuality may be an issue.

Animal husbandry and economy during the early Iron Age

Sheep

The fusion data from Phase 2 indicates that there are a number of neonatal and preterm lambs in the assemblage, and nearly 40% died before reaching 6–10 months of age (Table 4.7 and Fig. 4.8). Of the yearlings a further 40% were culled before reaching 28 months, and then a massive cull of over 80% of the flock apparently occured before they reach 36 months. There is no evidence for older, mature sheep, as all late fusing bones are unfused.

Evidence from tooth eruption (Silver 1969) and tooth wear patterns (Grant 1982) (Fig. 4.9) reflects the group of animals culled before reaching 12 months of age seen in the grouping on the left of the chart. The grouping to the right, while reflecting the high numbers of animals that died before reaching three years of age, also indicates the presence of adult animals on the site that would have been between three and six years of age before they died. There are

Table 4.7   Sheep/goat fusion data (Phase 2).

	Age (months)	Fused	Unfused	%Fused
Metacarpal P	0	23	4	85
Metatarsal P	0	20	2	91
Scapula	6–8	20	13	61
Pelvis	6–10	15	11	58
Humerus D	10	26	19	58
Radius P	10	31	5	86
1st phalanx	13–16	5	2	71
2nd phalanx	13–16	1		100
Metacarpal D	18–24	9	14	39
Tibia D	18–24	19	11	59
Metatarsal D	20–28	2	15	12
Ulna	30	2	9	18
Femur P	30–36		17	0
Calcaneum	30–36	4	7	36
Radius D	36	3	15	17
Femur D	36–42		17	0
Tibia P	36–42		3	0
Humerus P	36–42		9	0
Total		180	173	

still no very old animals alive after Mandible Wear Stage (MWS) 41. Such a difference between fusion and tooth wear data has also been noted at Lincoln, where younger animals were under represented by tooth wear analysis (Dobney *et al.* 1996). It is possible this is caused by environmental factors such as the type of fodder eaten, which may have caused premature wear on the occlusal surface of the teeth. Also, the eruption times of teeth in ancient populations may have been different from those observed in more modern sheep (Maltby 1978).

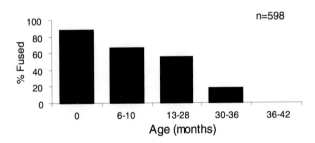

Figure 4.8   Sheep/goat fusion data, Phase 2.

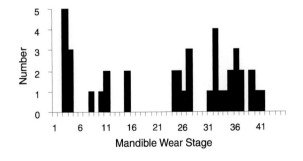

Figure 4.9   Sheep/goat tooth wear, Phase 2.

The presence of very young lambs suggests that sheep were kept in or around the site. The high mortality of animals before ten months old is reflected in wild or feral flocks, and is likely to be due to natural deaths (Noddle 1989; Ryder 1983; Wilson 1993), or a cull of animals excess to requirements (Maltby 1981). It is probable that most animals were culled at an age that reflects a compromise between meat and secondary product production, the majority being culled before reaching 36 months. At this age, the animals may have produced one season of wool (Maltby 1979) although the tooth wear evidence for older sheep implies their importance for milk or wool production.

The tooth wear patterns from Salford and Old Down Farm are similar to that seen at Fairfield Park, with two main groups before MWS 15, and after stage 33. This is interpreted in terms of a husbandry where animals were kept for their secondary products (milk and wool) before being culled for meat. The fusion data, meanwhile, is similar to the middle to late Iron Age sheep assemblage from West Stow, Suffolk, with high mortality in the first year, and a large number of juvenile deaths. This is suggested by Crabtree (1994) to be reflective of a subsistence husbandry, where animals were important for all the needs of the community, including both meat and secondary products. At Abingdon, there were few very young sheep who died before reaching 16 months of age, although a large number were culled before reaching 36 months, and only 18% of the assemblage were alive past this point. Other Iron Age sites such as Danebury, Dragonby, Groundwell Farm and Stansted generally have a higher proportion of mature and/or elderly animals, although at Danebury sheep also showed high mortality in the first year.

Due to the highly fragmentary nature of the assemblage, there were few bones complete enough to give suitable metrical evidence for analysis other than shoulder heights (Table 4.8), which range from 540 to 590 mm (Teichert in von den Driesch and Boessneck 1974), similar to those found at Abingdon, Danebury, Groundwell Farm, Old Down Farm and Salford. A large number of horned sheep were noted in the assemblage.

A number of pathological bones were found in the Phase 2 assemblage: two broken radii were present

Table 4.9   Cattle fusion data (Phase 2).

	Age (months)	Fused	Unfused	%Fused
Metacarpal P	0	29		100
Metatarsal P	0	37		100
Scapula	7–8	40	1	98
Pelvis	7–10	20	4	83
1st phalanx	13–15	18		100
Humerus D	15–18	38	1	97
Radius P	15–18	35	1	97
2nd phalanx	18	10	1	91
Metacarpal D	24–36	6	1	86
Tibia D	24–30	36	13	73
Metatarsal D	27–36	9	1	90
Calcaneum	36–42	4	7	36
Ulna	42	2	4	33
Femur P	42	2	3	40
Humerus P	42–48	7	2	78
Radius D	42–48	13	9	59
Femur D	42–48	12	5	71
Tibia P	42–48	5	10	33
Total		323	63	

which had rehealed within the animal's lifetime, and a thoracic vertebra with evidence of eburnation on the articular surface which is indicative of joint degeneration.

Cattle

There is no evidence for neonatal cattle (Table 4.9 and Fig. 4.10), and very few animals appear to have died before reaching 24 months of age. From 24 months there is a small but significant cull of approximately 20% of animals, which increases to 60% of the population reaching 36 months. A significant number (60%) of mature animals over 42 months are also present. This trend is reflected in the tooth wear and eruption data (Fig. 4.11).

Such a mortality pattern is indicative of animals brought to the site from elsewhere, as there are no neonates and very few calves younger than 15 months in the assemblage. Cattle at 24–36 months are nearly full-grown, and produce a prime meat

Table 4.8   Sheep/goat heights (Teichert 1974).

Bone	Shoulder height (mm)
Calcaneus	536
Calcaneus	536
Calcaneus	538
Metacarpal	543
Metacarpal	548
Astragalus	567
Astragalus	567
Metacarpal	586
Metacarpal	587

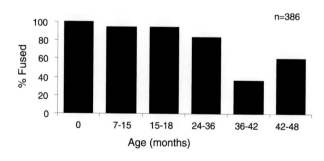

Figure 4.10   Cattle fusion data, Phase 2.

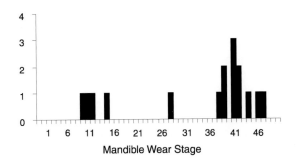

Figure 4.11   *Cattle tooth wear, Phase 2.*

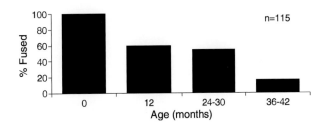

Figure 4.12   Pig fusion data, Phase 2.

yield. The significant number of older animals (over 42 months) is indicative of an economy based on secondary products such as milk or traction. It is therefore possible that the animal husbandry used in the production of cattle for the site balanced the use

Table 4.10   *Cattle heights (Fock 1966).*

Bone	Shoulder height (mm)
Tibia	1185
Metacarpal	1130
Radius	1126
Radius	1109
Metacarpal	1109
Metatarsal	1106
Metatarsal	1085
Tibia	1075
Metatarsal	1074
Metacarpal	1066
Humerus	1011

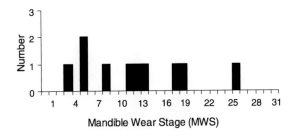

Figure 4.13   Pig tooth wear, Phase 2.

of animals for secondary products against the supply of beef. However, the absence of very young calves may suggest that dairying was not an important industry, as cows need to produce calves that would be excess to requirements if they were to be milked. However, the absence of these calves may be more indicative of the fact that very young animals were deposited nearer the place they were bred, elsewhere in the area.

Table 4.11   *Pig fusion data (Phase 2).*

	Age (months)	Fused	Unfused	%Fused
Metacarpal P	0	3		100
Metatarsal P	0	2		100
Scapula	12	8	3	73
Pelvis	12	5	1	83
Humerus D	12	1	2	33
Radius P	12	6	4	60
2nd phalanx	12	1	1	50
1st phalanx	24	1		100
Tibia D	24	6	3	67
Calcaneum	24–30		2	0
Metatarsal D	27	1	1	50
Ulna	36–42		7	0
Humerus P	42			0
Radius D	42		5	0
Femur D	42	1	1	50
Tibia P	42	1	2	33
Femur P	42		1	0
Total		36	33	

Table 4.12   *Horse fusion data (Phase 2).*

	Age (months)	Fused	Unfused
Metacarpal P	0	6	
Metatarsal P	0	5	
Scapula	9–12	9	
2nd phalanx	10–12		
Pelvis	10–12	5	
Metacarpal D	12–15	5	
1st phalanx	12–15	6	
Metatarsal D	12–20	3	
Humerus D	15–18	2	
Radius P	15–18	5	
Tibia D	24	8	
Calcaneus	36		
Femur P	36–42		
Humerus P	42	3	
Radius D	42	2	
Ulna	42	1	
Femur D	42		
Tibia P	42	2	
Total		62	0

Table 4.13   Horse heights (Keiswalter 1888).

Bone	Wither height	Hands
Metatarsal	1231 mm	12
Metacarpal	1295 mm	12.3
Metacarpal	1301 mm	12.3
Metatarsal	1301 mm	12.3
Metacarpal	1314 mm	13
Radius	1315 mm	13
Tibia	1391 mm	13.3

Table 4.14   Dog fusion data (Phase 2).

	Age (months)	Fused	Unfused	%Fused
Metacarpal P	0			
Metatarsal P	0			
Metatarsal D	5–6	2		100
Metacarpal D	5–6	1		100
1st phalanx	5–6		1	0
2nd phalanx	5–6			
Pelvis	6			
Scapula	6–8			
Humerus D	6–8		1	0
Radius P	6–8	2	1	67
Humerus P	12–18		1	0
Tibia D	14–15		1	0
Calcaneus	14–15		1	0
Ulna	15		1	0
Radius D	16–18	1	3	25
Femur P	18	1	1	50
Femur D	18		1	0
Tibia P	18		1	0
Total		7	13	

This pattern has also been noted at Salford, Stansted and Old Down Farm, which Maltby (1981) suggests may be because the very young animals were deposited elsewhere on the site. Abingdon also had a large number of subadult and mature animals in the cattle assemblage, although a number of animals died before 18 months. Other sites such as Danebury and Dragonby had much higher numbers of very young and immature animals.

As with the sheep assemblage there was not sufficient metrical data to investigate differences in male and female ratios, although a number of shoulder heights were calculated (after Fock 1966) which fell in the range of 1.00 and 1.13 m (Table 4.10). Similar sized animals have been found at Abingdon, Danebury, Dragonby, Groundwell Farm, Old Down Farm and Salford. Examples of short and small horned cattle were present in the assemblage (Armitage and Clutton-Brock 1976).

There were a number of pathological bones from Phase 2. Three phalanges showed signs of bony growths, and the distal articulation of a metatarsal showed splaying of the condyles. These injuries may be the indicative of animals used for traction (Dobney *et al.* 1996; Noddle 1989), an affliction also seen at Abingdon and Groundwell Farm. A number of bones exhibited other signs of joint degeneration. Eburnation was seen on the mandibular articular condyle, the proximal end of a metacarpal and distal articulation of two scapulae. Evidence of trauma was found on a long bone fragment which contained extra bony growth. Other pathologies came in the form of changes to the humerus suggesting an infection of the bone, a vestigial fifth metacarpal was fused to the proximal end of the animal's metacarpal, and a (probably congenital) 9 mm hole was noted in the parietal bone of a skull.

Pigs

The fusion data from Phase 2 (Table 4.11 and Fig. 4.12) provides no evidence for new-born piglets, although over 60% of the animals were culled before reaching 12 months of age. This cull continued in the second year, until less than 10% of the population were alive

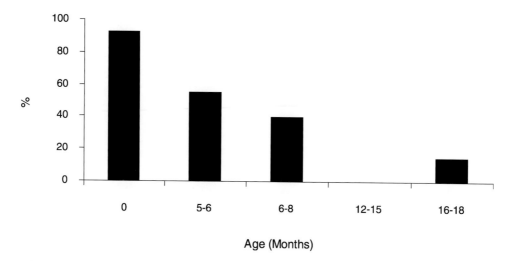

Figure 4.14   Dog fusion data, Phase 2.

as adults (over 42 months). The tooth wear and eruption evidence (Fig. 4.13) reflects the fusion data, with only one individual with a wear stage over 20, suggesting that most animals were younger than 36 months when they died (Hambleton 1999).

This is not an unusual example of pig husbandry, as traditionally their main yield is meat, and they are most productive between 12 and 24 months of age. The older animals in the assemblage may have been breeding stock or wild pigs. There was not sufficient metrical data to investigate the presence of wild pigs, or the morphology of the animals.

Similar mortality profiles are seen at Abingdon, Danebury, Dragonby, Groundwell Farm and Salford. At Old Down Farm, however, there were more older animals present.

Horses

There was no evidence for juvenile or subadult horses on the site, as all bones were fused (Table 4.12), and all teeth were in wear. The absence of juvenile horses has been noted at many Iron Age sites, including Abingdon, Danebury and Old Down

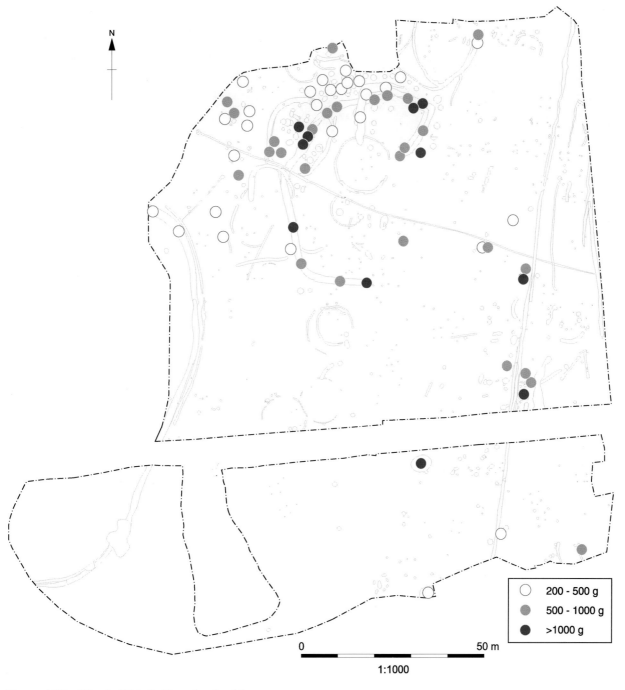

Figure 4.15   Site A. Distribution of animal bone.

Farm, and may indicate that they were bred away from the site. Wilson (1993) suggests that they may have been bred on specialist sites such as Dragonby, where evidence has been found for foals and juvenile animals, and traded to others with less expertise of horse breeding and training. It is likely that the horses on this site were important for riding and/or traction, before being used for meat.

The metrical data for the horse assemblage reveals the presence of animals between 12 and 13.3 hands, representing small to medium sized ponies

(Table 4.13) (Keiswalter 1888). Animals of similar sizes have also been found at Abingdon, Dragonby, Groundwell Farm, Old Down Farm and Salford. A scapula in Phase 2 showed signs of joint degeneration, with a large amount of bony growth around the glenoid process.

Dogs

There is evidence for puppies dying at less than 6, 8 and 18 months of age, although there are also a

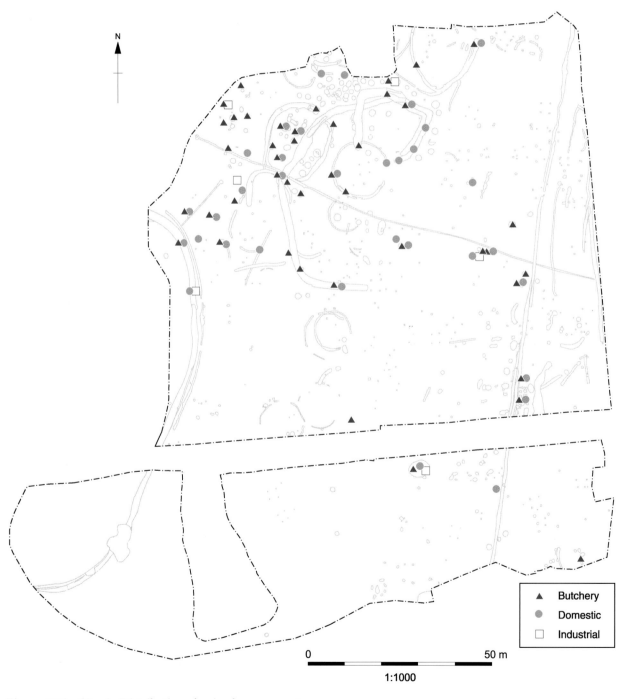

Figure 4.16   Site A. Distribution of animal carcass parts.

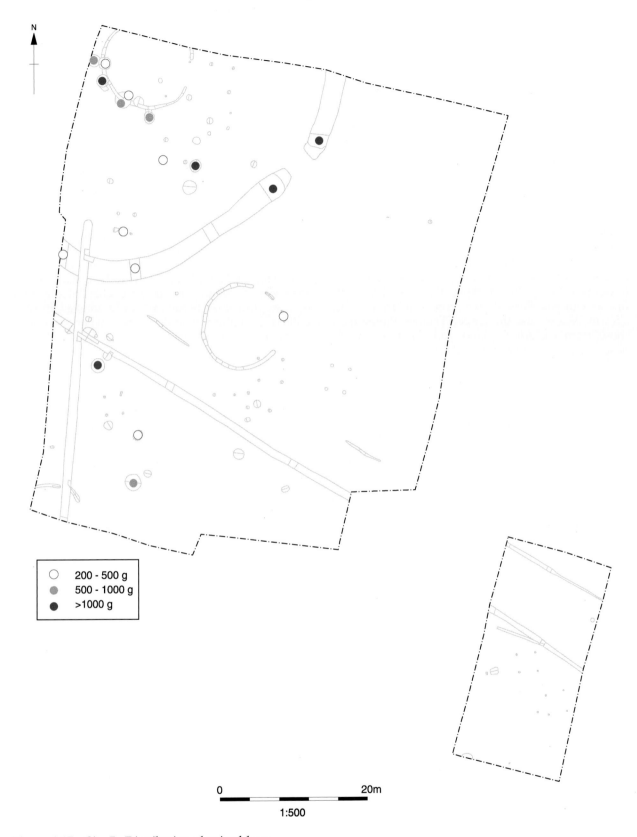

Figure 4.17   Site B. Distribution of animal bone.

number of fused bones from mature animals (Table 4.14 and Fig. 4.14). There were no bones complete enough for shoulder heights to be calculated.

Discussion

The animal husbandry of the early Iron Age settlement at Fairfield Park cannot be investigated in detail due to the highly fragmentary nature of the assemblage and the resulting dearth of bones complete enough for metrical analysis into sex and morphology. The metrical data that is available, however, implies that cattle and sheep fall into the general size ranges seen on other Iron Age sites. Evidence exists for horned species of cattle, goats and sheep.

The diet of the inhabitants would have consisted of beef, pork and lamb and, to a lesser extent, horsemeat. Generally speaking, the animal husbandry at Fairfield Park shares more similarities with sites in Wessex and the Upper Thames Valley than those from eastern England and the Great Ouse basin. Species proportions of the main domesticates (cattle, sheep and pig) fall between the ranges suggested by Hambleton (1999) to be representative of Iron Age assemblages from Wessex and the Upper Thames Valley. There are too many sheep in the assemblage to be comparable to early Iron Age sites to the east, where cattle typically predominate (Dawson 2000a).

The mortality profile of sheep at Fairfield Park is typical of a self sufficient subsistence economy where animals were bred on site, younger sheep were culled for meat and older animals used for wool and/or milk. The presence of a number of weaving tools from the site also suggests the use of sheep for wool. The number of sheep dying at 6–12 months is not large enough to imply the seasonal cull of animals suggested by Hambleton (1999) to be common on some Wessex and Upper Thames Valley sites, where yearlings were killed before winter after spending summer manuring fields. Instead, they fall into an alternative category of natural deaths more typical of sites with less intensive arable exploitation, where older animals were used for meat. This is again typical of both Wessex and Upper Thames Valley sites, but less so of sites from eastern England and the south Midlands.

The cattle assemblage was more typical of animals kept primarily for their secondary products, with a compromise apparent from a cull of a few subadult animals for meat. This regime is similar to that suggested by Hambleton (1999) to be typical of sites from Wessex where animals were killed later, as they were kept in small herds that could not sustain large culls of immature animals for beef when secondary products were important. Sites from the Upper Thames Valley and south Midlands were more indicative of beef production, where most animals were culled when immature.

It is evident from the presence of neonatal lambs that sheep were bred in close proximity to the site. Dogs also apparently whelped on the site, and appear to have had rather short life expectancies. Although there is no evidence of on-site breeding of cattle or horses, it is probable that they were kept and (at least in the case of cattle) bred in the surrounding environs. Pigs may also have been kept in close proximity to the site, as there is evidence for piglets.

Chapter 5: Environmental Evidence

CHARRED PLANT REMAINS
by Ruth Pelling

A series of bulk samples were taken during excavation for the extraction of charred plant remains. Following assessment of all samples (OA 2004b), 24 were selected for sorting and analysis on the basis of quantity and range of plant remains noted (Fig. 5.1). These comprised 22 samples of early Iron Age date (Phase 2)—of which 21 came from Site A and 1 from Site B—and 2 samples of probable medieval date (Phase 5) from Site A. Samples derived from pits, ditches and roundhouse eaves-gullies. Few published reports of charred plant remains are available from the area, and therefore the analysis allows us to move some way to developing a picture of the regional economy as well as providing a comparison with other parts of the country. The quantitative analysis of charred remains from archaeological sites provides the opportunity to establish the nature of arable activities at a site, and consequently can provide insights into the social organisation of a settlement as well as the cataloguing of species present.

Methodology

Each flot selected for sorting was first split into fractions using a stack of sieves (0.5 mm to 2 mm). Each fraction was sorted under a binocular microscope at magnification of ×10 to ×20. Any grain, chaff, seeds or other quantifiable plant parts were extracted. Identifications were made by morphological characteristics and by comparison with modern reference material. Nomenclature and taxonomic order of weeds or wild plants follows Clapham et al. (1989). Quantification of cereal grains is based on the presence of embryo ends. Chaff is quantified on the basis of glume bases or spikelet forks for hulled wheat, and rachis internodes for barley. Weed counts given are for seed, nutlet etc unless otherwise given.

Results

Detailed results are shown in Table 5.2 (for early Iron Age samples) and Table 5.3 (for medieval samples). The majority of samples produced small, mixed assemblages of cereal grain, chaff and weed seeds characteristic of background scatters of routine cereal processing waste. Eleven samples, all dating from Phase 2 (early Iron Age) produced larger assemblages with over 50 identified items (Table 5.1). These samples are discussed further in relation to sample composition below.

Cereal species

Two cereal species were positively identified, *Triticum spelta* (spelt wheat) and *Hordeum vulgare* (barley). The *Hordeum vulgare* includes hulled and asymmetric grain indicative of the hulled six-rowed variety. The ratio of asymmetric lateral grain to straight grain in six-row barley is 2:1 while two-row barley produces straight grain only. While the presence of asymmetric grain confirms the presence of six-row barley, the numbers of well-preserved grain were not sufficient to demonstrate the presence or absence of the two-row variety.

Triticum spelta is the dominant cereal crop of the Iron Age in southern Britain and its presence in the samples is to be expected. A second possible wheat species, *Triticum dicoccum* (emmer) was identified on the basis of two cereal grains and rare glume bases. Both wheat species are hulled wheats, in which the grain is tightly held in glumes. The separation of the grain from the glumes involves an additional stage of processing not required for free-threshing species. Emmer wheat is the dominant wheat of the earlier prehistoric period but was largely replaced by spelt in much of southern Britain by the beginning of the Iron Age. While emmer may have persisted as a crop on Iron Age sites in some areas, such as parts of Kent (eg Hillman 1982), Surrey (Murphy 1977; Pelling forthcoming a) and North Eastern England (van der Veen 1992), its presence at Fairfield Park is likely to be as a relic weed of the spelt crop.

A final possible crop present in the samples is *Avena* sp. (oats). In the absence of chaff it was not possible to establish if a cultivated or wild species was represented. Given the paucity of grain (six grains in total were identified) it is unlikely that oats contributed significantly to the cereal economy, and they may have been present as a weed of the barley crop.

Other food plants

Non-cereal food plants were rare in the samples but do include both cultivated and wild species. A single poorly preserved pea (*Pisum sativum*) was identified on the basis of the characteristic hilum still attached to a fragment of the seed. Pea is an ancient pulse crop present in Britain from the Neolithic, but not appearing in significant numbers until the Iron Age in some parts of the country or the Roman period in others. The remaining possible food crops are likely to have been harvested from the wild and include hazel (*Corylus avellana*) and sloe (*Prunus spinosa*), both identified from rare fragments of the nut shell

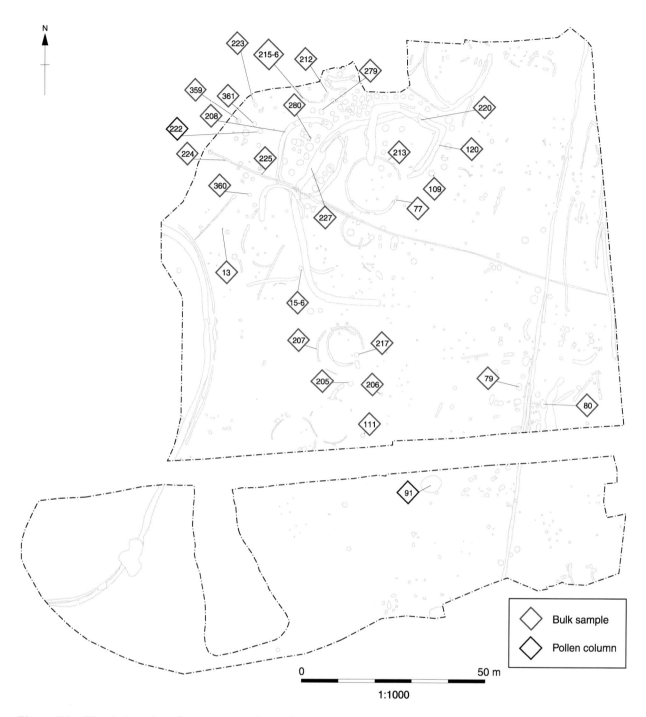

Figure 5.1 Site A. Location of environmental samples.

or stone. Indeterminate large fruit or nut fragments were also present.

Weed species

A range of wild herbaceous species were identified which suggest an evolving arable weed flora and the cultivation of a range of soils. The majority of species present are commonly associated with arable fields or ruderal habitats. *Plantago lanceolata*, *Galium* sp. and *Fallopia convolvulus* are amongst the oldest weed species, being consistently associated with cereal assemblages from the Neolithic onwards (Greig 1988). The assemblages also include species not normally regarded as arable weeds by modern phytosociological standards. *Eleocharis palustris* agg (common spikerush), *Carex* sp. (sedges) and *Scirpus* sp. (clubrush) are more usually associated with damp ground. *Eleocharis palustris* is normally associated with damp grazed grassland where its rhizomatous roots require being under water at least seasonally (Walters 1949). Similarly *Montia fontana* subsp. *chondrosperma* is

Table 5.1   Charrred plant remains: summary of components of samples with >50 items.

Sample	15	43	77	79	120	205	217	223	227	359	360
Total Grain	4	39	41	28	12	85	10	41	6	10	18
Total Chaff	2	104	37	12	22	86	15	53	42	143	110
Total Weeds	56	163	26	26	170	75	44	37	32	20	251
% of grain to weed seeds	6.7	19.3	61.2	51.9	6.6	53.1	18.5	52.6	15.8	33.3	6.7
Log ^{10} est. wheat grain/glume bases	0	−0.96	0.06	−0.63	−0.44	−0.54	−0.48	−0.69	−1.15	−1.15	−0.87
% of large weeds from all weed seeds	12.5	28.22	15.38	7.69	0	28	20.45	10.81	9.38	10	15.94
% of weed seeds to grain	93.33	80.69	38.81	48.15	93.41	46.88	81.48	47.44	84.21	66.67	93.31

usually associated with a high water table, especially in spring. While *E. palustris* and *Carex* sp. in particular are not regarded as arable weeds today, they are commonly associated with cereal remains on Iron Age sites (M K Jones 1978; 1984; Jones and Robinson 1993), and both were found with stored cereal grain in Roman granary deposits at South Shields, Tyne and Wear (van der Veen 1992). This regular association of *E. palustris* and *Carex* spp. with charred cereal grain assemblages indicates that they were weeds of arable fields in the past, suggesting the greater use of poorly drained arable fields (M K Jones 1984; 1988a; 1988b). Also not usually regarded as an arable weed, *Arrhenatherum elatius* (false oatgrass), identified on the basis of tubers, is characteristic of ungrazed grassland. *Arrhenatherum elatius* is a successful coloniser of abandoned arable and will continue to persist as an arable weed once cultivation resumes (Pfitzenmeyer 1962, 240), possibly indicating period of fallow or abandonment. Its presence in cereal assemblages from the Hampshire chalklands has been linked with the harvesting of crops by uprooting (Campbell 2000).

The majority of the wild plant species identified are regarded as typical weeds of arable fields. Several species tend to be associated with autumn sown crops such as *Galium aparine* (goosegrass), *Veronica hederifolia* (ivy-leaved speedwell), *Lithospermum arvense* (corn gromwell), *Agrostemma githago* (corn cockle) and *Ranunculus parviflorus* (small-flowered buttercup) (Fryer and Evans 1968; Silverside 1977). Such autumn germinating weeds are usually associated with autumn- or winter-sown wheat, in this case spelt wheat, while barley is traditionally sown in the spring.

Species indicative of both light, free-draining soils (*Papaver* sp., *Ranunculus parviflorus*, *Stellaria gramineae* and *Montia fontana*) and heavy calcareous soils (*Odontites verna*, *Galium aparine* and *Anthemis cotula*) were identified. This suggests that both the lighter gravel and alluvial soils and the heavier glacial till (Boulder Clay) soils were being utilised. An increase in weeds characteristic of heavy clay soils is noted at many Iron Age sites and is presumably associated with expansion of agriculture into new areas at this time. The evidence from Fairfield Park would suggest this had already occurred here by the latter stages of the early Iron Age.

Two weed species present in the samples are not commonly associated with cereal assemblages prior to the late Iron Age or Roman period in Britain (Greig 1988), although as more Iron Age sites are examined on a greater range of soils more examples are likely to be identified. *Agrostemma githago* is likely to be an introduction from the Mediterranean region (Clapham *et al.* 1989) and is particularly characteristic of Roman and later cereal assemblages. Its presence in an early Iron Age context is unusual and may indicate contamination from later deposits, or alternatively provides evidence for early contact with the continent. *Anthemis cotula* conversely may have been a rare native plant of calcareous soils, only becoming a common arable weed once heavy clay soils began to be more widely cultivated.

Seeds of low growing weed species such as *Odontites verna*, *Trifolium* sp., *Stellaria media* and *Sheradia arvensis* are present in the samples. If such seeds have derived from arable weeds then they cannot have entered the assemblages unless the crop had been reaped low on the straw. A similar pattern has been noted at sites within the Thames Valley (Stevens 2003) and may have been the norm in this period. Harvesting by uprooting would have limited both low-growing weeds and many taller weeds, favouring binding weeds (eg *Fallopia convolvulus* and the vetches: Hillman 1984, 27), while cutting high, or plucking the ear, would eliminate all but the taller growing weeds. As noted above, the presence of *Arrhenatherum elatius* tubers may however indicate harvesting by uprooting. It is possible therefore that both practices were used. Assuming the cereals were harvested low, the paucity of culm nodes (the growth nodes on the straw of grasses) must be due to either preservation biases or a taphonomic process which prevented the straw coming into contact with fire. Such processes could include use of straw for thatching, animal bedding or feed.

Large non-cereal grass seeds, including *Bromus* subsect *Eubromus*, are a fairly common component of the weed assemblages. The high concentration of *Bromus* seeds in some prehistoric assemblages has been suggested to be a result of deliberate harvesting (eg Hubbard 1975; M K Jones 1978; 1984; Knörzer 1967), or at least a tolerable impurity. Large weed seeds generally are removed from cereal crops at a late stage of processing by hand picking, and their presence may indicate that the crops were not yet fully cleaned.

Table 5.2 Charred Plant Remains from Phase 2.

Sample		15	77	79	111	120	205	207	208	212	213
Context		487	3267	3292	4115	3064	4316	4453	4491	4575	4595
Feature		484	3090	3285	4114	3058	4317	4452	4410	4440	3090
Feature Type		Pit	Eaves-gully (Str. 1)	Pit	Pit	Ditch (Encl. 4)	Pit	Eaves-gully (Str. 3)	Ditch (Encl. 2)	Eaves-gully (Str. 7)	Eaves-gully (Str. 1)
Site		A	A	A	A	A	A	A	A	A	A
Volume (litres)		80	40	40	40	40	40	40	40	40	40
Grain											
Spelt wheat	*Triticum spelta*	1	1	2	–	–	3	1	2	–	2
Emmer wheat	*Triticum dicoccum*	–	–	–	–	–	1	–	–	–	–
Spelt/emmer wheat	*Triticum spelta/dicoccum*	–	–	–	–	1	–	1	–	–	1
Wheat	*Triticum sp.*	–	8	–	1	4	–	2	1	–	1
Barley, hulled, lateral grain	*Hordeum vulgare*	1	–	2	–	–	2	–	–	–	1
Barley, hulled, straight grain	*Hordeum vulgare*	–	–	2	–	–	–	–	–	–	–
Barley, hulled grain	*Hordeum vulgare*	–	–	9	2	–	1	–	–	1	–
Barley, indeterminate grain	*Hordeum sp.*	–	–	5	–	2	7	2	1	3	2
Oats	*Avena sp.*	2	–	–	–	–	–	–	1	–	–
Cerealia indet.		–	32	8	5	6	71	9	4	6	4
Cereal size embryo		–	–	–	–	–	2	–	–	–	–
Total		4	41	28	8	12	85	15	9	10	10
Chaff											
Spelt wheat glume base	*Triticum spelta*	1	6	4	1	15	7	–	1	–	1
Emmer wheat glume base	*Triticum dicoccum*	–	–	–	–	–	1	–	–	–	–
cf. Emmer wheat glume base	*Triticum cf. dicoccum*	–	–	–	–	–	3	–	–	–	–
Spelt/emmer wheat glume base	*Triticum spelta/dicoccum*	1	28	8	3	3	73	2	–	2	2
Spelt/emmer wheat spikelet fork	*Triticum spelta/dicoccum*	–	1	–	–	2	–	–	–	–	–
Spelt/emmer wheat rachis	*Triticum spelta/dicoccum*	–	–	–	1	–	–	–	–	–	–
Barley rachis	*Hordeum sp.*	–	–	–	–	–	2	–	–	–	–
Cereal sized culm node	Cerealia indet.	–	1	–	–	–	–	–	–	–	–
Total		0	1	0	0	0	2	0	0	0	0
Other food plants											
Pea	cf. *Pisum sativum*	–	–	–	–	–	1	–	–	–	–
Indet. large fruit/nut fragment		–	1	–	–	–	2	–	–	–	–
Total		0	1	0	0	0	3	0	0	0	0
Weed/wild											
Small flowered buttercup	*Ranunculus cf. parviflorus*	1	–	–	–	–	–	–	–	–	–
Poppy	*Papaver sp.*	–	1	–	–	–	–	–	–	–	–
Chickweed	*Stellaria media agg.*	–	1	–	–	–	–	–	2	–	–

Agrostemma githago	Corn cockle	1	–	–	–	–	1	–	–	–	–
Caryophyllaceae indet		6	1	–	–	–	1	–	–	–	–
Montia fontana subsp. *chondrosperma*	Blinks	–	–	–	–	–	1	–	1	1	–
Chenopodium album	Fat hen	4	3	1	–	–	6	1	–	1	–
Atriplex sp.	Orache	1	4	1	–	1	2	1	4	4	–
Chenopodiaceae indet.		4	1	1	–	–	–	–	–	–	–
Vicia/Lathyrus sp. small seeded	Vetch/vetchling	–	4	2	1	1	–	–	–	–	1
Vicia/Lathyrus sp. large seeded	Vetch/vetchling	–	–	–	–	–	1	–	–	–	–
Medicago/Trifolium sp.	Medick/trefoil, clover etc	–	2	2	–	–	5	–	–	–	–
Umbelliferae indet.		1	–	–	–	–	–	–	–	–	–
Polygonum aviculare agg.	Knotgrass	–	1	1	–	1	–	–	–	–	1
Polygonum lapathifolium/persicaria	Pale persicaria/willow weed	1	–	–	–	–	–	–	–	–	–
Fallopia convolvulus		1	–	–	–	–	3	–	–	–	–
Rumex sp.	Docks	1	4	2	2	161	3	–	2	4	–
Polygonaceae indet.		1	–	1	–	1	3	–	1	2	–
Anagalis type	Pimpernel	–	1	–	–	1	1	–	–	–	–
Odontites verna/Eurphrasia sp.	Red bartsia/eyebright	3	1	1	–	–	–	–	–	–	–
Plantago media/lanceolata	Plantain	1	–	–	–	–	1	1	1	–	–
Galium aparine	Goosegrass	3	2	–	–	–	5	1	–	–	–
Valerinella dentata	Narrow-fruited corn-salad	–	–	–	–	1	2	–	–	–	–
Tripleurospermum inodorum	Scentless mayweed	–	–	–	–	–	5	–	–	–	–
Compositae small seeded		–	–	–	–	–	7	–	–	–	2
Eleocharis palustris type	Common spikerush	–	–	–	–	1	2	–	1	–	–
Carex sp. three sided	Sedge	–	–	–	–	1	–	–	–	–	–
Cyperaceae		1	3	–	–	–	–	–	–	–	–
Bromus subsect *Eubromus* sp.	Brome grass	1	2	2	–	–	6	–	1	2	–
Arrhenatherum elatius tuber	False oat grass	–	1	1	–	–	1	–	1	1	–
Gramineae (large)		12	1	1	–	–	4	–	1	1	–
Gramineae (small)		–	3	3	–	–	–	1	5	–	–
Indet. weeds large		13	1	1	–	–	–	–	–	–	–
Indet. weeds small		–	6	6	2	2	17	3	6	6	1
Total		56	26	26	5	170	74	6	25	15	5

Table 5.2 (Continued)

Sample	215	216	217	220	223	227	279	280	359	360	361	43
Context	4581	4584	4566	4661	4581	4954	5048	4994	5113	5106	5083	2091
Feature	4440	4440	4565	4663	4761	4700	5041	4996	5110	5029	5082	2043
Feature type	Eaves-drip gully (Str. 7)	Eaves-drip gully (Str. 7)	Pit	Ditch (Encl. 4)	Pit	Ditch (Encl. 3)	Pit	Pit	Pit	Pit	Pit	Pit
Site	A	A	A	A	A	A	A	A	A	A	A	B
Volume (litres)	40	40	40	40	40	40	40	40	40	40	40	40

Grain

	215	216	217	220	223	227	279	280	359	360	361	43
Triticum spelta — Spelt wheat	–	–	–	–	1	–	–	–	–	2	–	3
Triticum spelta/dicoccum — Spelt/emmer wheat	1	–	–	1	1	1	–	–	–	–	–	3
Triticum sp. — Wheat	–	–	1	–	3	1	1	–	2	2	1	–
Hordeum vulgare — Barley, hulled, lateral grain	–	–	–	–	–	–	–	–	–	–	–	2
Hordeum vulgare — Barley, hulled, straight grain	–	–	–	–	–	–	–	–	–	–	–	1
Hordeum vulgare — Barley, hulled grain	–	–	–	–	2	–	–	–	–	–	–	5
Hordeum sp. — Barley, indeterminate grain	1	2	1	2	11	2	1	–	–	3	–	7
Avena sp. — Oats	–	–	–	–	2	–	–	–	–	–	–	–
Cerealia indet.	4	5	8	5	21	2	5	3	8	11	3	18
Total	**6**	**7**	**10**	**8**	**41**	**6**	**7**	**3**	**10**	**18**	**4**	**39**

Chaff

	215	216	217	220	223	227	279	280	359	360	361	43
Triticum spelta — Spelt wheat glume base	1	–	5	1	5	6	1	–	16	16	1	46
Triticum cf. spelta — cf. Spelt wheat glume base	–	–	–	–	4	–	–	1	–	–	–	–
Triticum dicoccum — Emmer wheat glume base	–	–	–	–	–	–	1	–	–	–	–	–
Triticum cf. dicoccum — cf. Emmer wheat glume base	–	–	–	–	–	2	–	–	3	–	–	–
Triticum spelta/dicoccum — Spelt/emmer wheat glume base	9	2	10	2	40	26	6	1	91	86	7	48
Triticum cf. dicoccum — cf. Emmer wheat spikelet fork	–	–	–	–	–	4	–	–	1	–	–	–
Triticum spelta/dicoccum — Spelt/emmer wheat spikelet fork	3	–	–	–	2	–	–	1	15	4	–	4
Hordeum sp. — Barley rachis	–	–	–	–	–	–	–	–	1	–	–	2
Total	**0**	**0**	**0**	**0**	**0**	**0**	**0**	**0**	**1**	**0**	**0**	**2**

Other food plants

	215	216	217	220	223	227	279	280	359	360	361	43
Corylus avellana — Hazelnut shell fragment	–	1	–	–	–	–	–	–	–	–	–	–
Rubus sp. — Bramble/raspberry etc	–	–	–	–	–	–	–	–	1	–	–	–
Prunus spinosa — Sloe stone	–	–	–	2	–	–	–	–	–	–	–	–
Prunus sp. — Sloe/plum etc stone frag.	–	–	1	1	2	–	–	–	–	–	1	–
Indet. large fruit/nut fragment	–	–	–	–	–	–	–	–	–	–	–	–
Total	**0**	**1**	**1**	**3**	**2**	**0**	**0**	**0**	**1**	**0**	**1**	**0**

Weed/wild

Taxon	Common name													
Papaver sp.	Poppy	–	–	–	–	–	–	–	–	–	–	–	–	3
Stellaria media agg.	Chickweed	–	–	–	–	–	1	2	–	–	–	4	–	1
Silene sp	Campion/catchfly	–	–	–	–	1	1	–	–	–	1	–	–	–
Caryophyllaceae indet		–	–	–	–	–	–	–	–	–	1	–	–	2
Montia fontana subsp. *chondrosperma*	Blinks	1	–	1	–	1	1	1	1	–	1	18	–	1
Chenopodium album	Fat hen	6	1	5	1	1	7	2	2	2	1	7	–	15
Atriplex sp.	Orache	2	1	1	–	–	–	–	1	–	1	1	–	–
Chenopodiaceae indet.		–	–	1	–	–	1	1	–	–	–	1	–	7
Malva sp.	Mallow	–	–	–	–	–	1	1	–	–	–	–	–	2
Vicia/Lathyrus sp. small seeded	Vetch/vetchling	–	–	–	–	–	1	1	1	–	2	–	–	1
Vicia/Lathyrus sp. large seeded	Vetch/vetchling	–	–	1	–	–	–	–	–	–	–	–	–	3
Medicago/Trifolium sp.	Medick/trefoil, clover etc	–	–	–	–	–	4	4	4	–	–	23	–	6
Umbelliferae indet.		–	–	–	1	–	–	–	–	–	–	–	–	1
Polygonum aviculare agg.	Knotgrass	1	–	1	–	–	2	–	–	–	–	4	–	–
Fallopia convolvulus		1	–	1	–	–	–	–	–	–	–	1	–	–
Rumex sp.	Docks	1	–	1	–	2	4	1	1	–	1	8	1	11
Polygonaceae indet.		2	–	2	–	–	1	–	–	–	1	1	1	2
Urtica dioica	Common/stinging nettle	–	–	–	–	–	–	–	–	–	–	–	–	1
Lithospermum arvense (silica)	Corn gromwell	1	–	–	–	–	–	–	–	–	–	–	–	1
Veronica hederifolia	Ivy-leaved speedwell	–	–	–	–	–	–	–	–	–	1	–	–	–
Odontites verna/Eurphrasia sp.	Red bartsia/eyebright	–	–	–	–	–	1	4	–	–	–	2	–	2
Plantago media/lanceolata	Plantain	–	–	1	1	–	–	–	–	–	–	4	–	–
Galium aparine	Goosegrass	–	–	–	–	1	–	2	–	2	–	1	1	2
Galium sp.		–	–	–	–	–	–	–	–	–	1	3	–	1
cf. Rubiaceae indet.		–	–	–	–	–	–	–	–	–	–	–	1	3
Anthemis cotula	Stinking mayweed	–	–	–	–	–	–	–	–	–	–	–	–	–
Tripleurospermum inodorum	Scentless mayweed	–	–	–	–	–	1	1	1	–	–	1	–	5
Compositae small seeded		–	–	–	–	–	–	–	–	–	–	–	–	3
Eleocharis palustris type	Common spikerush	–	–	3	–	–	1	–	1	–	1	6	–	–
Juncus sp.	Rushes	–	–	–	–	–	–	–	–	–	–	1	–	1
Scirpus sp.	Club-rush	–	–	–	–	–	–	–	–	–	–	–	–	5
Carex sp. two sided	Sedge	–	–	–	–	–	–	–	–	–	–	2	–	–
Cyperaceae		–	–	–	–	–	1	–	–	–	–	–	–	–
Bromus subsect *Eubromus* sp.	Brome grass	1	–	5	–	5	2	1	–	–	–	5	–	19
cf. *Arrhenatherum elatius* tuber		–	–	–	–	1	–	–	–	–	1	–	–	–
Gramineae (large)		–	–	1	–	1	2	2	–	–	–	–	–	2
Gramineae (medium)		–	–	1	–	–	–	–	–	–	1	23	1	–
Gramineae (small)		1	–	12	2	2	7	7	5	2	5	72	1	44
Indet. weeds large		–	2	1	1	–	–	1	–	–	–	9	–	19
Indet. weeds small		4	2	6	2	4	4	11	5	2	5	53	5	–
Total		17	4	44	4	10	37	32	18	4	20	251	8	163

Table 5.3   Charred plant remains from Phase 5.

Sample		224	225
Context		4846	4872
Feature		4450	4450
Feature Type		Ditch	Ditch
Site		A	A
Volume (litres)		40	40
Grain			
Triticum cf. *dicoccum*	cf. Emmer wheat	–	1
Triticum sp.	Wheat	12	2
Hordeum sp.	Barley, indeterminate grain	–	2
Cerealia indet.		2	4
Total		14	9
Chaff			
Triticum spelta	Spelt wheat glume base	2	1
Triticum dicoccum	Emmer wheat glume base	2	–
Triticum spelta/ dicoccum	Spelt/emmer wheat glume base	15	21
Triticum spelta/ dicoccum	Spelt/emmer wheat spikelet fork	2	1
Cerealia indet.	Cereal sized culm node	–	1
Total		21	24
Weed/wild			
Stellaria gramineae	Lesser stichwort	–	1
Caryophyllaceae indet.		2	–
Chenopodium album	Fat hen	2	–
Vicia/Lathyrus sp. small seeded	Vetch/vetchling	1	–
Vicia/Lathyrus sp. large seeded	Vetch/vetchling	1	2
Polygonaceae indet.		1	–
Veronica hederifolia	Ivy-leaved speed well	1	–
Odontites verna/ Eurphrasia sp.	Red bartsia/eyebright	–	1
Galium aparine	Goosegrass	1	1
Anthemis cotula	Stinking mayweed	1	–
Cyperaceae		–	1
Bromus subsect *Eubromus* sp.	Brome grass	1	–
Gramineae (large)		1	–
Gramineae (small)		2	2
Indet weeds small		4	4
Total		18	12

Small seeded leguminous weeds (*Medicago/Trifolium* sp. and *Vicia/Lathyrus* sp.) were noted in several samples, as were seeds of *Odontites verna* (red bartsia). These taxa occurred in high numbers in late Iron Age to early Romano-British deposits at Stansted, Essex, decreasing in number by the later Romano-British

period. This phenomenon was suggested to be associated with declining soil fertility, with manuring in the late Romano-British period restoring fertility and resulting in the decline of these species (Carruthers forthcoming). The presence of these weeds has been associated with a decline in nitrogen levels on experimental wheat plots (Moss 2004). While it is not possible to plot long-term changes in weed flora at Fairfield Park, it is interesting to note the presence of these species in early Iron Age deposits, perhaps indicating nitrogen levels were already low.

In summary, the weed species suggest the cultivation of marginal wet soils, as well as expansion onto heavy clay soils, alongside cultivation of the lighter gravel and alluvial soils. There is some suggestion of harvesting techniques (by uprooting and/or harvesting low on the straw). Nitrogen levels may have been affected by levels of cultivation, although the indicator species may simply reflect the cultivation of heavy clay soils. Finally, the presence of large cereal sized weed seeds indicates incomplete processing of cereal grain. Generally, therefore, the weed evidence suggests expansion of agriculture onto heavy or wet soils had already started to occur by the latter stages of the early Iron Age in this area.

Sample composition

The processing of seed crops prior to milling and consumption is recognised to involve certain necessary steps or stages, each of which produces characteristic products and by-products (Hillman 1981; 1984; G E M Jones 1984). Such processing products and their waste tend to form the bulk of charred assemblages recovered from Northern European archaeological deposits (Knörzer 1971), preservation being biased towards denser, tougher parts of the plants (ie heavy chaff and seeds). The numerical analysis of the component parts of cereals and their associated weed seeds is frequently used to interpret the stage of crop processing activity or waste represented as well as the nature of the site being studied (Hillman 1984; G E M Jones 1984; 1987; M K Jones 1985; van der Veen 1992; Stevens 2003; van der Veen and Jones 2006). In the case of hulled wheats and barley—the only cereals represented in the samples—the basic processing stages are as follows (following Stevens 2003):

1. Threshing to break the ears into spikelets or separate the grain from the rachis and chaff;
2. Raking;
3. Winnowing to remove the light weed seeds and some chaff;
4/5. Coarse and fine sieving to remove weeds or chaff items which are either larger or smaller than the grain;
6. Pounding to release the grain from the glumes;
7. Second winnowing;
8. Sieving with a medium sieve to remove spikelet forks and unbroken spikelets;

9. Second fine sieving to remove glume bases, remaining small weed seed and tail grain;
10. Hand sorting to remove any grain-sized weeds.

Hulled wheats are thought to usually be stored in spikelet form following stages 4 and 5.

The majority of the assemblages from Fairfield Park produced low numbers of grain, cereal chaff and weed seeds. Such assemblages are characteristic of background scatters of cereal processing waste which have been distributed across the site, much of which is likely to be residual. The numbers of identifications in such samples are too low to enable any meaningful interpretation of ratios of grain to chaff or grains to processing waste. In order to examine aspects of the sample composition only those samples which contain 50 or more identifications are discussed in more detail. Limited non-cereal food remains were present in the samples but have been omitted from the following calculations and charts. The only field-crop other than cereals is represented by a single possible pea. While pulses follow similar processing stages to cereals, their paucity in the samples is such that it is not possible to assess their contribution. The other non-cereal food plants consist of nuts or fruits that must have entered the deposits by a different processing route, such as with firewood or by spitting or throwing of the waste into fires following consumption. The presence of such non-cereal components and the low density of remains indicates that the deposits consist of mixed assemblages burnt, for example, on domestic fires, rather than single burning events of pure deposits of cereals or cereal processing waste.

The total numbers of cereals, chaff and weed seeds were calculated for each sample with more than 50 items, all but one of which belong to Phase 2 (Table 5.1 and Fig. 5.2). Only three samples can be said to be dominated by any one category of remains. Samples 15 and 120 are dominated by weed seeds, while Sample 359 is dominated by cereal chaff. The overall number of weed seeds in Sample

15 is quite low, and they are dominated by small grass seeds and poorly preserved indeterminate seeds. The weed seeds in Sample 120 include 160 (out of a total of 170) seeds of *Rumex* sp. (docks). The seeds of *Rumex* sp. form in clusters which are held together until ripe. The presence of a large number of seeds of one genus like *Rumex* would suggest that a seed head or cluster is represented. A seed cluster would usually be broken up at the threshing stage and then removed by sieving. The fact that the seeds remained suggests that the first fine sieving stage had not taken place, the seeds therefore being stored with the grain until the later processing stages, or that the seeds were not ripe. Alternatively the *Rumex* seeds may have entered the deposit by some other means; they may have consisted of early processing waste or even have been a rodent store.

The remaining samples either produced mixtures of grain, chaff and weed seeds in similar proportions, or were rich in chaff and weed seeds with small numbers of grain, characteristic of cereal processing waste. No samples can be argued to be grain rich.

To further explore the crop processing stages three ratios were calculated: glumed wheat grain to chaff, cereal grain to weed seeds, and large to small weed seeds. The proportion of grain to weeds and the ratio of large to small weed seeds has been shown to be a useful method of identifying crop processing stages (Stevens 2003). This is particularly useful for charred remains where a bias towards grain over chaff is often observed due to differential preservation (Boardman and Jones 1990). In both spelt and emmer wheat crops the grain is held in spikelets where two grains are contained within two glume bases. Glume wheats are often stored in spikelet form in which grain and glume bases should be present in equal numbers. If the processing waste is present glume bases will outnumber grain. Following Stevens (2003, adapted from van der Veen 1992) the total number of *Triticum* grains was estimated by assigning unidentified cereal grain according to the proportion

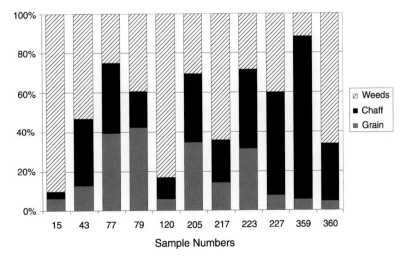

Figure 5.2   Relative proportions of grain, chaff and weed seeds in samples with >50 items.

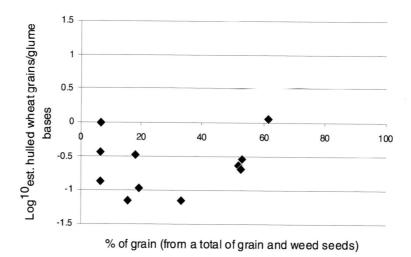

Figure 5.3 Log^{10} of the ratio of hulled wheat grain to glumes against the percentage of grain to grain and weed seeds.

of all wheat grains to those of barley for each sample. The number of glume bases is based on absolute counts where one spikelet fork is equivalent to two glume bases. The number of hulled wheat grains was divided by the number of glume bases for each sample and the log^{10} of the resultant figure was calculated. A negative figure would indicate a glume-rich sample and a positive one a grain-rich sample. Given the fact that differential preservation by charring is biased towards grain over chaff (Boardman and Jones 1990) a negative figure will always indicate processing waste, while a positive figure may be skewed by preservation biases. Figure 5.3 shows the number of grains to glumes plotted against the percentage of grain (from a total of grain and weed seeds).

All but two samples produced a negative figure and therefore indicate glume-rich samples. No samples can be considered grain-rich. The high proportion of glumes therefore suggests the burning of processing waste rather than stored crop. Furthermore, the majority of the samples are weed-rich or produced

grain and weeds in similar proportions. This further supports the interpretation that the samples contain processing waste from pounding (stage 6) and fine sieving (ie stages 8 and 9). Finally, the ratio of large to small weeds was plotted against the percentage of weeds to grain (Fig. 5.4) which demonstrates that small weed seeds dominated all samples. In a study by Stevens (2003) both these patterns were also found at several Iron Age sites in the Thames Valley. The high proportions of small weed seeds and glume bases compared to grain and large weed seeds suggest that the samples were generally derived from the waste of routine small-scale processing of spike-lets. If such processing activity is conducted regularly on a domestic level the waste is likely to be routinely used as fuel on domestic hearths. The presence of large numbers of small weed seeds suggests that early sieving stages may have been omitted and that spikelets were stored largely unprocessed or in a semi-clean rather than fully cleaned state.

Stevens (2003) suggests that the patterns observed are characteristic of sites where cereal processing,

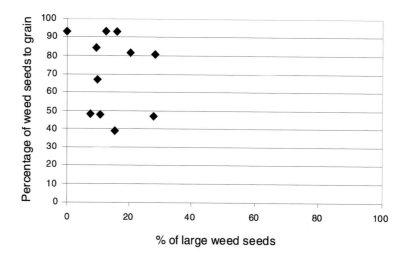

Figure 5.4 Percentage of weed seeds to grain plotted against the percentage of large weed seeds (from all weed seeds).

and presumably arable production, is conducted on a household level and where labour at harvest is limited. This contrasts with sites such as Ashville, Abingdon, in the Upper Thames Valley (Jones 1978), and Danebury Hillfort, Hants (Jones and Nye 1991), which produced grain-rich deposits suggested to indicate greater post-harvest bulk processing of crops prior to storage due to greater availability of labour (Stevens 2003). However, as van der Veen and Jones (2006) point out, the everyday processing of crops prior to use is likely to have taken place at all sites (with the exception of those where ceremonial or other large scale cereal processing may have taken place) and should therefore be expected as the norm. This is consistent with the pattern of background 'noise', which is likely to have built up through processing small-scale grain processing episodes. There is no evidence of burnt stored product, and the generally low density of remains would suggest a domestic scale of production.

Spatial and temporal distribution

The majority of the richer samples (with greater than 50 items present) were derived from the north-western part of Site A, where evidence for occupation was most dense. The richer samples were from pits, enclosure ditches and one roundhouse eaves-gully. This distribution would appear to support the interpretation of domestic-level processing of cereals. The four-post structures did not produce any significant deposits of plant remains and no posthole deposits produced sufficient material to merit sorting. While several samples from pits did produce rich deposits, the assemblages have all been interpreted as processing waste rather than stored grain or spikelets, suggesting that waste from domestic hearths was dumped into the emptied pits. The composition of the waste would suggest that storage of grain was in spikelet form and that processing prior to storage may have been minimal. No clear differences could be discerned between assemblages from Phases 2 and 5, though this may be due to redeposition of Iron Age material into putative medieval ditch 4450.

Discussion

The range of crop plants present at Fairfield Park is typical of much of Iron Age lowland Britain (Greig 1991). Spelt wheat dominates the assemblages while emmer may be present as a weed only. The importance of barley in the economy is difficult to establish but is likely to have been a significant second cereal crop.

The assemblages tend to be dominated by cereal processing waste (chaff and weed seeds), with some mixing of deposits evident. The density of remains is not suggestive of material burnt in storage, or of large-scale cereal production. It would appear that much of the material represents redeposited waste from day-to-day crop processing activities, possibly burnt as fuel in domestic hearths and fires.

A domestic scale of processing is seen at other early and middle Iron Age sites in eastern England such as Broom, Beds (Stevens 1997), Wandlebury, Cambs (Cyganowski 2004) and Stansted, Essex (Carruthers forthcoming). There is no evidence for the large-scale bulk processing of cereals seen on some sites elsewhere in southern Britain such as Ashville (M K Jones 1976; 1985) and Danebury (M K Jones 1985).

Weed seeds are common in the samples, as often seen in deposits of processing waste, especially fine sieving waste. It has been suggested that the predominance of small weed seeds is related to the degree of processing prior to storage (Stevens 2003). The Fairfield Park samples which were sufficiently rich to allow analysis of their composition are characterised by small seeded weeds, which would fit Steven's suggestion for limited processing prior to storage. A similar pattern is seen in some samples at Broom (Stevens 1997).

The weed evidence possibly provides more informative information about the nature of arable production at the site. As discussed above, the heavy Boulder Clay soils were probably being utilised for cereal cultivation, as well as seasonally waterlogged floodplain soils, indicated, for example, by the presence of *Eleocharis palustris*. Weed species characteristic of lighter soils are presumably derived from cultivation of the gravel or alluvial soils in the area. The cultivation of heavy clay and waterlogged soils by the latter stages of the early Iron Age would suggest that cereal cultivation was taking place on quite a significant scale. While the Iron Age is generally regarded as a period of arable expansion and the cultivation of such unfavourable or more difficult soils is widespread, it is often not evident until late in the period.

In contrast to Fairfield Park the evidence for the cultivation of heavy soils appears to be generally later elsewhere in the region, first occurring in the middle to late Iron Age (Webley forthcoming). For example, there is no evidence for cultivation of heavier soils from the Stansted sites until the later Iron Age/early Roman period (Carruthers forthcoming). It is likely that as more sites are available for detailed regional studies these patterns will become clearer. At this stage it is clear that even within particular regions the intensity of agriculture is likely to be varied.

Conclusions

The charred plant assemblages from Fairfield Park were dominated by cereal grain and its associated processing waste with occasional fruit or nut remains and a single pulse. The remains suggest an arable economy based on spelt wheat and barley, as seen across much of southern Britain. Few contemporary sites in Bedfordshire have produced good assemblages of charred plant remains, and as such the Fairfield Park material is of some significance. Charred remains recovered from the multi-period site of Biddenham Loop (Pelling forthcoming b) do indicate a similarly developed arable economy was well established by the late Bronze Age in parts of Bedfordshire, based on emmer wheat and barley with spelt wheat replacing emmer by the early Iron Age.

The pattern of a high proportion of chaff- and weed-rich assemblages amongst the samples has also been noted in many contemporary sites elsewhere in the country, including well-studied areas such as the Upper Thames Valley (Stevens 2003) and north-east England (van der Veen 1992). Such deposits appear to be typical of arable sites where routine domestic processing of spikelets of hulled wheat took place on a regular basis (Stevens 2003; van der Veen and Jones 2006). Cereal processing and presumably harvest at these sites is likely to have been conducted on a domestic or homestead level. Such sites are likely to be the norm but contrast strongly with those such as Danebury (Jones and Nye 1991) or Ashville (Jones 1978) where labour must have been more readily available and the scale of both harvest and cereal processing was much greater. Weed floras at many contemporary sites show remarkable similarities and indicate that crops were probably cultivated on a range of soils including those which would be regarded as too wet to cultivate today. It is possible that heavy clay soils were being utilised locally at some sites including Fairfield Park already in the latter stages of the early Iron Age, while elsewhere in eastern England this expansion occurred at a later date. Any regional patterns or trends will become more apparent as further sites in the area are excavated.

CHARCOAL
by Gill Thompson and Robert Francis

More than fifty flots were submitted for charcoal analysis with instructions to select and analyse ten of these. The samples chosen were selected to aid the broader project aims of investigating the social and economic status of the settlement and the general environment of the Iron Age. Identifying the fuel used for the cremations was also a priority. Examples of contexts associated with both funerary and settlement contexts (pits and gully fills) have been selected. None of these assemblages is interpreted as representing *in situ* burning.

Methods

The charcoal assemblage varied significantly between contexts, with some samples containing numerous and reasonably-sized fragments while others comprised significantly fewer, smaller fragments in a worse state of preservation. Nevertheless, some of these poorer samples came from contexts which might provide significant information, such as the cremation and the scatter of charcoal around the skeleton from pit 4761. These were examined, then, despite the difficulty in handling the material. In order to minimise any bias which can arise from analysing just large fragments, each sample was split into two size fractions (>4 mm and 2–4 mm) and material from both was analysed. Where possible, 100 fragments were analysed from each sample.

The charcoal was identified using conventional methods of splitting each fragment along three planes and viewing the wood anatomy under an epi-illuminating microscope at magnifications of up to ×500 (following Leney and Casteel 1975). Identification was carried out by comparing the anatomy of the archaeological charcoal with published wood atlases (Hather 2000; Schweingruber 1982) in conjunction with the reference collection from the Department of Archaeological Sciences at the University of Bradford.

Results

A total of 738 fragments have been examined and more than 90% were identified. As is typical of many British archaeological sites, oak was the commonest type of charcoal in the material analysed, being represented in all ten samples. The second in rank order is charcoal from the hedgerow taxa of Pomoideae (probably hawthorn-type though possibly apple or pear), then *Prunus* (possibly blackthorn) and *Corylus* (hazel) which each occur in seven of the ten samples analysed, followed by *Fraxinus* (ash) which is in half the samples. There were minor occurrences of *Acer* (maple, probably *Acer campestre*), *Salix/Populus* (willow/poplar) and *Cornus* (dogwood, probably *Cornus sanguinea*). The following types were also identified in just one sample: *Alnus* (alder), *Betula* (birch), *Hedera* (ivy) and *Ulmus* (elm), in each case at very low frequency.

The results from each sample are now outlined in turn. The summary data for all contexts are set out in Table 5.4.

Phase 1: late Bronze Age

Three of the analysed samples derived from Phase 1 cremation burials 407, 2094 and 2361. Sample <13> was one of three small flot samples recovered from cremation burial 407 and as with samples <12> and <14> which were not analysed, it contained very few tiny fragments of charcoal. There was no material in the >4 mm size category from this sample. The fragments examined were all 2–4 mm and all those identified were oak. The relatively high proportion of indeterminates here is a reflection of the small size of these fragments where it was often difficult to have a clear view of the wood anatomy. The other charcoal assemblages associated with cremated human bone were also dominated by oak. These were sample from cremation burial 2094, and from cremation burial 2361. In each of these samples oak made up more than 80% of the assemblage. The oak was accompanied in 2094 by small quantities of birch, hazel and *Prunus*, and Pomoideae with *Prunus* in 2361. The oak in sample had notably wide rings suggesting that

Table 5.4 Charcoal. Taxonomic composition of the assemblages.

Sample no.	13	44	75	16	77	79	80	223	359	57
Site	A	B	B	A	A	A	A	A	A	B
Context	408	2095	2362	488	3266	3292	3249	4762	5113	2223
Feature	407	2094	2361	484	3090	3285	3195	4761	5110	2186
Feature type	Cremation burial	Cremation burial	Cremation burial	Bell-shaped pit	Eaves-gully (Structure 1)	Bell-shaped pit	Concave pit	Pit containing inhumation	Bell-shaped pit	Enclosure ditch (Enclosure VIII)
Phase	1	1	1	2	2	2	2	2	2	2
Acer						2 (2%)	1 (1%)	1 (1%)	3 (7%)	
Alnus									3 (7%)	
Betula		1 (1%)								
Cornus				5 (5%)	3 (7%)					
Corylus		3 (3%)		1 (1%)	1 (2%)	1 (1%)	6 (7%)	2 (3%)		2 (3%)
Fraxinus					10 (23%)	59 (59%)	11 (12%)	2 (3%)	6 (15%)	2 (3%)
Hedera						1 (1%)				
Pomoideae			1 (1%)	3 (3%)	20 (45%)	13 (13%)	50 (56%)	21 (26%)	13 (33%)	10 (14%)
Prunus		3 (3%)	1 (1%)		4 (9%)		13 (14%)	15 (19%)	2 (5%)	3 (4%)
Quercus	31 (78%)	78 (87%)	73 (91%)	87 (87%)	2 (5%)	18 (18%)	4 (4%)	18 (23%)	2 (5%)	50 (68%)
Salix/Populus		1 (1%)				1 (1%)		2 (3%)	1 (2%)	
Ulmus									3 (7%)	
Indeterminate	9 (22%)	4 (4%)	5 (6%)	4 (4%)	4 (9%)	5 (5%)	5 (6%)	19 (24%)	7 (18%)	7 (9%)
Total no. of fragments analysed	40	90	80	100	44	100	90	80	40	74
No. of taxa identified	1	5	3	4	6	7	6	7	8	5

this particular wood had grown faster than the oak analysed from other areas of the site.

Phase 2: early Iron Age

Sample <223> was taken from a charcoal spread around an inhumation within pit 4761. The material was highly fragmented, distorted and generally in poor condition, reflected in the high proportion of the analysed material (24%) being listed as indeterminate. Despite this, the assemblage also contained a large array of taxa: Pomoideae, oak and *Prunus* each comprising about 20% of the assemblage, with smaller amounts of hazel, ash, willow/poplar and maple.

A fourth assemblage dominated by oak charcoal, which made up 87% of the examined material, was sample <16> from pit 484 at Site A. The annual rings in the oak from this context were relatively closely spaced in comparison with oak associated with the cremations, suggesting that it had been taken from a relatively slow-growing tree – or perhaps the trunk of a tree rather than a branch. The sample also included small quantities of dogwood, hazel and Pomoideae. The dogwood here is an interesting and unusual find. These five fragments of charcoal were all roundwood, with diameters between 4 and 7 mm, and each showed three growth rings, which may mean that they originally come from one piece of wood. This type of wood is particularly dense and consequently useful for turnery (Corkhill 1979, 146). In the past it was used for making skewers or spikes (Edlin 1956; Mabey 1996, 238–9) and is also reported as being used for making shuttles and bobbins (Corkhill 1979, 146). This pit had contained weaving tools (grooved/polished metapodials), and some of the charcoal, when excavated, was found in large fragments. We may, then, be looking at the remains of a burnt loom frame made from oak with other weaving tools made from dogwood.

This contrasts with charcoals from other pits at Fairfield Park, which most probably contained domestic fuel debris and waste. Two of these were examined, both from Site A: sample <79> from pit 3285 and <359> from bell-shaped pit 5110. The material from 5110 was comminuted and smaller than 4 mm. Nevertheless, both of these samples had diverse assemblages with seven charcoal types recognised in 3285 and eight taxa in 5110. The material from 3285 is unusual in being dominated by ash charcoal while that from 5110 has an even greater mixture of taxa, with Pomoideae being the most common. We see fuel refuse here from fires burning a variety of woods, or perhaps the refuse from several different burns, deposited together within each pit.

One charcoal sample from an enclosure ditch (Enclosure VIII, Site B) was examined: sample <57> from 2186. The most common taxon was oak (68%), followed by Pomoideae, *Prunus*, hazel and ash. Sample <77> had been taken from the eaves-gully of Structure 1, and was another highly fragmented sample, with only four fragments in the >4 mm fraction. This diverse assemblage, with six types of wood identified, was dominated by Pomoideae, followed by ash, *Prunus*, dogwood, oak and hazel. These are not the result of *in situ* burning and probably represent debris from domestic fires washed or swept into the features.

Discussion

The charcoal assemblages thus show that a variety of woody taxa was being exploited within the vicinity of the later prehistoric settlement at Fairfield Park. Woodland trees such as oak, ash and elm are represented, together with shrubby taxa like hazel and willow/poplar which could have been managed by coppicing. Unusual finds at this site include ivy which may have been climbing around an ash branch which was burnt and eventually found its way into a fill of pit 3285. Dogwood (probably *Cornus sanguinea*), a shrub which often grows in scrub, along woodland edges and in hedgerows, was found in two samples: pit 484 and gully 3090. In the hedgerows it may have been growing with the Pomoideae shrubs/small trees and *Prunus* trees.

The most focused selection of wood noted in this group of samples is the residue from Phase 1 cremation burial 408 which is entirely oak, perhaps selected as this wood burns to a high temperature or because a single tree may be sufficient to fuel a pyre. By contrast, the other assemblages are more diverse, especially those associated with domestic activities. It is perhaps noteworthy that 18% of the charcoal from pit 5110 was unidentified, and high proportions of indeterminate charcoals have been noted elsewhere to be associated with iron-working debris where charcoal rather than wood had been the fuel (Wheeler *et al.* 2003). This is because charcoal-fuelled fires burn at higher temperatures than wood-fuels causing greater distortion of the anatomy making it harder to identify the taxon. Finally, the charcoals from pit 484 may be the remains of a burnt oak loom with associated wooden weaving tools.

POLLEN
by Sylvia Peglar

Monolith samples from early Iron Age hollow 3545 (column 91; Fig. 2.22) and early Iron Age pit 4635 (column 222) were submitted for pollen analysis. Incremental subsamples were taken from each monolith as shown by Table 5.5. All samples were prepared using a standard chemical procedure (method B of Berglund and Ralska-Jasiewiczowa (1986)), using HCl, NaOH, sieving, HF, and Erdtman's acetolysis, to remove carbonates, humic acids, particles > 170 microns, silicates, and cellulose, respectively. The samples were then stained with safranin, dehydrated in tertiary butyl alcohol, and the residues mounted in 2000 cS silicone oil. Slides were examined at a magnification of 400 × (1000 × for critical examination) by equally-spaced traverses across a slide to reduce the possible effects of differential dispersal on the slide (Brooks and Thomas 1967).

Table 5.5   Summary of palynological samples.

Feature	Sample	Context
3545	<91> 10 cm	3587
	35 cm	3588
	58 cm	3589
	71 cm	3746
4635	<222> 20 cm	4634
	30 cm	4634
	40 cm	4669
	52 cm	4669

The aim was to obtain a pollen count of at least 100 grains. Pollen identification was made using the keys of Moore *et al.* (1991), Faegri and Iversen (1989), and a small modern pollen reference collection. Andersen (1979) was followed for identification of cereal-type grains. Indeterminable grains were also recorded as an indication of the state of the pollen preservation. Plant nomenclature follows Clapham *et al.* (1989).

Results

The results are presented in Table 5.6 as percentages of the total pollen sum, SumP (trees + shrubs + herbs + ferns). *Sphagnum* and indeterminable grains are presented as percentages of the SumP + *Sphag-Sphagnum*, and SumP + sum indeterminable, respectively. Pollen was rather poorly preserved in all samples, with indeterminable pollen values varying from 18.8–35.5%. All slides contained large quantities of microcharcoal particles which were not quantified.

Pit 4635 <222>

The two basal samples (40 and 52 cm, context 4669) have very high grass pollen values (56.7 and 47.4%); dandelion-type (Compositae (Liguliflorae)) which could include, among others, dandelions (*Taraxacum*), hawk's-beard (*Crepis*), mouse-eared hawkweed (*Pilosella*), hawkweed (*Hieracium*), and hawkbit (*Leontodon*); and daisy-type (*Aster*-type) possibly including daisy (*Bellis*), and ragwort (*Senecio*). These taxa are indicative of grassland and pastures. The pollen assemblages also include high cereal values, 5.7 and 9.4%, including wheat (*Triticum*) and/or oats (*Avena*), and barley (*Hordeum*). There are also many weeds of arable fields, waysides, and rough and waste ground such as *Aster*-type which could include ragwort (*Senecio*), butterbur (*Petasites*), and colt's foot (*Tussilago*); dandelion-type, (Compositae (Liguliflorae)) which could include, among others, dandelions (*Taraxacum*), chicory (*Cichorium*), oxtongue (*Picris*), goat's-beard (*Tragopogon*), sow-thistle (*Sonchus*), and lettuce (*Lactuca*); the pink family (Caryophyllaceae) which includes the chickweeds; the goosefoot family (Chenopodiaceae); and knotgrass-type (*Polygonum aviculare*-type). These pollen assemblages, including very little tree and shrub pollen (mainly hazel

(*Corylus*)), therefore suggest an open environment with pastures, arable fields, waysides, and waste and disturbed ground, when this fill was deposited.

The two upper samples (20 and 30 cm, context 4634) have very similar pollen assemblages probably originating from a similar environment. However, herb pollen values are slightly lower, with a concomitant slight increase in total tree and shrub pollen, and Pteridophyte spore values. Total cereal values are less (with barley (*Hordeum*) absent), and both dandelion-type and daisy-type, which may represent many weeds of waste and disturbed ground, are higher, together with the spores of bracken (*Pteridium*) which may grow in woodland or on old pastures and open acidic ground. This may represent a slight decrease in farming and an increase in waste land, but this evidence is from a very small pollen assemblage, with rather poorly preserved pollen, and this interpretation is therefore questionable.

Hollow 3545 <91>

Samples were taken from each discrete context within the fill of hollow 3545 apart from the basal one (3747) which was unavailable. Pollen assemblages from all samples are dominated by herb pollen as in pit 4635, but total tree and shrub and Pteridophyte values are higher. Again many weed species characteristic of pastures, arable fields, waysides and waste and disturbed ground are present. This suggests that the environment was dry and open. The small pollen sums mean that caution must be taken with interpretation.

The basal sample, 71 cm (context 3746), has no cereal pollen. However, this sample is particularly corroded (35.5% indeterminable pollen) and the interpretation is questionable. It has high values of grass and ribwort plantain pollen which may indicate that pastures were prevalent at the time of fill. Certainly most woodland around the site appears to have been cleared, probably with only a few scattered trees and bushes of alder (*Alnus glutinosa*) and hazel (*Corylus avellana*) within the area.

The fill from context 3589 (58 cm), however, is rather different from all the other samples analysed. It is still dominated by herb pollen (41.5%), but has much higher total tree and shrub pollen (35.1%) and Pteridophyte (23.4%) spore values. Trees represented include birch (*Betula*), pine (*Pinus sylvestris*), oak (*Quercus*) (6%), alder (*Alnus glutinosa*)(19.5%), lime (*Tilia*) and hazel (*Corylus avellana*), together with spores of bracken (*Pteridium aquilinum*) and other ferns (*Dryopteris*-type). Cereal pollen grains are present though at low values (including wheat and/or oats, and barley), and the pollen of many weeds is found. This assemblage appears to indicate that this fill was laid down when some deciduous woodland, including ferns in the field layer, was growing in the area, but with a lot of cleared ground, or it may be that this fill includes material (perhaps from cereal crops) brought into the site from fields

Table 5.6   *Results of palynological assessments as percentages of total terrestrial pollen and spores (SumP = sum of trees + shrubs + herbs + ferns). Sphagnum and indeterminable pollen and spores are given as percentages SumP + Sphagnum, and SumP + sum indeterminable, respectively. und. = undifferentiated.*

Column		91	91	91	91	222	222	222	222
Context		3587	3588	3589	3746	4634	4634	4669	4669
mm from top		100	350	580	710	200	300	400	520
Trees & Shrubs									
Betula	Birch	1.7		0.8					
Pinus sylvestris	Pine		1.0	1.6	1.0		0.8		
Quercus	Oak			6.0		0.8			
Ulmus	Elm						0.8		
Alnus glutinosa	Alder		2.0	19.5	4.0	2.5	0.8		0.8
Tilia	Lime			0.8			0.8		
Corylus avellana	Hazel	1.7	6.0	6.0	5.0	1.7	3.1	0.9	3.2
Salix	Willow				1.0				
Herbs									
Gramineae	Grass family	25.2	33.0	20.3	44.0	45.4	31.6	47.4	56.7
Cereal und.	Cereal-type	0.9	2.0	1.6		0.8	0.8	1.9	0.8
Avena/Triticum	Oats /wheat		3.0	0.8		1.7		4.7	4.1
Hordeum-type	Barley-type	1.9		0.8				2.8	0.8
Cyperaceae	Sedge family	2.6		1.6	2.0			0.9	
Compositae (Tubuliferae) und.	Daisy family und.	0.9	1.0		1.0	3.4	1.7	1.9	
Aster-type	Daisy-type	4.4	1.0	1.6	4.0	3.4	6.0	2.8	
Achillea-type	Yarrow-type	0.9							
Centaurea cyanus	Cornflower					0.8			
Centaurea-type und.	Knapweed				1.0		0.8		
Cirsium-type	Thistle-type			0.8					0.8
Compositae (Liguliflorae)	Dandelion-type	50.5	24.0	7.8	11.0	24.4	34.7	15.8	17.0
Caryophyllaceae	Pink family			0.8	1.0			2.8	2.4
Chenopodiaceae	Goosefoot family	0.9					0.8	0.9	0.8
Cruciferae	Cabbage family	0.9	1.0		2.0				
Dipsacaceae	Scabious family							1.9	
Melampyrum	Cow-wheat				0.8				
Leguminosae	Pea family								0.8
Plantago lanceolata	Ribwort plantain		3.0	1.6	7.0	2.5	6.9	4.7	6.5
Plantago major/ P. media	Greater/hoary plantain	0.9	1.0		2.0		0.8	1.9	
Polygonum aviculare-type	Knotgrass-type		1.0					1.9	0.8
Potentillia-type	Cinquefoil-type					0.8			
Ranunculus acris-type	Meadow buttercup-type		4.0	0.8		4.2	0.8	2.8	0.8
Rumex acetosa-type	Sorrel-type			2.3	3.0	3.4	0.8	0.9	
Umbelliferae	Carrot family				1.0				
Urtica	Nettle						0.8		
Ferns and fern allies									
Polypodium vulgare agg.	Polypody fern			0.8					
Pteridium aquilinum	Bracken	5.1	14.0	17.2	4.0	5.0	5.4	2.8	3.2
Dryopteris-type	Und. ferns	1.7	2.0	5.5	5.0	0.8	0.8	0.9	
Sphagnum	Bog moss		1.9		2.0	0.8	0.8		0.8
Indeterminable pollen & spores		25.8	18.8	20.0	35.5	21.3	20.7	20.3	21.7
Sum Trees & Shrubs		3.4	9.0	35.1	11.0	4.8	6.4	0.9	4.0
Sum Herbs		89.6	74.0	41.5	80.0	89.6	87.2	95.5	92.8
Sum Ferns		7.0	16.0	23.4	9.0	5.6	6.4	3.6	3.2
No. of grains in pollen sum		115	99	128	100	119	130	108	123

closer to woodland, and therefore including higher pollen values of trees and shrubs. Most of the tree pollen increase is due to an increase in *Alnus* pollen and it is possible that a small piece of anther was included in the sample.

Sample 35 cm (context 3588) is again dominated by herb pollen including grasses, cereals and many weeds, but with less tree and shrub pollen and Pteridophyte spores than in sample 58 cm. This may indicate further woodland clearance.

Sample 10 cm (context 3587) has less grass, ribwort plantain, buttercup, and total cereal pollen values suggesting a decrease in arable fields and pasture, but with large increases in dandelion- and daisy-types, which suggests an increase in disturbed and waste ground.

If the fills of pit 3545 are natural, then the sequence represents an almost treeless local environment with dry, open conditions at the base, possibly followed by some regrowth of deciduous woodland in the area (context 3589), and then further woodland clearance. However, apart from 58 cm (context 3589), the fills of pit 3545 are very similar to those from the fills of pit 4635. Significant quantities of pottery and bone were found throughout the fills of both pits, and it may be that all the fills are connected with cereal processing activities and rubbish disposal.

Conclusions

The pollen analyses from the fills of the early Iron Age pits represented by columns <222> and <91> show that the local environment was open and dry during the periods of sediment deposition, with pastures, arable fields, and much disturbed and waste ground. Some deciduous woodland was probably still extant at some distance. These interpretations concur with the results of the analyses of the charred plant remains and mollusca from the site.

LAND SNAILS
by Elizabeth Stafford

The soil conditions at Fairfield Park were not generally conducive to preservation of mollusc shell and no samples were retrieved from the excavations specifically for land snails. However, the superficial geology of the site is quite variable and in places discrete pockets of more calcareous material were noted. Consequently the samples processed for charred plant remains were also scanned for the presence of molluscan remains. The burrowing snail *Cecilioides acicula* was very numerous in most of the samples. However, this species burrows deeply and provides no useful information on conditions as a sediment or soil formed. The shells were generally well preserved and likely to be of relatively recent origin. Identifiable molluscan fragments of other species were recovered from five contexts, all early Iron Age pit fills from Site A (3049, 4114, 4317, 4318 and 5110). However, concentrations were extremely

Table 5.7 Molluscan assemblages.

Feature number		3049	4114	4317	4318	5110
Context number		3052	4115	4316	4379	5113
Sample number		109	111	205	206	359
Volume processed (l)		40	40	40	10	40
Vallonia costata (Müller)	O		+			
Vallonia excentrica (Sterki)	O	+	++	++	++	+
Vallonia pulcella (Müller)	O		+			
Vallonia spp.	O		+	+	+	+
cf. *Clausilia bidentata* (Ström)	S			+		
Vitrea spp.	C			+		
Trichia hispida (Linné)	C		+	+		
Total		+	++	+++	++	++

Abundance: +1–3, ++ 4–10, +++ 11–25, S = Shade-loving species, C = Catholic species, O = Open-country species.

low considering the large volumes of sediment processed. The results are presented in Table 5.7. Nomenclature follows Kerney (1999) and habitat groupings follow the scheme of Evans (1972; 1984).

The assemblages were dominated by open country Valloniidae, particularly *V. excentrica*, although *V. costata* and *V. pulcella* were also present, along with the catholic species *Trichia hispida* and *Vitrea* spp. Shade-loving species were almost entirely absent apart from single fragment of *Clausilia* cf. *bidentata* in context 4316. The assemblages indicate dry, open conditions, probably grassland, in the locality during the in-filling of these features. At the very least, if the pits were deliberately back-filled, the material may derive from a soil formed under these conditions. There is no evidence from the molluscan remains to suggest woodland or scrub in the locality. Equally there is no evidence to suggest the features contained seasonal standing water. However, it is quite possible, given the very low numbers of shells in the samples, together with the presence of modern roots and abundance of *Cecilioides acicula*, that a component of the assemblages may represent intrusive elements.

CHEMISTRY AND MAGNETIC SUSCEPTIBILITY OF SOILS AND SEDIMENTS
by John Crowther

An initial assessment of 40 bulk soil and sediment samples from Site A had suggested that soil phosphate and magnetic susceptibility data were likely to provide considerable insight into the character, origin and mode of development of the secondary fills of features on the site (OA 2004b). As a consequence, the analytical work was extended to cover a further 152 samples from Site A, and also to include the determinations of loss-on-ignition (which provides an estimate of organic matter concentration) on all 192 samples. The majority of the samples (180 in total) are from the lower secondary fills of different types of feature (pits, ditches, gullies, eaves-gullies and postholes) located in various areas of the site. The remaining 12 samples (of topsoil, subsoil and 'natural') were taken as control samplesand are from four modern soil profiles at the site.

Both phosphate and magnetic susceptibility areroutinely determined in archaeological site investigation:

Phosphates: Phosphates are present in all organic material (plant tissue, excreta, bone, etc.). As they are released by organic decomposition processes, they tend to form insoluble compounds and thus become 'fixed' within the mineral fraction of soils and sediments. Many forms of human activity lead to phosphate enrichment and, under favourable conditions, this may remain detectable for 10^2–10^3 years (see reviews by Bethel and Máté 1989; Crowther 1997; Heron 2001).

Magnetic properties: χ (low frequency mass-specific magnetic susceptibility) in soils and sediments largely reflects the presence of magnetic forms of iron oxide

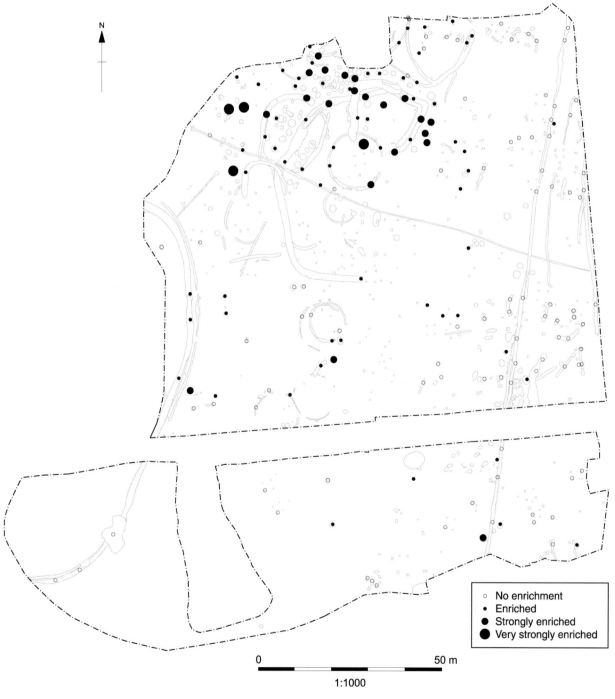

○ No enrichment
• Enriched
● Strongly enriched
⬤ Very strongly enriched

0   50 m

1:1000

Figure 5.5   Site A. Phosphate survey results.

(eg maghaemite) – this being dependent upon the presence of iron (Fe) and occurrence of alternating reduction-oxidation conditions that favour the formation of magnetic minerals. Enhancement is particularly associated with burning, but is also caused by microbial activity in topsoils (see reviews by Clark 1990 and Scollar *et al.* 1990). χmax is a measure of maximum potential magnetic susceptibility, determined by subjecting a sample to optimum conditions for susceptibility enhancement in the laboratory. In general it will tend to reflect the overall iron concentration of a sample. χconv (fractional conversion), which is expressed as a percentage, is a measure of the extent to which the potential susceptibility has been achieved in the original sample, viz: $(\chi/\chi max) \times 100.0$ (Tite 1972; Scollar *et al.* 1990). In many respects this is a better indicator of magnetic susceptibility enhancement than raw χ data, particularly in cases where soils or sediments have widely differing χmax values (Crowther and Barker 1995; Crowther 2003).

Only a brief summary of the most significant results of the analysis are presented here (further details are provided in the Appendix). The phosphate samples could be ascribed to four categories: 'no enrichment', 'enriched', 'strongly enriched' and 'very strongly

Figure 5.6 Site A. Magnetic susceptibility survey results.

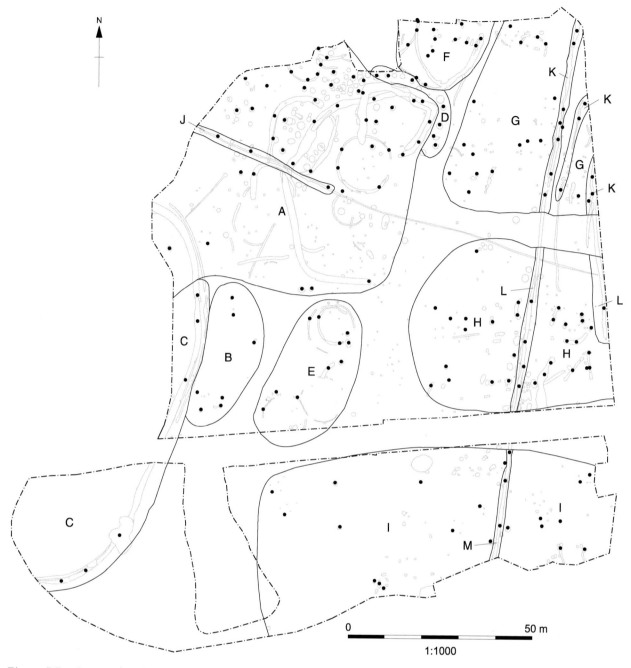

Figure 5.7 Areas referred to in discussion of phosphate and magnetic susceptibility surveys.

enriched'. The magnetic susceptibility samples were similarly ascribed to four categories ranging from 'no enhancement' to 'very strongly enhanced'. The distribution of the samples and their levels of phosphate enrichment and magnetic susceptibility enhancement are shown by Figures 5.5 and 5.6.

The evidence confirms the impression that the north-western settlement area (area A on Fig. 5.7) saw the most intensive human activity. In particular, the zone to the west of Enclosures II and V produced three of the four 'very strongly enriched' phosphate samples and the only 'very strongly enhanced' magnetic susceptibility sample. At least some of the fills in all the other sampled areas of the site show clear signs of phosphate enrichment and/or magnetic susceptibility enhancement, with the notable exception of gullies 3100, 3110, 3130 and 3280 at the eastern periphery of the site (areas K–M on Fig. 5.7).

Chapter 6: Discussion

The various phases of fieldwork at Fairfield Park— including geophysical survey, fieldwalking, evaluation trenching and open area excavation—have between them provided significant insights into the long-term history of the hilltop (Table 6.1). This concluding chapter begins with a summary of the overall sequence of occupation. A more detailed discussion of the late Bronze Age activity and early Iron Age settlements will then follow.

THE SEQUENCE OF OCCUPATION AT FAIRFIELD PARK

No features predating the late Bronze Age were encountered in any of the investigations. Although some residual flintwork was recovered from Sites A and B, probably ranging in date from the Mesolithic to the early Bronze Age, the quantities were quite small. Furthermore, very little worked flint was recovered in the surrounding areas during fieldwalking and evaluation trenching. Use of the hilltop during early prehistory may thus have been limited to sporadic, low-level visitations.

Late Bronze Age activity is recorded at Site A in the form of a large suboval enclosure, a small cluster of pits and an un-urned cremation burial. Two further un-urned cremation burials were found at Site B, one of which has been radiocarbon dated to around the 9th century cal BC. Following the late Bronze Age, there may have been a hiatus in activity at both sites. It is possible that this gap in the occupation sequence can be filled by the cluster of pits found during the evaluation at Site C, although the pottery from these features can only be broadly dated to the late Bronze Age/early Iron Age.

During the latter stages of the early Iron Age, settlements were established at both Sites A and B. In both cases these settlements consisted of small enclosures, roundhouses, four-post structures and numerous pits. Some limited continuity into the middle Iron Age occurred at Site A, evinced mainly by material from the upper fills of early Iron Age ditches and pits. During the Late Iron Age, the focus of activity shifted westwards, to Site C. The excavated evidence from evaluation Trench 10 suggests that a rectilinear enclosure system was laid out. Little Roman material was associated with these ditches, but the recovery of significant amounts of Roman pottery from the area of Site C during fieldwalking indicates that settlement continued beyond the conquest. A richly furnished cremation burial dating to *c* AD 75–120 was found in Trench 10, cutting one of the earlier ditches. Elsewhere on the hilltop, evidence for Romano-British activity was limited. Site B was crossed by a double-ditched trackway, containing pottery dated to the 2nd century AD, while at Site A only two small pits or gullies occurred. There was also an almost total absence of Roman pottery from the fieldwalking and evaluation trenching beyond the three identified sites. This evidence suggests that the immediate hinterland of the late Iron Age to Romano-British settlement at Site C saw no more than agricultural use.

During the earlier Anglo-Saxon period, a substantial double-ditched earthwork was constructed along the eastern edge of the hilltop, running for a distance of at least 325 m. It is unclear whether this formed part of an enclosure around the hilltop or represents a linear landscape boundary. However, it can be noted that an estate charter of AD 1007, granting land in neighbouring Norton to St Albans Abbey, describes the western boundary of this grant as running "from Wilbury Hill along Stotfold dyke, then along Stotfold boundary" (Doggett 1983). This 'dyke' has never been identified, but could conceivably be a reference to the double-ditched earthwork, which may well still have been visible as a landscape feature.

No evidence for medieval or early post-medieval activity was found beyond agricultural features such as furrows and boundary gullies. This supports the historical and cartographic evidence that the hilltop formed part of the open fields of Stotfold parish, prior to enclosure in 1848 and the subsequent foundation of Fairfield Hospital.

LATE BRONZE AGE ENCLOSURE AND BURIAL

Enclosure

Enclosure I would have had an imposing presence in the landscape, measuring *c* 100 m in diameter and occupying a prominent position on the highest part of the hilltop. Initial construction of the enclosure probably occurred during the late Bronze Age, to judge by the small quantity of pottery recovered from the initial cut of the ditch; certainly, the absence of Iron Age material strongly suggests that it predates the closely adjacent early Iron Age settlement. The later recut of the ditch is of more uncertain date. A radiocarbon date of 1250–1230 cal BC/1220–1010 cal BC (NZA-21952: 2916 ± 25 BP) from a middle fill may suggest that this recut was also constructed in the late Bronze Age, but pottery from the lower fills of the feature elsewhere along the circuit suggests an early Iron Age attribution (see Chapter 2). The enclosure ditch was of moderate size, with a surviving depth of no more than 1 m. There was no evidence for the location of any upcast bank.

Interpreting the role of the enclosure is difficult, as its most striking feature is its apparent emptiness. No late

Table 6.1   Summary of the long-term use of the hilltop.

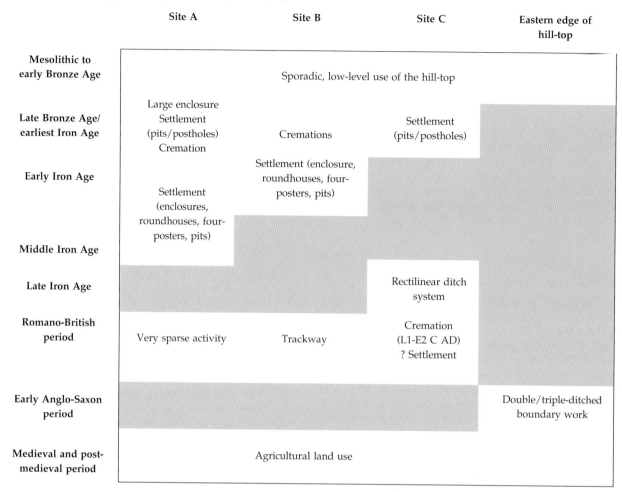

	Site A	Site B	Site C	Eastern edge of hill-top
Mesolithic to early Bronze Age	Sporadic, low-level use of the hill-top			
Late Bronze Age/ earliest Iron Age	Large enclosure Settlement (pits/postholes) Cremation	Cremations	Settlement (pits/postholes)	
Early Iron Age	Settlement (enclosures, roundhouses, four-posters, pits)	Settlement (enclosure, roundhouses, four-posters, pits)		
Middle Iron Age				
Late Iron Age			Rectilinear ditch system	
Romano-British period	Very sparse activity	Trackway	Cremation (L1-E2 C AD) ? Settlement	
Early Anglo-Saxon period				Double/triple-ditched boundary work
Medieval and post-medieval period	Agricultural land use			

Bronze Age features were present within the enclosed area, and there seems to have been little contemporary deposition of material culture into the ditches. In contrast to the emptiness of the interior of the enclosure, some activity did occur immediately to the east of it. This took the form of a small cluster of shallow pits and postholes, which yielded modest quantities of late Bronze Age pottery and animal bone along with a copper alloy awl. These features need not represent more than a single brief episode of occupation.

Assuming a late Bronze Age origin, Enclosure I can be paralleled by a number of similarly-sized, broadly contemporary hilltop enclosures from across southern England. The earliest of these seem to date to the closing centuries of the 2nd millennium BC. The best example is the well-known site at Rams Hill, Oxon, where an oval enclosure with a ditch and internal bank measuring *c* 120 x 75 m has been found. Radio-carbon evidence places the first phase of the enclosure in the 13th to early 11th centuries cal BC. Occupation in the form of pits and post-built structures was present in the interior, although it is not clear how much of this was contemporary with the enclosure itself (Bradley and Ellison 1975; Needham and Ambers 1994). Bradley and Ellison (1975) have cited several further possible examples of middle Bronze

Age 'Rams Hill-type' enclosures, including South Lodge Camp, Wiltshire; Martin Down, Hampshire; Highdown Hill, Sussex; and Norton Fitzwarren, Somerset. However, at each of these sites there are uncertainties surrounding the dating evidence and interpretation of the structural remains (Needham and Ambers 1994). Some further possible parallels have however come to light in recent years. These include a site at Camp Gardens, Stow-on-the-Wold, Gloucestershire, where a large ditch interpreted as belonging to a hilltop enclosure has produced two radiocarbon dates of 1400–990 cal BC and 1390–1005 cal BC respectively (Parry 1999). Meanwhile, a 1.2 ha hilltop enclosure at Thundersbarrow Hill, Sussex, has produced a very early radiocarbon date of 1670–1320 cal BC from antler from a basal ditch fill, although the possibility of residuality is clearly an issue (Hamilton and Manley 1997).

A slightly later group of hilltop enclosures date from *c* 1050 BC onwards. These include the final phase of the Rams Hill enclosure, dating to the late 11th–10th centuries BC, when a double palisade was set into the now infilled ditch (Needham and Ambers 1994). At Castle Hill, Oxon, a subcircular hill-top enclosure measuring *c* 100 m in diameter contained late Bronze Age 'plain ware' pottery, and has produced four radiocarbon determinations with date ranges falling between the late 11th and 9th centuries cal BC (Allen *et al.* forthcoming a). At Taplow, Buckinghamshire, an enclosure probably measuring *c* 160 m long and 80–100 m across has been found on a bluff overlooking the River Thames. The enclosure ditch contained late Bronze Age plain ware, and an optically stimulated luminescence (OSL) date of 1070–790 BC has been obtained from the lower silts (Allen *et al.* forthcoming b). At Carshalton, Surrey, a circular enclosure *c* 150 m in diameter has produced plain ware pottery from its ditch (Adkins and Needham 1985), and recent small-scale excavation has produced evidence for pits both inside and outside the enclosure (Groves and Lovell 2002). A similar circular enclosure at Thrapston, Northamptonshire, is around 110 m in diameter and has produced late Bronze Age material; again, occupation in the form of pits was found both within and outside the enclosed area (Hull 2001).

Fairfield Park may thus be an example of a more widespread class of later Bronze Age hilltop enclosures, which show a fair degree of consistency in their size and in their oval to circular form (Allen *et al.* forthcoming a). The limited extent of excavation means that the function of these enclosures remains uncertain, although there are few indications that they were major foci for settlement. The evidence from Fairfield Park perhaps instead suggests a role as a venue for periodic gatherings of a kind that did not leave substantial material residues.

Burial

A single un-urned cremation burial occurred immediately to the north of Enclosure I. Two similar cremation burials were also found at Site B, one of which produced a radiocarbon date of 920–790 cal BC (NZA-22062; 2687 ± 40 BP). This is significantly later than the date obtained from the enclosure ditch, and thus whether Enclosure I was still in use when the burials were interred is uncertain.

The late Bronze Age in southern England has traditionally been characterised as a period in which 'formal' burials were rare (Brück 1995). However, a decade ago Needham (1995) drew attention to a few rare examples of cremation burials contained within or associated with post-Deverel-Rimbury vessels, and speculated that the 'invisibility' of the bulk of the population may be due to a tradition of cremation burial without associated grave goods. This has been borne out in recent years, as un-urned and unaccompanied cremation burials have been found at a number of late Bronze Age sites in south-east England. Aside from Fairfield Park, examples have been found within Bedfordshire at Biddenham Loop (Luke forthcoming), Broom (Cooper and Edmonds forthcoming) and High Barns Farm, Great Barford (Webley forthcoming). Elsewhere, examples include Gadebridge, Herts (Bryant 1997; Gibson 2001), Stone, Bucks (Gibson 2001), Reading Business Park, Berks (Moore and Jennings 1992), White Horse Stone,

Table 6.2   Radiocarbon determinations post-dating 1100 BC from un-urned cremation burials in south-east England.

Site	Date (cal BC)	Reference
Fairfield Park, Beds.	920–790	This volume
Broom, Beds.	1000–820	Cooper and Edmonds forthcoming
Stone Hall, Essex	980–810	Timby *et al.* forthcoming
Stone Hall, Essex	1040–820	Timby *et al.* forthcoming
Ongar Road, Essex	910–790	Timby *et al.* forthcoming
Gadebridge, Herts.	1055–885	Gibson 2001
White Horse Stone, Boxley, Kent	1010–830	Hayden and Stafford 2006

Kent (Hayden and Stafford 2005) and several sites in Essex (Brown 1988; Timby *et al.* forthcoming) and Surrey (Cotton 2004, 29). These cremation burials are typically found singly or in small groups, without any obvious form of enclosure. A number of radiocarbon dates have now been obtained which fall within the 11th–9th centuries cal BC (Table 6.2). Overall, the evidence now suggests a coherent tradition of late Bronze Age cremation burial which has previously been overlooked, due to the insubstantial nature of the deposits and their lack of associated datable finds.

The landscape

Knowledge of the contemporary landscape surrounding Fairfield Park is limited. However, small amounts of pottery broadly dated to the late Bronze Age/early Iron Age have been recovered from excavations at Letchworth Cemetery (1.5 km to the south: Edmondson *et al.* 2002), Blackhorse Road, Letchworth (3 km to the east-south-east: Moss-Eccardt 1988) and Etonbury Farm, Arlesey (3 km to the north: Hillelson 2004) (see Fig. 6.1 for site locations). These limited finds may represent small-scale and perhaps shifting communities, for whom the hilltop enclosure at Fairfield Park might have served as a focal point in the landscape.

IRON AGE SETTLEMENT

Early Iron Age settlement in eastern England is relatively poorly understood at present. There have been few large-scale, modern excavations of sites of this period, in contrast to the large numbers of middle to late Iron Age sites investigated in recent years. Fairfield Park thus has considerable potential to advance our understanding of how early Iron Age communities were organised, moving us beyond a reliance on models derived from Wessex and the Upper Thames Valley.

The landscape setting

The landscape within which the early Iron Age settlements were situated can be characterised as

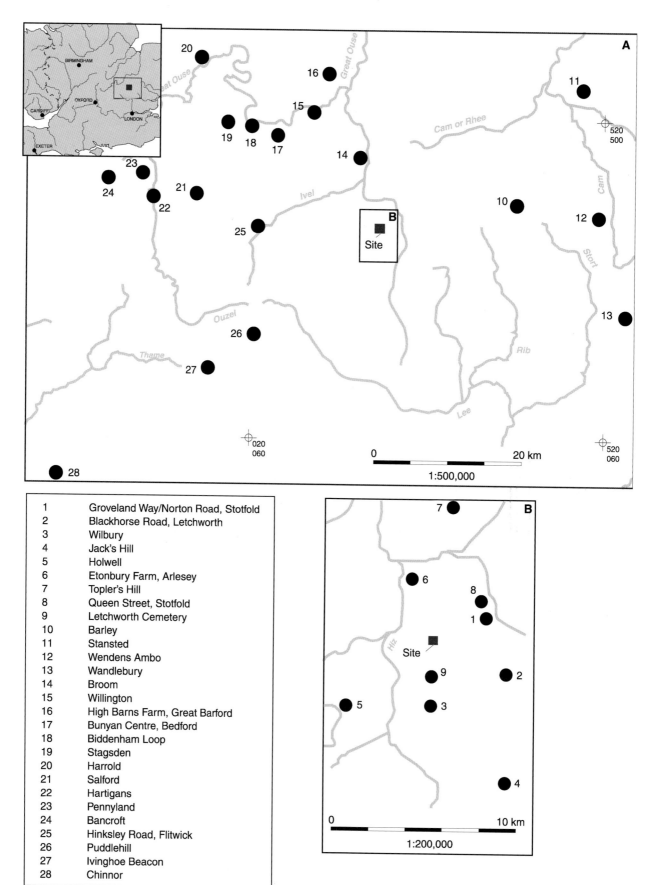

1	Groveland Way/Norton Road, Stotfold
2	Blackhorse Road, Letchworth
3	Wilbury
4	Jack's Hill
5	Holwell
6	Etonbury Farm, Arlesey
7	Topler's Hill
8	Queen Street, Stotfold
9	Letchworth Cemetery
10	Barley
11	Stansted
12	Wendens Ambo
13	Wandlebury
14	Broom
15	Willington
16	High Barns Farm, Great Barford
17	Bunyan Centre, Bedford
18	Biddenham Loop
19	Stagsden
20	Harrold
21	Salford
22	Hartigans
23	Pennyland
24	Bancroft
25	Hinksley Road, Flitwick
26	Puddlehill
27	Ivinghoe Beacon
28	Chinnor

Figure 6.1 Location of early-middle Iron Age sites mentioned in the text.

essentially open. The pollen and mollusc analyses at Site A indicate a local environment of arable fields, grassland and disturbed ground, with any woodland being some distance away. This picture of a largely open and 'tamed' landscape appears to be typical of the first millennium BC within the wider region (Wiltshire 2005, 153–4).

Environmental reconstruction of the landscape provides only half the story, of course, as the *experience* of the landscape would have been informed by history and myth. In this context, the location of the Site A settlement adjacent to the pre-existing late Bronze Age enclosure is worth noting. It is unclear whether the enclosure was still in active use at the time that the settlement was established, but at the very least it still existed as an earthwork, and would thus have continued to shape people's perception of place (Barrett 1999). Even if the original purpose of the enclosure was long forgotten, it is likely to have engendered a sense that previous agents (either human or supernatural) had been at work on the hilltop in the distant past. Continued awareness of the enclosure is suggested by the fact that it effectively bounded the western side of the Iron Age settlement at Site A, with only a single pit transgressing this line. Whether the presence of the enclosure played any role in the initial choice of location for the settlement is unclear. However, examples do exist elsewhere in the region of Iron Age sites deliberately sited on or adjacent to earlier earthwork monuments, particularly barrows (Bradley 2002, 135–41).

Chronology

The dating evidence suggests that the main occupation of Site A (Phase 2) occurred during a relatively brief period in the latter stages of the early Iron Age. The pottery can be compared with assemblages from elsewhere in the region which have produced absolute dates of the 5th–4th centuries BC. Other closely datable objects are few in number, but generally fit this picture. The La Tène I brooch from Structure 17a can be ascribed to the 4th–3rd centuries BC. The rotary querns from pit 4565 are unusually early in a regional context, but are compatible with evidence from elsewhere in southern England for a 5th–4th century BC introduction of such artefacts. Similarly, the iron 'poker' from pit 156 is consistent with the suggested 4th century BC date for the introduction of this artefact type to Britain (see Chapter 3). The radiocarbon dating evidence is discussed in Chapter 2, but the salient point is that all six dates from Phase 2 contexts are compatible with occupation during the 4th century BC.

Some continuity of occupation into the middle Iron Age (Phase 3) did however occur at Site A, represented by small quantities of material in stratigraphically late contexts. This included scored ware pottery (Elsdon 1992), and an involuted brooch of a type dating from the late 3rd century BC onwards.

The radiocarbon dating programme for Site B unfortunately yielded only a single acceptable determination from an Iron Age context, from pit 2327, and even this produced a relatively broad date range of 730–690 cal BC/540–380 cal BC (NZA-22005; 2376±40 BP). The upper limit of this range just overlaps with two of the determinations from Phase 2 features at Site A, but falls short of the remaining four. This could suggest a slightly earlier inception for the settlement at Site B. However, it would of course be unwise to place too much emphasis on a single radiocarbon date. The pottery assemblage from Site B shows marked similarities to that from Site A, and the emphasis must again be on the latter stages of the early Iron Age. It is particularly notable that sherds from almost identical bowls with a highly unusual rim-top decoration of hatched triangles were found at both Sites A and B (pits 4757 and 2043 respectively). This provides a hint that the two sites may have been occupied at the same time. Unlike Site A, however, Site B produced no evidence for continuity in activity into the middle Iron Age.

To summarise, the main occupation of Site A fell towards the end of the early Iron Age, probably centring around the 4th century BC. Settlement at Site B might have begun slightly earlier in the early Iron Age, but the main occupation is again likely to have been during the latter stages of the period. While it cannot be proven that occupation of the two sites overlapped, the ceramic evidence suggests that it may well have done.

The structure of settlement space

Lying 550 m apart, it must be assumed that Sites A and B were separate settlement foci rather than parts of a single agglomeration. The total extent of each settlement is unknown, as in both cases occupation continued beyond the limit of excavation. This problem is exacerbated by the fact that the evaluation fieldwork did not cover the areas immediately to the north and west of Site A, or that to the north, north-east and west of Site B. However, the available evidence would suggest that we are dealing with 'hamlet'-sized communities (Fig. 6.2).

The core of the settlement at Site A was a roughly north-south aligned row of roundhouses. Seven definite and five possible roundhouses have been identified (Structures 1–12), though no more than seven of these buildings could have stood at any one time. At the northern end of the row of roundhouses lay a series of curvilinear and subrectangular enclosures, measuring between 10 and 50 m across. These show a stratigraphic sequence, with Enclosure II replaced by Enclosure III, which was in turn succeeded by Enclosures IV and V. Enclosure II cut two storage pits, indicating that a period of unenclosed activity preceded this sequence. Enclosure III may have been laid out around a pair of roundhouses, Structures 1 and 2; certainly, Structure 1 was abandoned by the time that Enclosure IV was

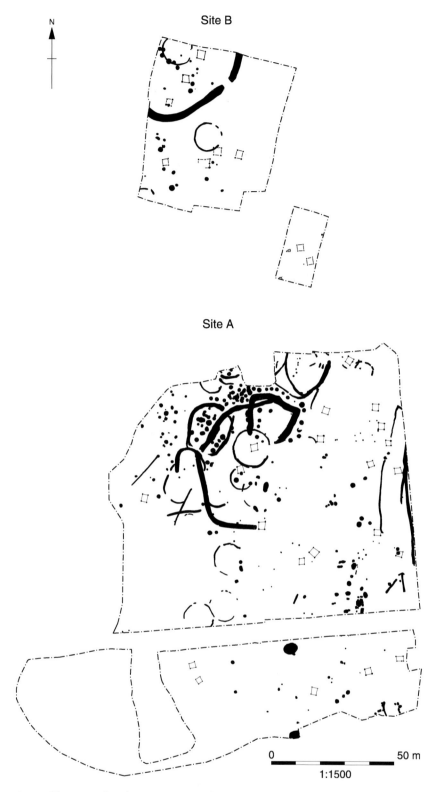

Figure 6.2   Comparison of layouts of early Iron Age settlements at Sites A and B.

constructed. To the north of this group of enclosures lay a further compound, Enclosure VI, which again may have enclosed a roundhouse (Structure 11). The area around Enclosures II–VI—and particularly that to the north and west of Enclosure III—was

characterised by large numbers of pits, including storage pits. The density of features in this area of the site suggests that it was a major focus of activity, an impression confirmed by the artefact distribution plots (Figs 3.11 and 4.15) and the phosphate and magnetic susceptibility surveys (Figs 5.5–6). Notably, three of the four 'very strongly enriched' phosphate samples came from pits clustered together in a small area to the west of Enclosures II and V. This resonates with the fact that one of these features was noted to have a greenish 'cess-like' fill (pit 4635). Middens or latrines may thus have been located in this area.

The area to the east and south-east of the enclosures and roundhouses was characterised by more dispersed pits and numerous four-post 'granaries', suggesting an emphasis on storage rather than habitation. Two large hollows—possibly ponds—were located in the south-eastern corner of the site. Most of the other pits in this south-eastern area were shallow, and showed relatively low phosphate levels, suggesting that some could in fact be of natural origin. At the eastern limit of the excavated area, a group of north-south aligned gullies were found that might represent boundary features at the settlement periphery, although their dating was uncertain. The south-western corner of the excavated area was devoid of early Iron Age features, and it would seem that the edge of the settlement has been defined here.

The smaller area excavated at Site B means that much less can be said about the spatial organisation of the early Iron Age occupation. However, the basic elements of the settlement are similar to those at Site A. There were three roundhouses, again roughly arranged in a north-south aligned row. The northernmost roundhouse was placed within a curvilinear ditched enclosure, which had an east-facing entrance and had been recut at least once. Pits, storage pits and four-post structures were scattered across the site, with no clear concentrations, although the north-eastern corner of the excavated area was largely devoid of features.

Comparisons for the settlement layout at Fairfield Park are few, given the paucity of contemporary excavated sites in eastern England. However, the majority of early Iron Age settlements in the region appear to have consisted of unenclosed clusters or swathes of roundhouses, ancillary structures and pits, as at the Bunyan Centre, Bedford (Steadman 1999), and the early phases at Puddlehill (Matthews 1976). The small, subrectangular or suboval ditched enclosures at Fairfield Park are most easily paralleled in late early Iron Age and middle Iron Age contexts, as at Broom (Cooper and Edmonds forthcoming) and Groveland Way, Stotfold (Steadman forthcoming). Meanwhile, the north-south linear arrangement of the roundhouses at Fairfield Park can be paralleled at the early to middle Iron Age site at Salford, Beds (Dawson 2005), and the middle Iron Age site at Bancroft, Bucks (Williams and Zeepvat 1994).

Settlement architecture

Buildings

The roundhouses at Sites A and B were all represented by penannular eaves-gullies, with little or no trace of the buildings themselves surviving. Similar 'eaves-gully houses' are common within the region from the latter stages of the early Iron Age onwards, replacing buildings of the early first millennium BC which had more robust structural posts and generally lacked a surrounding drainage ditch. Various explanations have been proposed for the paucity of evidence for house superstructures during this period, including turf or earth 'mass wall' construction, or the use of small stakes to form a 'basketwork' structure that did not penetrate the subsoil (Knight 1984, 143). Clearly, any vertical posts within the Fairfield Park roundhouses must have been shallow-set or placed on stone pads, given that so many postholes belonging to four-post structures survived on the site. Some trace of the roundhouses may have survived in the form of burnt daub, moderate amounts of which were recovered. However, it is notable that at Site A the largest concentrations of daub and structural fired clay were found in pits located some distance away from the roundhouses, at the eastern periphery of the settlement.

Ranging between 8.3 and 13.9 m in diameter, the house gullies from Fairfield Park are comparable in size to those from contemporary sites elsewhere in the region (Fig. 6.3), with Structure 1 falling at the upper limit for buildings of this type. Entrance orientations fell between east and south-east (Fig. 6.5), as typical for Iron Age roundhouses in the region (Knight 1984, 144–5; Oswald 1997).

Evidence for internal fixtures within the roundhouses is sparse. However, small clay-lined pits were concentrated in and around the roundhouses. Within Structure 1, one such 'cooking pit' was placed just within the entrance, on the left side when looking out of the building, and a second example may also have been placed in a similar location within Structure 3. These pits often contained significant quantities of burnt or heat-cracked stones, although the clay linings never showed any evidence of heating. Similar pits have been identified at a number of other sites in the region dating from the late Bronze Age to middle Iron Age, and are thought to have been used for heating water or boiling food (eg Williams 1993).

The placing of clay-lined 'cooking pits' within the left hand side of roundhouses finds many parallels at late Bronze Age to middle Iron Age sites across southern England. In fact, of at least 29 examples of roundhouses containing clay-lined pits from ten different sites, in all but two cases the pits are located in the left side of the building (Table 6.3 and Fig. 6.4). The strength of this pattern suggests that the clay-lined pits were indeed internal fixtures of the houses, even though (given the absence of preserved floors) there is no stratigraphic evidence to demonstrate the contemporaneity of building and pit in any single case. This seems to be a previously unidentified tradition in the use of domestic space, which was followed by communities stretching from Gloucestershire in the west to Essex and Cambridgeshire in the east.

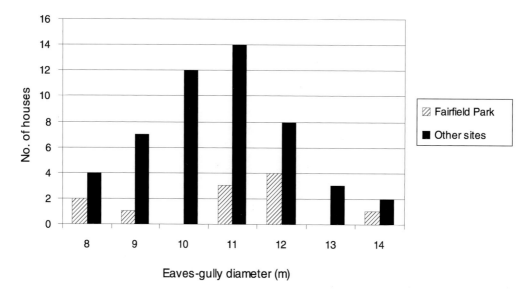

Figure 6.3 House size (eaves-gully diameter) at Fairfield Park compared to other early and middle Iron Age settlements in the region. 'Other sites' include Groveland Way (Steadman forthcoming) and Salford (Dawson 2006), Beds., Bancroft (Williams and Zeepvat 1994) and Pennyland (Williams 1993), Bucks., and Wendens Ambo, Essex (Hodder 1982); combined total 49 houses.

The other recognisable class of building at Fairfield Park was the 'four-post structure', of which 20 were identified at Site A and 8 at Site B. While such structures have traditionally been interpreted as raised granaries, it is possible that they could have served a range of different functions (Ellison and Drewett 1971). The alignment of the four-post structures tended to fall around the cardinal points, a different principle to that followed by the roundhouses (Fig. 6.5).

Enclosures

The nature of enclosure and the purposes it may have served has been a recurring theme in discussions of Iron Age settlement in the region (eg Knight 1984; Dawson 2000a; forthcoming). The enclosures at Fairfield Park varied significantly in their size, form, entrance orientation and ditch dimensions, suggesting that the activities associated with them are also likely to have differed. Notably, a pattern can be seen whereby all of the east-facing enclosures (III, VI and VIII) contained roundhouses, while enclosures facing in other directions (II, IV and VII) did not. This corresponds with the fact that the roundhouses themselves all faced east or south-east.

It is now widely accepted that settlement enclosure during the Iron Age cannot be explained simply in functional terms, as serving for defence or stock-management; it also had a symbolic aspect (Bowden and McOmish 1987; Hingley 1990). Site A illustrates this point, as the open-sided nature of Enclosures III and IV makes them seem more of a 'statement' than a practical means of containing livestock or excluding enemies. The symbolic dimension of the enclosures is underlined by the pit row which partially surrounded Enclosure IV. The pits seem to have been rapidly back-filled, though not before human corpses were placed within two of them. The procedure of digging and then filling these pits

Table 6.3 Roundhouses containing clay-lined 'cooking' pits from southern England.

Site	Date	No. of houses	Reference
Broom (Beds.)	LBA or EIA	2	Cooper and Edmonds forthcoming
Fairfield Park, Stotfold (Beds.)	EIA	1–2	This volume
Bancroft (Bucks.)	MIA	2	Williams and Zeepvat 1994
Pennyland (Bucks.)	MIA	4	Williams 1993
King's Dyke West, Whittlesey (Cambs.)	LBA	1	Knight 1999
Eldons Seat, Encombe (Dorset)*	EIA	1	Cunliffe and Phillipson 1968
Little Waltham (Essex)	MIA	1	Drury 1978
Claydon Pike, Lechlade (Gloucs.)	MIA	11	Miles *et al.* forthcoming
Weekley (Northants.)	MIA	1	Jackson and Dix 1987
Gravelly Guy, Stanton Harcourt (Oxon.)	E-MIA	5	Lambrick and Allen 2005

* = less certain example.

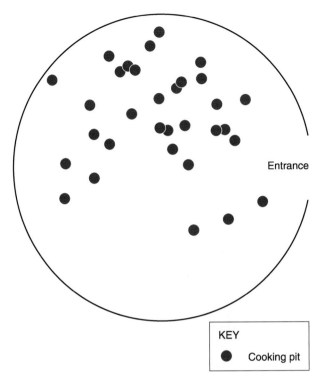

Figure 6.4 Location of clay-lined 'cooking pits' within roundhouses at ten sites in southern England.

would appear to have served no purpose beyond emphasising the enclosure boundary.

The sequence of enclosures in the north-western part of Site A seems to represent an enduring concern with marking the distinctiveness of this particular area of the settlement. As well as making a visual statement, the enclosure ditches perhaps also served to guide or formalise appropriate paths of movement around this locale. The significance of this particular area may also be reflected in the fact that it

contained the largest roundhouse at the site, and was a focus for deposition, including both human and animal burials (see below).

Pits

Numerous deep, bell-shaped or cylindrical pits were found at Sites A and B, a few of which showed traces of clay lining. Pits of this kind are argued to have been used for storage of seed corn, grain for consumption being more likely to have been stored above ground (Reynolds 1979). The pits were typically back-filled fairly soon after they had gone out of use, although the back-fill deposits were sometimes interleaved with episodes of natural slumping, suggesting that the process could be punctuated by hiatuses. The back-fill deposits often included dumps of midden material and 'placed' deposits of artefacts, animal bone or human remains (see *Depositional practices* below).

Similar storage pits are a common feature of early to middle Iron Age sites in the region, although they are generally absent from those located on poorly-drained clay soils (eg Salford: Dawson 2005). In the Chilterns, dense clusters of storage pits often occur at early to middle Iron Age settlements, at sites such as Puddlehill (Matthews 1976), Barley (Cra'ster 1960; 1965) and Blackhorse Road, Letchworth (Moss-Eccardt 1988). A notable feature of the storage pits from these sites, seen also at Fairfield Park, is how rarely they intercut. This may suggest that the location of the pits was remembered or marked in some way after they had been backfilled.

It is difficult to ascribe specific functions to the numerous shallower pits found at Fairfield Park. While some of the more irregular examples may relate to clay or gravel extraction, this can hardly explain all of them. However, it is possible that many of these pits were not 'functional' in the usual sense of the word. The pit row surrounding Enclosure IV,

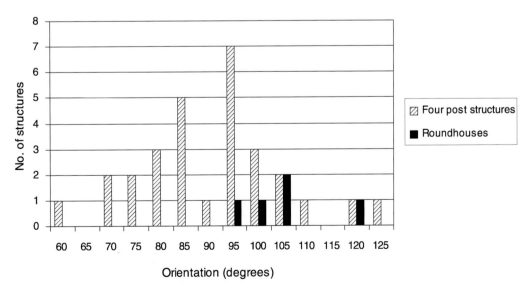

Figure 6.5 Orientations of roundhouse entrances and four-post structures (eastern side) at Fairfield Park.

discussed above, may have served no purpose beyond demarcating space and receiving human remains. 'Structured' or placed deposits also occurred in shallow pits elsewhere on the site (see below). In such cases, the suspicion must be that the pits were dug for no other reason than to receive these deposits.

Making a living

The community at Fairfield Park was engaged in mixed farming. The importance of cereals is attested both by the abundant charred plant remains and by a number of saddle and rotary querns. Spelt and barley were grown, possibly along with oats and peas. The weed taxa suggest that a range of soils were cultivated, including both the lighter gravel soils and the heavier boulder clays (till) around the settlements. Cereal processing took place within the settlement, apparently on a fairly small-scale, 'domestic' level. Livestock are also well attested, with sheep, goats, cattle, pigs, horses and dogs all kept by the community. Caution is needed when interpreting the relative abundance of species, as depositional practices at the site clearly involved the structured and selective treatment of animal remains (see below). However, it is notable that Fairfield Park differs from many other Iron Age sites within the region, in that sheep/goats rather than cattle were dominant (Hambleton 1999). Overall, Holmes (Chapter 4) argues that the nature of the animal husbandry at Fairfield Park was more similar to contemporary sites in Wessex and the Upper Thames Valley than to sites in eastern England. As is typical, wild foodstuffs seem to have been of minimal importance, although hazelnuts and sloes may have been gathered. There are no indications that hunting took place, as only small quantities of wild animal bone were recovered, aside from deer antler which was probably collected after it had been shed.

A typical range of 'craft' activities were pursued within the community. Weaving is evinced by the grooved metapodials from Site A (Pls 3.2–3.3), and possibly also by fired clay 'loomweights' (Fig. 3.9). Evidence for spinning is scarcer, though Site A yielded a single bone spindle whorl (Fig. 3.12). At both sites, waste pieces from antler and bone working were present. Finds of hearth bottoms show that iron smithing occurred, although the paucity of slag indicates that this must have been carried out on a small scale. Expedient flint knapping to produce simple tools probably also occurred. Although no direct evidence was found for ceramic manufacture, the pottery fabrics are consistent with local production, as typical for sites in the region (Morris 1996).

Depositional practices and the treatment of the dead

A considerable degree of patterning is apparent in where and in what manner different types of objects were deposited within the settlements at Fairfield Park. This provides evidence for the significance of different areas within the settlements. It may also inform us about the categorisation of artefacts, animals and people, and concepts of their appropriate treatment once their lifecycles had come to an end.

The nature of depositional practices within Iron Age settlements is an issue that has attracted considerable interest in recent years. For example, there has been much work on the apparently 'structured' nature of the deposits often found in storage pits (eg Cunliffe 1992; Hill 1995a; Hamilton 1998). Finds of near-complete artefacts, human remains or articulated animal burials in such pits have been suggested to represent offerings, forming part of propitiatory rites intended to maintain agricultural fertility (Cunliffe 1992; Cunliffe and Poole 1995). However, most discussion of such practices has focussed on Wessex and neighbouring areas, and the extent to which similar practices occurred in eastern England is at present unclear. Re-examination of older published reports suggests that 'placed' storage pits deposits similar to those seen in Wessex—including animal skeletons and complete querns—may have occurred at a number of early and middle Iron Age sites in the Chilterns (eg Puddlehill, Beds: Matthews 1976; Barley, Herts: Cra'ster 1960). In the absence of detailed contextual information, however, these observations cannot be pursued very far. The evidence from Fairfield Park may help us to more fully address such questions of regionality in depositional practice.

Depositional practices at Fairfield Park: general considerations

While the notion of 'structured deposition' has undoubtedly been very useful in advancing our understanding of the Iron Age, the application of this concept in many recent site reports has arguably been somewhat simplistic. Typically, certain deposits which seem striking or unusual to the author are picked out as 'special' or 'ritual', while the rest of the material from the site is apparently still considered as mundane rubbish. This is an unhelpful approach which reveals more about our perceptions as modern observers than it does about the beliefs or behaviours of prehistoric people. Instead, the approach pursued here will be to consider depositional practices in the round, acknowledging that there may be no clear distinction between what we might label as ritualistic and pragmatic acts (Brück 1999).

The distribution plots of the main finds categories give an overall sense of the density of artefact-rich deposits at Sites A and B (Figs 3.7–8, 4.15 and 4.17). Most of the finds-rich deposits were relatively mixed and fragmented, and of a character consistent with general domestic 'waste' or midden material, although some of them also incorporate apparently freshly-broken items or articulated human or animal bone (see below). To some extent the 'high spots' in the distribution plots merely reflect the distribution of deep pits and ditches. Nevertheless, it can be noted that at Site A, large artefact assemblages are not restricted to the 'core' area around the houses and enclosures, but also occur in features in the peripheral areas to the east and south-east (such as the very large assemblage from pit 3285). Furthermore, the levels of attrition of the material, as measured by the mean sherd weight of pottery, shows no clear patterning across the site; some deposits of relatively 'fresh' material again occur in the eastern peripheral areas. This could perhaps have been the result of deliberate clearance of material away from the settlement 'core'.

The very largest assemblages of finds were recovered from pits, particularly storage pits. The most striking example was pit 2043 at Site B, which contained a huge assemblage of finds, including 10.7 kg of pottery. The bulk of the material from pits seems to have been deposited in the course of the deliberate back-filling of these features. Human remains or articulated animal bone deposits were found within the back-fill deposits in several of the pits, and indeed were largely restricted to pit contexts (see below).

While work in Wessex and Sussex has indicated patterning in the vertical placement of items within storage pits, with pit bases often favoured for 'placed' deposits (Cunliffe and Poole 1995; Hill 1995a; Hamilton 1998), this is not the case at Fairfield Park. Different artefact categories in fact seem to show an essentially even distribution (Table 6.4), with the caveat that any deposits made in the very uppermost parts of the pits are likely to be missing due to truncation. The one possible exception to this even distribution is metal artefacts, which seem to favour the upper fills of pits, but the sample is very small. There were also no recurrent associations of particular artefact categories occurring together within the same pit.

The distribution of material in ditch and gully contexts tended to follow the pattern commonly seen at Iron Age settlements, in which the entrances to enclosures and roundhouses form a focus for deposition (Hill 1995a). The ditches of Enclosures III, VI and VIII and the eaves-gullies of Structures 4 and 35 all showed increased quantities of finds adjacent to the entrance, when compared to the rest of the

circuit (Figs 3.7–8, 4.15 and 4.17). Furthermore, raised phosphate levels relative to the rest of the circuit can be seen at the entrances to Structures 1, 4 and 7 (Fig. 5.5), suggesting greater deposition of organic material.

The deposition of specific artefact categories

Pottery was by far the most abundant artefact type at both sites. No entirely complete vessels were recovered, but a few deposits of unusually large and fresh sherds were observed, which may represent a different depositional pathway from the norm (see *Pottery*, Chapter 3). Relative to animal bone, pottery was significantly more abundant in pits than in ditches, a pattern consistent at both Sites A and B (Fig. 6.6). This may indicate selective patterns of deposition, although it is also possible that greater attrition of pottery in open ditches (see Table 3.4) has lead to under-representation in the recovered assemblage.

A few patterns can be discerned in the distribution of particular classes of small finds at Site A. Some of the more 'functional' objects seem to have been clustered around the core of the settlement. This includes worked bone implements, which were all found around the north-western enclosure group (Fig. 3.13). Complete or near-complete querns meanwhile seem to have had a particularly close association with roundhouses, although smaller fragments occur more widely across the site, often reused as post-packing (Fig. 3.16). In contrast to the distributions of such 'functional' objects, dress accessories made from copper alloy or jet exclusively occurred at the eastern periphery of the site (Fig. 3.13). This implies that it was thought appropriate to treat such items differently from more everyday, domestic objects. This matches observations elsewhere in southern England that high-status metalwork and items of personalia are generally disassociated from the domestic sphere in their context of deposition. Most were disposed of away from settlements, for example in watery places such as rivers, while those that were deposited in settlements often occupied peripheral or boundary locations (Hill 1995a; Haselgrove 1997).

Two particularly unusual deposits deserve further mention. The first is the collection of 49 burnt weaving tools made from sheep/goat metapodials recovered from the middle fill of storage pit 484. Similar items have been found at many other Iron Age settlements in southern England, but they have only previously occurred singly or in small numbers, suggesting that an atypical mode of deposition lay behind the much larger group from Fairfield Park. Substantial pieces of oak and dogwood charcoal were also found in the same context, raising the possibility that a complete burnt loom or set of weaving equipment had been placed in the pit (see *Charcoal*, Chapter 5).

The second is the iron 'poker' from pit 156, which appears to have been deliberately bent in half prior to deposition (Fig. 3.19). This is paralleled at

Table 6.4 Vertical location of selected artefact types from Phase 2 pits containing more than one fill.

	Pit third			Total
	Lower	*Middle*	*Upper*	
Human remains	2	2	2	6
Articulated animal bone	4	3	3	10
Metal artefact	0	1	3	4
Worked bone/antler artefact	2	0	1	3
Loomweight	1	1	2	4
Large pottery group (>500 g)	8	6	8	22

Site A

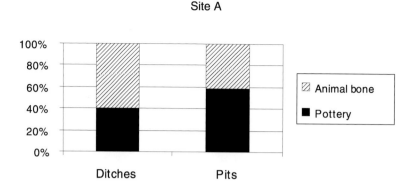

Site B

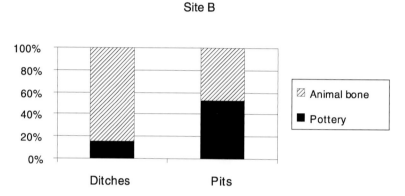

Figure 6.6 Relative proportions (by weight) of pottery and animal bone in pit and ditch contexts.

Billingborough, Lincs, where a similar iron poker was broken in half prior to deposition in a ditch, the two parts of the object being formally laid out alongside each other (Fitzpatrick and Bacon 2001). Such acts are reminiscent of the 'ritual killing' of weaponry and high-status artefacts seen at votive sites such as Llyn Cerrig Bach (Fox 1946), and may suggest that iron 'pokers' had significance beyond a prosaic function in tending fires.

The deposition of animal remains

As noted above, animal bone formed the most abundant category of find from ditch contexts, but were significantly less abundant than pottery in pit contexts (Fig. 6.6). Despite this, the thirteen articulated animal deposits were entirely restricted to pits (Table 6.5). This contrast ties in with some marked differences in the treatment of different species. The articulated deposits from the pits included sheep/goats, pigs and dogs; cattle and horse were absent. At the same time, the data for the bone assemblage as a whole shows that most of the sheep/goat, pig and dog bone was found in pits, while cattle and horse bone was more often found in ditches (Fig. 4.5). This does not appear to be the result of taphonomic factors (Chapter 4). Thus, different species show contrasts in both the context and manner of deposition.

A greater emphasis on sheep/goats in pits and on cattle and horse in ditches is a pattern seen at many Iron Age sites across southern England (Maltby 1996). Maltby argues that the greater representation of cattle in ditches relates to butchery at the periphery of settlements, but this does not apply at Fairfield Park where most ditches belonged to small enclosures located within the settlement core. Instead, we must regard these patterns of deposition as relating to the categorisation of animals and concepts of their appropriate treatment.

Comparing Sites A and B, there is a contrast in the animal species represented in the articulated deposits, with nine sheep/goats and one dog at Site A, compared to three pigs, two sheep/goats and one dog at Site B. Within Site A, articulated animal deposits show a similar distribution to that of human remains, being clustered around the north-western enclosure group.

The deposition of human remains

Two distinct practices in the deposition of human remains can be discerned at Fairfield Park, with children and adults treated differently. Neonates and children are represented by complete or partially complete inhumations, of which there were four from Site A and one from Site B. The two most complete inhumations were placed within shallow pits forming part of pit row 3530, while the remaining examples were all placed in storage pits. Adults, meanwhile, were only represented by individual disarticulated bones, comprising three femurs, a rib and a parietal fragment. Again, there were four examples from Site A and one from Site B. All were from storage pits, except for one femur from a ditch. These two different practices may relate to different ways of treating the dead prior to deposition. While the adults are likely to have been excarnated, with certain individual bones subsequently selected for retrieval, possible curation, and ultimate deposition within the settlement (Carr and Knüsel 1997), the children may have been subject to a briefer cycle of mortuary ritual, being buried relatively promptly. Similar distinctions in the treatment of neonates and adults have been noted at some other Iron Age sites in southern England (Cunliffe 1992). Age may also have influenced burial location at Fairfield Park, as at both Site A and Site B, the child inhumations were placed to the north of the adult bone deposits. Differential treatment according to gender is harder to judge, as only some of the remains could be sexed, but it is clear that both men and women are represented among the adult disarticulated bones.

An unusual aspect of the human bone deposits from Fairfield Park is the fact that all eight of the deposits of disarticulated or semi-articulated human bone consist solely of parts of the left side of the body. There can be little doubt that this was the result of a deliberate process of selection. The exclusive deposition of left-sided elements is not mirrored in the animal bone deposits from the site, and cannot be paralleled in the human bone assemblages from other Iron Age sites in the region. Nevertheless, that the 'sidedness' of the body could carry symbolism in some Iron Age societies is suggested by Parker Pearson's (1999) work on inhumation burials in East Yorkshire, which has revealed complex patterning in the orientation of the body and the choice of left- or right-sided animal parts as grave goods.

There is some evidence from other Iron Age sites in southern England that disarticulated human bones could be curated for a significant length of time before their ultimate deposition. A good example comes from a middle Iron Age settlement at High Barns Farm, Great Barford, Beds, where an articulated skeleton and three skull fragments were formally laid out within a single ditch fill. Radiocarbon dating has indicated that one of the skull fragments is at least 20 years earlier than the articulated skeleton, and is thus likely have been curated prior to its burial (Webley forthcoming). At Fairfield Park, one of the female femur shafts is rounded and polished at one end, suggesting that it had been kept and used for presumably ritual purposes for a period between the excarnation of the body and the final deposition of the bone. It is perhaps no coincidence that the single clearly utilised bone from the site was deposited in a different context to the other human remains, being found in an enclosure ditch rather than a pit. This femur is an unusual find, as deliberately worked or utilised human bone is not commonly recovered from Iron Age sites, and those examples that do occur tend to be skull fragments (Wilson 1981). Notably, however, "part of a human (possibly female) femur worked to a rough point" has been reported from the early Iron Age site at Jack's Hill, 6.5 km to the south-west (Tebbutt 1931, 371). It is therefore conceivable that there was a local tradition in this area of the ritual use of human femurs.

Why the disarticulated bones of certain individuals were selected for retention and ultimate deposition in settlements, while those of others were not, is currently unclear. It could be that the practice relates to 'ancestor cults', with the remains of particularly revered members of the community being selected for special treatment. Equally, it is possible that the bones of defeated enemies from other communities were retained for ritual purposes. Such issues are difficult to disentangle, but it may be pertinent that in the one case from Fairfield Park in which a cause of death is apparent, the individual seems to have met a violent end. This is the woman represented by the parietal from pit 153, who had received a heavy blow to her head.

Social organisation: household, community and society

For the purposes of discussion, three levels of social organisation will be considered: the household, the community and the wider society. Of course, these levels are to some extent arbitrarily defined, and may have been crosscut by other organising principles or institutions.

The household

It seems likely that in many Iron Age societies, the household was the basic unit of social organisation (Hill 1995b). The clearest manifestation of the household group at Fairfield Park was, of course, the roundhouses. It is often stated that roundhouses should not be assumed to be dwellings, and could in some cases have served as craft workshops or as byres, but good evidence for such specialised functions has failed to emerge even though the number of excavated examples has exploded in recent years. It will therefore be assumed that all of the roundhouses from Fairfield Park were broadly 'domestic' in character, although this does not preclude some variation in the ranges of activities associated with each structure.

In some other parts of southern England, it has been argued that early Iron Age settlements were often characterised by a residential unit of paired roundhouses, one possibly associated with food storage and preparation and the other with food consumption (Fisher 1985; Parker Pearson 1996).

The only possible hint of a similar unit at Fairfield Park is the fact that Structure 1 was located closely adjacent to the much smaller Structure 2, which could perhaps have served as an outbuilding. However, investigation of any relationship between these buildings is hindered by the paucity of associated artefacts (see Table 2.4).

It seems likely that food preparation was associated with the individual household group, given that clay-lined 'cooking pits' cluster in and around roundhouses (see *Roundhouses* above). As noted above, the examples from Fairfield Park follow a pattern seen across the wider region, in which cooking pits tend to be placed in the left-hand side of roundhouses (Fig. 6.4). The consistency of this pattern suggests that there was a strong concern with the 'proper' organisation of the household, in spatial and perhaps also social terms. The evidence from this region contradicts Parker Pearson's (1999) generalising model for domestic organisation during the Iron Age, in which food preparation and other 'daytime' activities are supposed to have occurred in the right side of the roundhouse and sleeping in the left side (Webley 2007).

Further possible evidence that food preparation was associated with the household group comes from the fact that finds of complete or near-complete querns also seem to have a close association with roundhouses. Caution is needed here, given the highly structured nature of much of the artefact deposition occurring at the site (see *Depositional practices* above), although it is conceivable that heavy items such as querns would have been less likely to be moved far from their location of use.

The extent to which other activities were organised on a household basis is unclear. Pelling (Chapter 5) suggests that the small-scale nature of cereal processing at the site would be consistent with 'household level' organisation. However, it is notable that the distribution of storage pits and four-post 'granaries' shows no clustering around individual roundhouses. This makes it difficult to judge how far households were in control of their own agricultural resources.

The community

For the purposes of discussion, the community is defined as those inhabiting the hilltop as a whole. Issues of interest here include the social relationships that may have existed within the community, both between households and between the two settlement areas at Sites A and B.

Investigation of relationships between households is hampered by the lack of finds associated with individual buildings. The only possible hint of 'status' differences between households is the variation in size shown by the roundhouses. It is notable that the two largest roundhouses—Structures 1 and 34—were both further distinguished by being located within substantial ditched enclosures. The possible associations of enclosure with status during the Iron Age have been discussed by Hingley (1990).

Historical and ethnographic parallels would suggest that certain skilled tasks are likely to have been carried out on a semispecialist basis by a limited number of people within the community, rather than by every household. This includes production of the finer pottery—if this was indeed made within the local community—and iron working. Although distinct 'craft working areas' are not apparent, at Site A iron smithing waste was restricted to the north-west corner of the excavated area (see *Slag* above). This may simply reflect the *deposition* of waste in this area, but could also provide a hint of specialisation.

It is unfortunate that we cannot be certain whether the settlements at Sites A and B were directly contemporary, although there are indications that they were (see *Chronology* above). In either case, however, it is interesting to note the similarities and differences in the activities attested at each site. The relative abundance of most categories of artefacts was similar at the two sites, suggesting that a broadly comparable range of activities was pursued in both settlements (Fig. 6.7). However, some subtle differences between the assemblages can be identified. The faunal remains from Site B show significantly more cattle and slightly more pig than Site A. The presence of articulated pig burials at Site B but not at Site A is potentially interesting in the light of arguments that pigs and pork had status associations during the Iron Age (Parker Pearson 1999).

Connections to wider social networks

The community at Fairfield Park would not, of course, have existed in isolation. Contact with other communities would have occurred in connection with the exchange of goods, livestock and people (in marriage), and through participation in wider gatherings and festivities.

The artefact assemblages from Fairfield Park provide some evidence for links with neighbouring communities. The faunal assemblage shows a lack of young cattle and horse remains, suggesting that these animals were only brought to the site once they had reached maturity. This may simply mean that cattle and horses were bred by the community elsewhere in the local landscape, but the possibility exists that contacts with other groups were relied upon to maintain stocks of these animals. Artefact styles are of course a further indirect source of evidence for contact with other groups, with the fineware pottery in particular showing close similarities to other sites along the Chiltern ridge (the so-called 'Chinnor-Wandlebury style': Cunliffe 1991). Unfortunately, the generic nature of the fabric inclusions makes the pottery difficult to source, and hence the extent to which vessels were exchanged with other communities is uncertain.

A few items from the site were of very distant origin, although they are likely to have passed

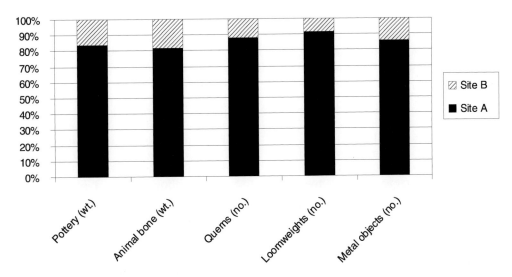

Figure 6.7   Comparison of artefact assemblages from Sites A and B.

through many hands before reaching Fairfield Park. Two of the rotary querns were made from Spilsby Sandstone, which outcrops *c* 125 km away in Lincolnshire, although glacial transport of the stone cannot be ruled out. The jet object (Fig. 3.17.6) probably comes from the Whitby area of North Yorkshire, *c* 275 km to the north. Most exotic of all are the coral studs from the copper alloy pin (Fig. 3.17.2), which must ultimately have come from the Mediterranean. Finds of such rare materials as jet and coral might be taken to imply that the community at Fairfield Park had a greater than usual access to exchange networks of exotic goods, and hence was relatively 'high status'. However, caution is needed here. The number of potentially 'high status' objects from the site is low when considered against the large size of the total artefact assemblage. Furthermore, it seems somewhat dubious to use the frequency of such objects as a measure of settlement status, given that the norm was to deposit them in non-settlement contexts during this period (see *Depositional practices* above).

Other settlements in the valleys below would almost certainly have been visible from the hilltop, which can only have heightened the inhabitants' sense of belonging to a wider world and to wider social networks. The surrounding landscape appears to have been relatively densely occupied, with

a number of potentially contemporary excavated settlements lying within a 5 km radius of the site (Fig. 6.1). These include the sites at Blackhorse Road, Letchworth (early to middle Iron Age: Moss-Eccardt 1988), Holwell (early to middle Iron Age: Applebaum 1934; Shepherd *et al.* forthcoming), Topler's Hill (early and/or middle Iron Age: Luke 2004), Queen Street, Stotfold (middle Iron Age: Wessex Archaeology 2006) and Groveland Way, Stotfold (probably middle Iron Age: Steadman forthcoming). At some of these sites the character of the occupation is unclear, but most seem to represent small communities with a mixed agricultural basis. With no obvious signs of any kind of settlement 'hierarchy', we may be dealing with units essentially similar in their organisation, any differences in social position being differences of degree rather than kind.

Fairfield Park also lies only 2.5 km to the north of the 'hillfort' at Wilbury, a univallate enclosure approximately 200 m in diameter sited on the Chiltern ridge. Although Wilbury is located on only slightly higher ground than Fairfield Park (*c* 85 m AOD), the two sites would have been intervisible, provided that there was little tree cover on the intervening ground. The role of the hillfort is poorly understood, as fieldwork has been limited to small-scale investigations carried out many years ago

Table 6.5   Summary of main patterns in artefact and bone deposition at Fairfield Park.

Material	Depositional context
Juvenile human remains	Pits at northern end of site; all articulated or semi-articulated burials
Adult human remains	Area to south of juvenile remains; no articulated burials present
Sheep/goat, pig and dog remains	Mainly in pits; articulated burials present
Cattle and horse remains	Relatively more common in ditches; no articulated burials present
Querns	Complete/near-complete examples concentrated around roundhouses
Worked bone objects	Limited to main north-west settlement area of Site A
Dress accessories	Limited to eastern periphery of Site A

(Applebaum 1933; 1949; Moss-Eccardt 1964). The enclosure was probably first constructed during the terminal Bronze Age or earliest Iron Age, although middle and late Iron Age material has also been recovered from the site. It seems that some parts of the interior of the enclosure saw activity during the early Iron Age in the form of pits and artefact spreads, while other parts were empty.

Wilbury is one of a series of hillforts fairly evenly spaced along the eastern Chiltern ridge, 7–12 km apart (Bryant 1995). The even spacing of the hillforts led some earlier researchers to propose that they served as territorial centres, dominating the surrounding area. A number of earthwork dykes run across the Chiltern ridge, and it has been argued that these served as boundaries between neighbouring territories (Dyer 1961; Bryant and Burleigh 1995; Cunliffe 1991, 361). However, it should be stressed that the evidence for the dating and development of both the hillforts and the dykes is limited, and thus the notion of discrete, hillfort-dominated territories remains unproven. The discovery of a substantial Anglo-Saxon boundary feature on the hilltop at Fairfield Park is significant as it raises the possibility that the Chiltern dykes could, in fact, be of varying dates.

Clearly, current evidence gives little basis for assessing the relationship between the hillfort at Wilbury and neighbouring settlements such as Fairfield Park. However, recent work elsewhere in southern England has highlighted the probable role of many hillforts as focal places in regions where settlements were small-scale and dispersed. By acting as a venue for collective gatherings and rituals, hillforts could have provided an element of higher-level integration in societies which otherwise emphasised the independence of smaller social groups (Hill 1995b; Hamilton and Manley 2001). A similar situation could have pertained to the dispersed communities of the eastern Chilterns.

Bibliography

Adkins, L, and Needham, S, 1985 New research on a late Bronze Age enclosure at Queen Mary's Hospital, Carshalton, *Surrey Archaeol Collect* **76**, 11–50

Allen, T, Cramp, C, Lamdin-Whymark, H, and Webley, L, forthcoming a *Castle Hill and the surrounding landscape, Little Wittenham, Oxfordshire*, Oxford Archaeology

Allen, T, Hayden, C, and Lamdin-Whymark, H, forthcoming b *Excavations at Taplow Court, Buckinghamshire*, Oxford Archaeology

Andersen, S T, 1979 Identification of wild grasses and cereal pollen, *Danmarks Geologiske Undersøgelse* **1978**, 69–92

Applebaum, E S, 1933 Excavations at Wilbury Hill in 1933, *J British Archaeol Soc* **39**, 352–61

Applebaum, E S, 1934 An early Iron Age site at Holwell, Hertfordshire, *Antiq J* **14**, 383–8

Applebaum, E S, 1949 Excavations at Wilbury Hill, an Iron Age hillfort near Letchworth, Hertfordshire, *Archaeol J* **106**, 12–45

Armitage, P L, and Clutton-Brock, J, 1976 A system for classification and description of the horn cores of cattle from archaeological sites, *J Archaeol Sci* **3**, 329–48

Arnold, D E, 1985 *Ceramic theory and cultural process*, Cambridge

Ball, D F, 1964 Loss-on-ignition as an estimate of organic matter and organic carbon in non-calcareous soils, *J Soil Sci* **15**, 84–92

Barclay, A, 2001 The prehistoric pottery, in A prehistoric enclosure at Eynsham Abbey, Oxfordshire (A Barclay, A Boyle and G D Keevill), *Oxoniensia* **66**, 105–62

Barrett, J, 1980 The pottery of the later Bronze Age in lowland England, *Proc Prehist Soc* **46**, 297–319

Barrett, J, 1999 The mythological landscape of the British Iron Age, in *Archaeologies of landscape* (eds W Ashmore and A B Knapp), 253–65, Oxford

Barrett, J, Freeman, P W, and Woodward, A, 2000 *Cadbury Castle, Somerset: the later prehistoric and early historic archaeology*, London

BCAS 1997 Fairfield Hospital, Stotfold: archaeological field evaluation, unpubl., Bedfordshire County Archaeology Service

Berglund, B E, and Ralska-Jasiewiczowa, M, 1986 Pollen analysis and pollen diagrams, in *Handbook of Holocene palaeoecology and palaeohydrology*, (ed. B E Berglund), 455–84, Chichester

Bethell, P, and Máté, I, 1989 The use of phosphate analysis in archaeology: a critique, in *Scientific Analysis in Archaeology* (ed. J Henderson), 1–29, Oxford

Birley, M, 1988 Iron Age [pottery], in Moss-Eccardt 1988, 79–84

Boardman, S, and Jones, G E M, 1990 Experiments on the effects of charring on cereal plant components, *J Archaeol Sci* **17**, 1–11

Bowden, M, and McOmish, D, 1987 The required barrier, *Scot Archaeol Rev* **4**, 76–84

Bradley, R, 2002 *The past in prehistoric societies*, London

Bradley, R, and Ellison, A, 1975 *Rams Hill: a Bronze Age defended enclosure and its landscape*, BAR Brit Ser **19**, Oxford

Brickley, M, and McKinley, J, 2004 *Guidelines to the standards for recording human remains*, Southampton

British Museum, 1925 *A guide to antiquities of the early Iron Age*, 2 edn, London

Britnell, W J, 2000a Grooved and polished sheep/goat metapodials, in Barrett *et al.* 2000, 186

Britnell, W J, 2000b Small pointed blades, in Barrett *et al.* 2000, 183–6

Bronk Ramsey, C, 1995 Radiocarbon calibration and analysis of stratigraphy: the OxCal program, *Radiocarbon* **37/2**, 425–30

Bronk Ramsey, C, 2001 Development of the radiocarbon program OxCal, *Radiocarbon* **43/2A**, 355–63

Brooks, D, and Thomas, K W, 1967 The distribution of pollen grains on microscope slides: the non-randomness of the distribution, *Pollen Spores* **9**, 621–9

Brooks, S, and Suchey, J M, 1990 Skeletal age determination based on the os pubis: a comparison of the Acsadi-Nemeskeri and Suchey-Brooks methods, *Human Evolution* **5**, 227–38

Brothwell, D, 1981 *Digging up bones*, 3 edn, New York

Brown, L, 1984 Objects of stone, in Cunliffe 1984, 407–26

Brown, N, 1988 A late Bronze Age settlement on the boulder clay: excavations at Broads Green 1986, *Essex Archaeol Hist* **19**, 7–14

Brown, N, 2004 Late Bronze Age, early and middle Iron Age pottery, in Havis and Brooks 2004, 39–54

Brück, J, 1995 A place for the dead: the role of human remains in late Bronze Age Britain, *Proc Prehist Soc* **61**, 245–77

Brück, J, 1999 Ritual and rationality: some problems of interpretation in European archaeology, *Eur J Archaeol* **2**, 313–44

Brudenell, M, forthcoming The prehistoric pottery, in Cooper and Edmonds forthcoming

Bryant, S, 1995 The late Bronze Age to the middle Iron Age of the north Chilterns, in Holgate (ed.) 1985, 17–27

Bryant, S, and Burleigh, G, 1995 Later prehistoric dykes of the eastern Chilterns, in Holgate (ed.) 1985, 92–5

Bryant, S, 1997 Iron Age, in *Research and archaeology: a framework for the eastern counties. 1. Resource assessment* (ed. J Glazebrook), 23–34, Scole

Buckley, D G, 1979 The stone, in *Gussage All Saints. An Iron Age Settlement in Dorset* (G J Wainwright), 89–97, London

Campbell, G, 2000 Plant utilisation: the evidence from charred plant remains, in *The Danebury Environs*

Programme. *The prehistory of a Wessex landscape, volume 1: introduction* (B Cunliffe), English Heritage and Oxford University Committee for Archaeology Monogr **48**, 45–59, Oxford

Carr, G, and Knüsel, C, 1997 The ritual framework of excarnation by exposure as the mortuary practice of the early and middle Iron Ages of central southern Britain, in Gwilt and Haselgrove (eds), 167–73

Carruthers, W, forthcoming Stansted Airport: the charred, mineralised and waterlogged plant remains, unpubl., Oxford Archaeology

Chamberlain, A, 1994 *Human remains*, London

Champion, T C, and Collis, J R (eds), 1996 *The Iron Age in Britain and Ireland: recent trends*, Sheffield

Clapham, A R, Tutin T G, and Moore, D M, 1989 *Flora of the British Isles*, 3rd ed, Cambridge

Clark, A J, 1990 *Seeing beneath the soil*, London

Cohen, A, and Serjeantson, D, 1996 *A manual for the identification of bird bones from archaeological sites*, rev. edn, London

Coles, J M, 1987 *Meare Village East: the excavations of A Bulleid and H St George Gray 1932–1956*, Somerset Levels Papers **13**

Cooper, A, and Edmonds, M, forthcoming *Past and present: land and time on the Broom gravels*, Cambridge

Corkhill, T, 1979 *A glossary of wood*, Southampton

Cotterell, B, and Kamminga, J, 1987 The formation of flakes, *American Antiquity* **52**, 675–708

Cotton, J, 2004 Surrey's early past: a survey of recent work, in *Aspects of archaeology and history in Surrey: towards a research framework for the county* (eds J Cotton, G Crocker and A Graham), 19–38, Guildford

Coy, J, 1982 The animal bones, in Excavation of an Iron Age enclosure at Groundwell Farm, Blunsdon St. Andrew (C Gingell), *Wiltshire Archaeol Natur Hist Mag* **76**, 68–73

Crabtree, P, 1994 Animal exploitation in East Anglian villages, in *Environment and economy in Anglo-Saxon England* (ed. J Rackham), CBA Res Rep **89**, 40–54

Cra'ster, M, 1960 The Aldwick Iron Age settlement, Barley, Hertfordshire, *Proc Cambridge Antiq Soc* **54**, 22–46

Cra'ster, M, 1965 Aldwick, Barley: recent work at the Iron Age site, *Proc Cambridge Antiq Soc* **58**, 1–11

Crowther, J, 1997 Soil phosphate surveys: critical approaches to sampling, analysis and interpretation, *Archaeol Prospection* **4**, 93–102

Crowther, J, 2003 Potential magnetic susceptibility and fractional conversion studies of archaeological soils and sediments, *Archaeometry* **45**, 685–701

Crowther, J, and Barker, P, 1995 Magnetic susceptibility: distinguishing anthropogenic effects from the natural, *Archaeol Prospection* **2**, 207–15

Cunliffe, B, 1984 *Danebury: an Iron Age hillfort in Hampshire. Vol. 2. The excavations 1969–78: the finds*, London

Cunliffe, B, 1991 *Iron Age communities in Britain*, 3 edn, London

Cunliffe, B, 1992 Pits, preconceptions and propitiation in the British Iron Age, *Oxford J Archaeol* **11**, 69–83

Cunliffe, B, and Phillipson, D, 1968 Excavations at Eldon's Seat, Encombe, Dorset, *Proc Prehist Soc* **34**, 191–237

Cunliffe, B, and Poole, C, 1995 Pits and propitiation, in *Danebury: an Iron Age hillfort in Hampshire. Vol. 6. A hillfort community in perspective* (B Cunliffe), CBA Res Rep **102**, 249–75, London

Cyganowski, C, 2004 The macro-botanical remains from a selection in exterior/interior pits, in French, 49–53

Dawson, M, 2000a The Ouse Valley in the Iron Age and Roman periods: a landscape in transition, in *Prehistoric, Roman and post-Roman landscapes of the Great Ouse Valley* (ed. M Dawson), 107–30, London

Dawson, M, 2000b *Iron Age and Roman settlement on the Stagsden Bypass*, Bedfordshire Archaeological Monogr **3**, Bedford

Dawson, M, 2005 *An Iron Age settlement at Salford, Bedfordshire*, Bedfordshire Archaeological Monogr **6**, Bedford

Dawson, M, forthcoming Late Bronze Age to Roman period, in *Research and archaeology: a framework for Bedfordshire* (ed. M Oake)

Dick, W A, and Tabatabai, M A, 1977 An alkaline oxidation method for the determination of total phosphorus in soils, *J Soil Sci Soc America* **41**, 511–14

Dobney, K M, Jaques S D, and Irving, B G, 1996 *Of butchers and breeds*, Lincoln Archaeological Studies **5**, Lincoln

Doggett, N, 1983 Stotfold parish survey, unpublished report held by Bedfordshire SMR

von den Driesch, A, 1976 *A guide to the measurement of animal bones from archaeological sites*, Cambridge (Massachusetts)

von den Driesch, A, and Boessneck, J, 1974 Kritische Anmerkungen zur Wideristhohenberechnung aus Langemassen vor- und frühgeschichtlicher Tierknochen, *Saugtierkundliche Mitteilungen* **22**, 325–48

Drury, P, 1978 *Excavations at Little Waltham 1970–71*, CBA Res Rep **26**, London

Dyer, J, 1961 Dray's Ditches, Bedfordshire, and early Iron Age territorial boundaries in the eastern Chilterns, *Antiq J* **41**, 32–43

Dyer, J, 1971 Excavations at Sandy Lodge, Bedfordshire, *Bedfordshire Archaeol J* **6**, 9–16

Dunning, G C, 1935 The swan's neck and ring-headed pins of the early Iron Age in Britain, *Archaeol J* **91**, 269–95

Eagles, B N, and Evison, V, 1970 Excavations at Harrold, Bedfordshire, 1951–53, *Bedfordshire Archaeol J* **5**, 17–56

Edlin, H L, 1956 *Trees, woods and man*, London

Edmondson, G, Dicks, S, and Edwards, D, 2002 Arlesey, Letchworth Cemetery extension, *South Midlands Archaeol* **32**, 1

Ellison, A, and Drewett, P, 1971 Pits and postholes in the British early Iron Age: some alternative explanations, *Proc Prehist Soc* **37**, 183–94

Elsdon, S, 1992 East Midlands scored ware, *Trans Leicestershire Archaeol Hist Soc* **66**, 83–91

Elsdon, S, and Knight, D, 2003 Pottery, in Field and Parker Pearson 2003, 87–92

Evans, J G, 1972 *Land snails in archaeology*, London

Evans, J G, 1984 Stonehenge: the environment in the late Neolithic and early Bronze Age and a beaker burial, *Wiltshire Archaeol Natur Hist Mag* **78**, 7–30

Faegri, K, and Iversen, J, 1989 *Textbook of modern pollen analysis*, 4 edn, Chichester

Fell, C, 1936 The Hunsbury hill-fort, Northants: a new survey of the material, *Archaeol J* **93**, 57–100

Field, N, and Parker Pearson, M, 2003 *Fiskerton: Iron Age timber causeway with Iron Age and Roman votive offerings*, Oxford

Fisher, A R, 1985 Winklebury hillfort: a study of artefact distributions from subsoil features, *Proc Prehist Soc* **51**, 167–80

Fitzpatrick, A P, and Bacon, J F, 2001 Iron objects, in *Excavations at Billingborough, Lincolnshire, 1975–8: a Bronze-Iron Age settlement and salt-working site* (P Chowne, R Cleal and A P Fitzpatrick), 23–4, Salisbury

Fock, J, 1966 *Metrische Untersuchungen an Metapodien einiger europaischer Rinderrassen*, dissertation, University of Munich

Ford, S, 1987 Chronological and functional aspects of flint assemblages, in *Lithic analysis and later British prehistory* (eds A Brown and M Edmonds), BAR Brit Ser **162**, 67–81, Oxford

Ford, S, Bradley, R, Hawkes, J, and Fisher, P, 1984 Flint-working in the metal age, *Oxford J Archaeol* **3**, 157–73

Fox, C, 1946 *A find of the early Iron Age from Llyn Cerrig Bach, Anglesey*, Cardiff

French, C, 2004 Evaluation, survey and excavation at Wandlebury Ringwork, Cambridgeshire, 1994–7, *Proc Cambridge Antiq Soc* **93**, 15–66

Fryer, J D, and Evans, S A, 1968 *Weed control handbook*, Oxford

Gent, H, 1983 Centralized storage in later prehistoric Britain, *Proc Prehist Soc* **49**, 243–67

George, T J, 1917 *Hunsbury, with a description of the relics found*, Northampton

Gibson, C, 2001 Late Bronze Age to Roman site at the former Nurses Home, Oxford Road, Stone, Buckinghamshire, *Rec Buckinghamshire* **41**, 47–62

Graham, I D G, and Scollar, I, 1976 Limitations on magnetic prospection in archaeology imposed by soil properties, *Archaeo-Physika* **6**, 1–124

Grant, A, 1982 The use of toothwear as a guide to the age of domestic ungulates, in *Ageing and sexing animal bones from archaeological sites* (eds B Wilson, C Grigson, and S Payne), BAR Brit Ser **109**, 91–108, Oxford

Grant, A, 1984 Animal husbandry, in Cunliffe 1984, 496–548

Gray, H St G, 1966 *The Meare lake village: a full description of the excavations and relics from the eastern half of the west village, 1910–1933*. Vol. 3, privately printed

Green, S H, 1984 Flint arrowheads: typology and interpretation, *Lithics* **5**, 19–39

Greig, J, 1988 Traditional cornfield weeds – where are they now? *Plants Today*, Nov-Dec 1988, 183–91

Greig, J, 1991 The British Isles, in *Progress in Old World palaeoethnobotany* (eds W van Zeist, K Wasylikowa and K-E Behre), 229–334, Rotterdam

Groves, J, and Lovell, J, 2002 Excavations within and close to the late Bronze Age enclosure at the former Queen Mary's Hospital, Carshalton, 1999, *London Archaeol* **10**, 13–19

Gwilt, A, and Haselgrove, C (eds), *Reconstructing Iron Age societies*, Oxford

Hambleton, E, 1999 *Animal husbandry regimes in Iron Age Britain: a comparative study of faunal remains from British Iron Age sites*, BAR Brit Ser **282**, Oxford

Hamilton, S, 1998 Using elderly databases: Iron Age pit deposits at the Caburn, East Sussex, and related sites, *Sussex Archaeol Collect* **136**, 23–39

Hamilton, S, and Manley, J, 1997 Points of view: prominent enclosures in 1st millennium BC Sussex, *Sussex Archaeol Collect* **135**, 93–112

Hamilton, S, and Manley, J, 2001 Hillforts, monumentality and place: a chronological and topographic review of first millennium BC hillforts of south-east England, *Eur J Archaeol* **4**, 7–42

Harding, D W, 1972 *The Iron Age in the Upper Thames Basin*, London

Harding, P, 1990 The worked flint, in *The Stonehenge environs project* (ed. J Richards), *passim*, London

Harman, M, 1996 Mammalian bones, in *Dragonby: report on excavations at an Iron Age and Romano-British settlement in north Lincolnshire* (J May), 141–63, Oxford

Hartley, B R, 1957 The Wandlebury Iron Age hillfort: excavations of 1955–56, *Proc Cambridge Antiq Soc* **50**, 1–27

Haselgrove, C, 1997 Iron Age brooch deposition and chronology, in Gwilt and Haselgrove (eds), 51–72

Hather, J, 2000 *The identification of the northern European woods*, London

Hattatt, R, 1989 *Ancient brooches and other artefacts*, Oxford

Hattatt, R, 2000, *A visual catalogue of Richard Hattatt's ancient brooches*, Oxford

Havis, R, and Brooks, H, 2004 *Excavations at Stansted Airport 1986–91*, E Anglian Archaeol Rep **107**

Hayden, C, and Stafford, E, 2006 *The prehistoric landscape at White Horse Stone, Boxley, Kent*, CTRL Integrated Site Report Series, Archaeology Data Service (http://ads.ahds.ac.uk/)

Heron, C, 2001 Geochemical prospecting, in *Handbook of archaeological sciences* (eds D R Brothwell and A M Pollard), 565–73, Chichester

Hill, J D, 1995a *Ritual and rubbish in the Iron Age of Wessex: a study on the formation of a specific archaeological record*, BAR Brit. Ser. **242**, Oxford

Hill, J D, 1995b How should we understand Iron Age societies and hillforts? A contextual study from southern Britain, in *Different Iron Ages: studies on the Iron Age in temperate Europe* (eds J D Hill and C Cumberpatch), 45–66, BAR Int Ser **601**, Oxford

Hill, J D, 1996 The identification of ritual deposits of animal bones: a general perspective from a specific study of 'special animal deposits' from the southern English Iron Age, in *Ritual treatment of human and animal remains* (eds S Anderson and K Boyle), 17–32, Oxford

Hill, J D, 2004 Pottery, in French 2004, 37–43

Hillelson, D, 2004 A multi-period site at Etonbury Farm, Arlesey, Bedfordshire, *South Midlands Archaeol* **34**, 2–4

Hillman, G C, 1981 Reconstructing crop husbandry practices from charred remains of crops, in *Farming practice in British prehistory* (ed. R Mercer), 123–62, Edinburgh

Hillman, G C, 1982 *Late Iron Age glume wheats from Wilmington Gravel-pit, Kent,* Ancient Monuments Laboratory Report **3611**

Hillman, G C, 1984 Interpretation of archaeological plant remains: the application of ethnographic models from Turkey, in *Plants and ancient man* (eds W van Zeist and W A Casparie), 1–41, Rotterdam

Hillson, S, 1996 *Dental anthropology,* New York

Hingley, R, 1990 Boundaries surrounding Iron Age and Romano-British settlements, *Scott Archaeol Rev* **7**, 96–103

Hodder, I, 1982 *Wendens Ambo: the excavation of an Iron Age and Romano-British settlement,* London

Hodge, C A H, Burton, R G O, Corbett, W M, Evans, R, and Seale, R S, (eds) 1984 *Soils and their use in eastern England,* Soil Survey of England and Wales Bulletin **13**

Holgate, R (ed.), 1995 *Chiltern archaeology: recent work. A handbook for the next decade,* Dunstable

Hoppa, R D, 1992 Evaluating human growth: an Anglo-Saxon example, *Int J Osteoarchaeol* **2**, 275–88

Hopson, P M, Aldiss, D T, and Smith, A, 1996 *Geology of the country around Hitchin: memoir for 1:50 000 geological sheet 221*

Hubbard, R N K B, 1975 Assessing the botanical component of human palaeo-economies, *Bull Inst Archaeol London* **12**, 197–205

Hull, G, 2001 A late Bronze Age ringwork, pits and later features at Thrapston, Northamptonshire, *Northamptonshire Archaeol* **29**, 73–92

Hull, M R, and Hawkes, C F C, 1987 *Corpus of ancient brooches in Britain: pre-Roman bow brooches,* BAR Brit Ser **168**, Oxford

Hutton, R, 2004 Animal bone, in Havis and Brooks 2004, 54–65

Ingle, C, 1994 The quernstones from Hunsbury hill-fort, Northamptonshire, *Northamptonshire Archaeol* **25**, 21–35

Inizan, M-L, Reduron-Ballinger, M, Roche, H, and Tixier, J, 1999 *Technology and terminology of knapped stone,* Bordeaux

Jackson, D, and Dix, B, 1987 Late Iron Age and Roman settlement at Weekley, Northants, *Northamptonshire Archaeol* **21**, 41–94

Jackson, D, and Knight, D, 1985 An early Iron Age and Beaker site near Gretton, Northants, *Northamptonshire Archaeol* **20**, 67–85

Jones, G E M, 1984 Interpretation of archaeological plant remains: ethnographic models from Greece, in *Plants and ancient man* (eds W van Zeist and W A Casparie), 43–61, Rotterdam

Jones, G E M, 1987 A statistical approach to the archaeological identification of crop processing, *J Archaeol Sci* **14**, 311–23

Jones, M K, 1978 The plant remains, in Parrington 1978, 93–110

Jones, M K, 1984 The ecological and cultural implications of carbonized seed assemblages from selected archaeological contexts in southern Britain, Unpubl. DPhil Thesis, University of Oxford

Jones, M K, 1985 Archaeobotany beyond subsistence reconstruction, in *Beyond domestication in prehistoric Europe* (eds G Barker and C Gamble), 107–28, London

Jones, M K, 1988a The phytosociology of early arable weed communities with special reference to southern England, in *Der prähistorische Mensch und seine Umwelt* (ed. H Kuster), Forschungen und Berichte zur Vor- und Frühgeschichte in Baden-Wurttemburg **31**, 43–51, Stuttgart

Jones, M K, 1988b The arable field: a botanical battleground, in *Archaeology and the flora of the British Isles* (ed. M K Jones), 86–92, Oxford

Jones, M K, and Nye, S, 1991 The plant remains, in *Danebury: an Iron Age hillfort in Hampshire. Vol. 5. The excavations 1979–1988: the finds* (B Cunliffe and C Poole), London

Jones, M K, and Robinson, M, 1993 The carbonised plant remains, in *The prehistoric landscape and Iron Age enclosed settlement at Mingies Ditch, Hardwick-with-Yelford, Oxon* (eds T G Allen and M Robinson), 120–3, Oxford

Jope, M, 1965 Faunal remains: frequencies and ages of species, in *Windmill Hill and Avebury: excavations by Alexander Keiller 1925–39* (I F Smith), 142–5, Oxford

Keiswalter, L, 1888 Skelettmessungen am Pferde als Beitrag zur theoretischen Grundlage der Beurteilungslehre der Pferdes, dissertation, University of Leipzig

Keller, P T, 1988 Quern production at Folkestone, south-east Kent: an interim report, *Britannia* **20**, 193–201

Kerney, M, 1999 *Atlas of land and freshwater molluscs of Britain and Ireland,* Colchester

Knight, D, 1984 *Late Bronze Age and Iron Age settlement in the Nene and Great Ouse basins,* BAR Brit Ser **130**, Oxford

Knight, M, 1999 Prehistoric excavations at King's Dyke West, Whittlesey, Cambridgeshire, unpubl., Cambridge Archaeological Unit

Knörzer, K H, 1967 Die Roggentrespe (*Bromus secalinus* L.) als prähistorische Nutzpflanze, *Archaeo-Physika* **2**

Knörzer, K H, 1971 Urgeschichtliche Unräuter im Rheinland: ein Beitrag zur Entstehungsgeschichte der Segetalgesellschaften, *Vegetatio* **23**, 89–111

Lambrick, G, 1984 Pitfalls and possibilities in Iron Age pottery studies: experiences in the Upper Thames Valley, in *Aspects of the Iron Age in central southern Britain* (eds B Cunliffe and D Miles), 162–77, Oxford

Lambrick, G, and Allen, T, 2005 *Gravelly Guy, Stanton Harcourt: the development of a prehistoric and Romano-British community*, Oxford

Lambrick, G, Barclay, A, and Duncan, D, 2005 Final Bronze Age to middle Iron Age pottery, in Lambrick and Allen, 259–303

La Niece, J, and Slowikowski, A, 1999 Ceramics, in Steadman, 19–24

Larsen, C S, 1997 *Bioarchaeology: interpreting behaviour from the human skeleton*, Cambridge

Leney, L, and Casteel, R W, 1975 Simplified procedure for examining charcoal specimens for identification, *J Archaeol Sci* **2**, 153–9

Lovejoy, C O, Meindl, R S, Pryzbeck, T R and Mensforth, R P, 1985 Chronological metamorphosis of the auricular surface of the ilium: a new method for determination of adult skeletal age-at-death, *American J Physical Anthrop* **68**, 15–28

Luke, M, 2004 The investigation of an early-middle Iron Age settlement and field system at Topler's Hill, *Bedfordshire Archaeol* **25**, 23–54

Luke, M, forthcoming *Excavations on the Biddenham Loop*, Albion Archaeology

Lyman, R L, 1994 *Vertebrate taphonomy*, Cambridge

Mabey, R, 1996, *Flora Britannica*, London

MacDonald, P, 2005 The 'poker', in *Conderton Camp, Worcestershire: a small middle Iron Age hillfort on Bredon Hill* (N Thomas), 153–6, London

Maltby, M, 1978 *The animal bones from the Iron Age settlement at Chilbolton Down*, Ancient Monuments Laboratory Report **2645**

Maltby, M, 1979 *Faunal studies on urban sites: the animal bones from Exeter, 1971–5*, Exeter Archaeol Rep **2**, Sheffield

Maltby, M, 1981 The animal bones, in Excavations at Old Down Farm, Andover (S Davies), *Proc Hampshire Fld Club Archaeol Soc* **37**, 81–163

Maltby, M, 1985 The animal bones, in *The prehistoric settlement at Winnall Down, Winchester* (P J Fasham), Hampshire Fld Club Monogr **2**, 97–138

Maltby, M, 1996 The exploitation of animals in the Iron Age: the archaeozoological evidence, in Champion and Collis (eds) 1996, 17–28

Martin, E, 1999 Suffolk in the Iron Age, in *Land of the Iceni: the Iron Age in northern East Anglia* (eds J Davies and T Williamson), 45–99, Norwich

Matthews, C L, 1976 *Occupation sites on a Chiltern ridge, part 1: Neolithic, Bronze Age and Early Iron Age*, BAR Brit Ser **29**, Oxford

McSloy, E, 1996 The ceramics assemblage, in Plantation Quarry, Willington: Excavations 1988–1991 (M Dawson), *Bedfordshire Archaeol* **22**, 2–49

McSloy, E, 1999 The pottery, in An enclosed, pre-'Belgic' Iron Age farmstead with later occupation at Hinksley Road, Flitwick (M Luke), *Bedfordshire Archaeol* **23**, 43–87

Meindl, R S, and Lovejoy, C O, 1985 Ectocranial suture closure: a revised method for the determination of skeletal age at death based on the lateral-anterior sutures, *American J Physical Anthrop* **68**, 29–45

Miles, D, 1965 Socio-economic aspects of secondary burial, *Oceania* **35**, 161–73

Miles, D, Palmer, S, Smith, A, and Jones, G P, forthcoming *Iron Age and Roman settlement in the Upper Thames Valley: excavations at Claydon Pike and other sites within the Cotswold Water Park*, Oxford

Miracle, P, Corrado, A, and Hanks, B, 2004 The faunal remains, in French 2004, 43–7

Moore, J, and Jennings, D, 1992 *Reading Business Park: a Bronze Age landscape*, Oxford

Moore, P D, Webb, J A, and Collinson, M E, 1991 *Pollen analysis*, Oxford

Moorees, C F A, Fanning, E A, and Hunt, E E, 1963 Age variation of formation stages for ten permanent teeth, *J Dental Res* **42**, 1490–502

Morris, E, 1996 Iron Age artefact production and exchange, in Champion and Collis (eds) 1996, 41–66

Moss, S, 2004 The Broadbalk long-term experiment at Rothamsted: what has it told us about weeds? *Weed Science* **52**, 864–73

Moss-Eccardt, J, 1964 Excavations at Wilbury Hill, an Iron Age hill-fort near Letchworth, Herts, 1959, *Bedfordshire Archaeol J* **2**, 34–41

Moss-Eccardt, J, 1988 Archaeological investigations in the Letchworth area, 1958–1974, *Proc Cambridge Antiq Soc* **77**, 35–103

Murphy, P, 1977 Early agriculture and environment on the Hampshire chalklands: *c* 800 BC–400 AD, unpubl. MPhil thesis, University of Southampton

Needham, S, 1986 Late Bronze Age artefacts, in *Baldock: the excavation of a Roman and pre-Roman settlement, 1968–72* (I M Stead and V Rigby), Britannia Monogr **7**

Needham, S, 1993 The structure of settlement and ritual in the late Bronze Age of south-east Britain, in *L'habitat et l'ocupation du sol a l'Age du Bronze en Europe* (eds C Mordant and A Richard), Paris, Editions du Comite des Travaux Historiques et Scientifiques, Documents Prehistoriques **4**

Needham, S, 1995 A bowl from Maidscross, Suffolk: burials with pottery in the post-Deverel-Rimbury period, in *Unbaked urns of rudely shape: essays on British and Irish pottery for Ian Longworth* (eds I Kinnes and G Varndell), Oxbow Monogr **55**, 159–72

Needham, S, and Ambers, J, 1994 Redating Rams Hill and reconsidering Bronze Age enclosure, *Proc Prehist Soc* **60**, 225–43

Noddle, B, 1989 Flesh on the bones. Some notes on animal husbandry of the past, *Archaeozoologia* **3**, 25–50

OA, 1992 Oxford Archaeology fieldwork manual, unpubl.

OA, 2001 Fairfield Hospital, Stotfold, Bedfordshire: Archaeological evaluation, unpubl.

OA, 2002 Fairfield Hospital, Stotfold, Bedfordshire, Zone 3: Archaeological evaluation, unpubl.

OA, 2004a Fairfield Hospital, Stotfold, Bedfordshire: archaeological watching brief report, unpubl.

OA, 2004b Fairfield Hospital, Stotfold, Bedfordshire: post-excavation assessment and updated project design, unpubl.

Olsen, S L, 1994 Exploitation of mammals at the early Bronze Age site of West Row Fen (Mildenhall 165), Suffolk, England, *Annals of Carnegie Museum* **63.2**, 115–53

Onhuma, K, and Bergman, C, 1982 Experimental studies in the determination of flake mode, *Bull Inst Archaeol London* **19**, 161–71

Oswald, A, 1997 A doorway on the past: practical and mystical concerns in the orientation of roundhouse doorways, in Gwilt and Haselgrove (eds), 87–95

Parker Pearson, M, 1996 Food, fertility and front doors in the first millennium BC, in Champion and Collis (eds) 1996, 117–32

Parker Pearson, M, 1999 Food, sex and death: cosmologies in the British Iron Age with particular reference to east Yorkshire, *Cambridge Archaeol J* **9**, 43–69

Parrington, M, 1978 *The excavation of an Iron Age settlement, Bronze Age ring-ditches and Roman features at Ashville Trading Estate, Abingdon, Oxfordshire, 1974–76*, CBA Res Rep **28**, London

Parry, C, 1999 Excavations at Camp Gardens, Stow-on-the-Wold, Gloucestershire, *Trans Bristol Gloucestershire Archaeol Soc* **117**, 75–87

Payne, S, 1985 Morphological distinctions between the mandibular teeth of young sheep and goats, *J Archaeol Sci* **12**, 139–47

PCRG, 1997 *The study of later prehistoric pottery: general policies and guidelines for analysis and publication*, Prehistoric Ceramics Research Group occasional papers 1 and 2, Oxford.

Peacock, D P S, 1986 Iron Age and Roman quern production at Lodsworth, West Sussex, *Antiq J* **67**, 61–85

Pelling, R, forthcoming a. Charred plant remains, in *The excavation of a late Iron Age/early Roman settlement enclosure and prehistoric and early/middle Saxon deposits at Battlebridge Lane, Merstham, Surrey 1999* (M J Saunders and S Weaver), Thames Valley Archaeological Services

Pelling, R, forthcoming b. Charred plant remains, in Luke forthcoming

Pettigrew, J, Reynolds, R, and Rouse, S, 1998 *A place in the country: Three Counties Asylum, 1860–1998*, Luton

Pfitzenmeyer, C D C, 1962 Arrhenatherum elatius (L.) J. and C. Presl, *J Ecol* **50**, 235–45

Poole, C, 1984 Objects of baked clay, in Cunliffe 1984, 398–407

Poole, C, 1991 Objects of baked clay, in *Danebury: an Iron Age hillfort in Hampshire. Vol. 5. The excavations, 1979–1988: the finds* (B Cunliffe), 382–404, London

Prummel, W, 1988 Distinguishing features on post-cranial skeletal elements of cattle and red deer, *Schriften aus der archäologisch-zoologischen Arbeitsgruppe Schleswig-Kiel* **12**, 3–52

Prummel, W, and Frisch, H, 1986 A guide for the distinction of species, sex and body side in bones of sheep and goat, *J Archaeol Sci* **13**, 567–77

Reimer, P J, Baillie, M G L, Bard, E, Bayliss, A, Beck, J W, Bertrand, C, Blackwell, P G, Buck, C E, Burr, G, Cutler, K B, Damon, P E, Edwards, R L, Fairbanks, R G, Friedrich, M, Guilderson, T P, Hughen, K A, Kromer, B, McCormac, F G, Manning, S, Bronk Ramsey, C, Reimer, R W, Remmele, S, Southon, J R, Stuiver, M, Talamo, S, Taylor, F W, van der Plicht, J, and Weyhenmeyer, C E, 2004 INTCAL04 terrestrial radiocarbon age calibration, 0–26 cal kyr BP, *Radiocarbon* **46**, 1029–58

Reynolds, P J, 1979 *Iron Age farm: the Butser experiment*, London

Richardson, K M, and Young, A, 1951 An Iron Age 'A' site on the Chilterns, *Antiq J* **31**, 131–48

Rigby, V, 2004 *Pots in pits: the British Museum Yorkshire settlements project, 1988–92*, East Riding Archaeologist **11**

Roberts, A, 2005 Animal bone, in Dawson 2005, 146–9

Roberts, C, and Manchester, K, 1995 *The archaeology of disease*, 2 edn, New York

Rodwell, W, 1976 Iron pokers of La Tène II–III, *Archaeol J* **133**, 43–9

Ryder, M, 1983 *Sheep and man*, London

Saunders, C, 1972 The pre-Belgic Iron Age in the central and western Chilterns, *Archaeol J* **128**, 1–30

Saville, A, 1981 Iron Age flint working: fact or fiction? *Lithics* **2**, 6–9

Scheuer, J L, Musgrave, J H, and Evans, S P, 1980 The estimation of late fetal and perinatal age from limb bone length by linear and logarithmic regression, *Annals of Human Biology* **7**, 257–65

Schmid, E, 1972 *Atlas of animal bones*, Amsterdam

Schweingruber, F, 1982 *Microscopic wood anatomy*, 2 edn, Teufen (Switzerland)

Scollar, I, Tabbagh, A, Hesse, A, and Herzog, I, 1990 *Archaeological prospecting and remote sensing*, Cambridge

Sellwood, L, 1984 Objects of bone and antler, in Cunliffe 1984, 371–95

Serjeantson, D, 1996 The animal bones, in *Runnymede Bridge research excavations, volume 2. Refuse and disposal at Area 16 East, Runnymede* (S Needham and T Spence), 194–223, London

Shepherd, N, Phillips, M, and Wells, J, forthcoming *Excavations at Holwell Quarry, Hertfordshire*

Silver, A, 1969 The ageing of domestic animals, in *Science in archaeology* (eds D Brothwell and E S Higgs), 283–302, London.

Silverside, A J, 1977 A phytosociological survey of British arable weed and related communities, unpubl. PhD thesis, University of Durham

Slowikowski, A, 2005 The pottery, in Dawson 2005, 95–117

Smith, A, and Rose, J, 1997 A new find of Quaternary quartzite-rich gravel near Letchworth, Hertfordshire, south-eastern England, *Proc Geol Assoc* **108**, 317–26

Stead, I M, 1991, *Iron Age cemeteries in East Yorkshire*, Engl Heritage Archaeol Rep **22**

Steadman, S, 1999 A later Neolithic and Bronze Age mortuary complex and Iron Age settlement at the Bunyan Centre, Bedford, *Bedfordshire Archaeol* **23**, 2–31

Steadman, S, forthcoming *Iron Age, Roman and Saxon settlement at Stotfold, Bedfordshire*, Albion Archaeology

Stevens, C, 1997 Charred plant remains, in Investigations of a prehistoric landscape at Broom, Bedfordshire: post-excavation assessment (R Mortimer), Cambridge Archaeological Unit Report **202**, unpubl.

Stevens, C, 2003 An investigation of agricultural consumption and production models for prehistoric and Roman Britain, *Environ Archaeol* **8**, 61–76

Stuart-Macadam, P, 1991 Anaemia in Roman Britain: Poundbury Camp, in *Health in past societies: Biocultural interpretations of human skeletal remains in archaeological contexts* (eds H Bush and M Zvelebil), BAR Int. Ser. **567**, 101–13, Oxford

Tebbutt, C F, 1931 Early Iron Age settlement on Jack's Hill, Great Wymondley, Herts, *Proc Prehist Soc East Anglia* **6**, 371–4

Timby, J, Brown, R, Biddulph, E, Hardy, A, and Powell, P, forthcoming *A slice of rural Essex: recent archaeology along the A120 between Stansted and Braintree*, Oxford

Tite, M S, 1972 The influence of geology on the magnetic susceptibility of soils on archaeological sites, *Archaeometry* **14**, 229–36.

Tite, M S, and Mullins, C, 1971 Enhancement of magnetic susceptibility of soils on archaeological sites, *Archaeometry* **13**, 209–19

Tyrell, R, 1994 Querns and millstones, in Williams and Zeepvat 1994, 370–1

van der Veen, M, 1992 *Crop husbandry regimes: an archaeobotanical study of farming in northern England 1000 BC–AD500*, Sheffield

van der Veen, M, and Jones, G, 2006 A re-analysis of agricultural production and consumption: implications for understanding the British Iron Age, *Vegetation History and Archaeobotany* **15**, 217–28

Vigne, J-D, 1991 The meat and offal (MOW) method and the relative proportions of ovicaprines in some ancient meat diets from the north-western Mediterranean, *Rivista di Studi Liguri A* **57**, 21–47

Wait, G A, 1985 *Ritual and religion in Iron Age Britain*, BAR Brit Ser **149**, Oxford

Walters, M, 1949 Eleocharis palustris (L.) R. Br. Em R. and S., *J Ecol* **37**, 194–202

Watts, A B, McKerrow, W S, and Richards, K, 2005 Localized Quaternary uplift of south-central England, *J Geol Soc London* **162**, 13–24

Webley, L, 2005 Evaluation, survey and excavation at Wandlebury Ringwork, Cambridgeshire, 1994–7: part II, the Iron Age pottery, *Proc Cambridge Antiq Soc* **94**, 39–46

Webley, L, 2007 Using and abandoning roundhouses: a reinterpretation of the evidence from late Bronze Age-early Iron Age southern England, *Oxford J Archaeol* **26**, 127–44

Webley, L, forthcoming. The first settlers: the prehistoric landscape of Great Barford, in *Settlement on the Bedfordshire claylands: recent archaeology along the A421 Great Barford Bypass* (J Timby, R Brown, A Hardy, S Leech, C Poole and L Webley), Oxford Archaeology

Wells, J, 2004 The artefact assemblage, in Luke 2004, 39–43

Wells, J, forthcoming. Ceramics phases 10–17, in Steadman forthcoming

Wessex Archaeology 2006 Land at Queen Street, Stotfold, Bedfordshire: post-excavation assessment and updated project design, unpubl.

Wheeler, J, Thompson, G, McDonnell, G, Clay, G, and Spence, B, 2003 *Smelting and smithing: medieval charcoal for ironworking at Myers Wood, West Yorkshire*, poster presented at the conference 'Walking and working in the footsteps of ghosts', Sheffield Hallam University, May 2003

Whimster, R, 1981 *Burial practice in Iron Age Britain (700 BC–AD 43)*, BAR Brit Ser **90**

Williams, R J, 1993 *Pennyland and Hartigans*, Aylesbury

Williams, R J, and Zeepvat, R J, 1994 *Bancroft: a late Bronze Age/Iron Age settlement, Roman villa and temple-mausoleum*, Aylesbury

Wilson, B, 1978 The animal bones, in Parrington 1978, 110–45, London

Wilson, B, 1979 The vertebrates, in *Iron Age and Roman riverside settlements at Farmoor, Oxfordshire* (G Lambrick and M Robinson), 128–33, London

Wilson, B, 1993 Bone and shell evidence, in *The prehistoric landscape and Iron Age enclosed settlement at Mingies Ditch, Hardwick with Yelford, Oxon* (T Allen and M Robinson), Oxford

Wilson, B, 1996 *Spatial patterning among animal bones in settlement archaeology*, BAR Brit Ser **251**

Wilson, C E, 1981 Burials within settlements in southern Britain during the pre-Roman Iron Age, *Bull Inst Archaeol Univ London* **18**, 127–69

Wiltshire, P E J, 2005 Palynological analysis of pond deposits, in Dawson 2005, 149–54

Young, R, and Humphrey, J, 1999 Flint use in England after the Bronze Age: Time for a re-evaluation? *Proc Prehist Soc* **65**, 231–42

Appendix: Phosphate and Magnetic Susceptibility Analysis

By John Crowther

Methods

Analysis was undertaken on the fine earth fraction (i.e. <2 mm) of the samples. LOI (loss-on-ignition) was determined by ignition at 375 °C for 16 hours (Ball 1964), previous experimental studies having shown that there is no significant breakdown of carbonate at this temperature. Phosphate-P (total phosphate) was determined following alkaline oxidation of the sample with NaOBr, using the procedure described by Dick and Tabatabai (1977). A Bartington MS1 meter was used for magnetic susceptibility measurements. χmax was achieved by heating samples at 650 °C in reducing, followed by oxidising conditions. The method used broadly follows that of Tite and Mullins (1971), except that household flour was mixed with the soils and lids placed on the crucibles to create the reducing environment (after Graham and Scollar 1976; Crowther and Barker 1995). χmax determinations were made on 30 samples, half of these being representative samples with the highest χ values, and the remainder being chosen at random. Relationships between χ, χmax and χconv were investigated in order to establish the extent to which variations in χ are attributable to variations in magnetic susceptibility enhancement (χconv). These relationships were examined using Pearson product-moment correlation coefficients (r). Since it is usually the few samples with enhanced values that are of greatest archaeological interest, $\log_{10}$ transformations were not applied to reduce skewness when examining these particular relationships (see Crowther 2003). For other correlations reported, $\log_{10}$ transformations have been applied to data sets with skewness <1.00 in order to increase parametricity. Mann-Whitney U tests have been used to establish the statistical significance of differences in mean values between different data sets. Statistical significance has been assessed at the 95% confidence level (i.e. $\alpha = 0.05$). Spatial plots of the phosphate-P and magnetic susceptibility data are presented in Figures 5.5 and 5.6 respectively.

General character of soils

The soils in the area are mapped as being of the Wantage 2 association, which are dominated by typically well-drained, calcareous, grey rendzinas formed on chalk rubble or chalky drift (Hodge *et al.* 1984).

Results

Comparison of control soils and feature fills

Organic matter (LOI)

The four control soils investigated show quite marked variability in organic matter concentration in the topsoil (LOI: range, 4.33–8.11%; Table A1.1), which seems likely to be attributable to differences in drainage characteristics and/or modern-day land use (assuming that that the samples taken are truly representative of the topsoil horizons). The LOI figures recorded for the subsoil and natural are consistently

Table A1.1 *Chemistry and magnetic susceptibility of soils and sediments. Summary data for control samples: topsoil, subsoil and natural.*

	n	Mean	Minimum	Maximum	Std dev.
LOI (%)					
Topsoil	4	5.74	4.33	8.11	1.66
Subsoil	4	3.30	2.88	3.77	0.451
Natural	4	2.80	2.23	3.87	0.767
Phosphate-P (mg g^{-1})					
Topsoil	4	0.858	0.511	1.16	0.326
Subsoil	4	0.751	0.312	1.42	0.472
χ(10^{-8} SI)					
Topsoil	4	49.3	35.8	79.8	20.7
Subsoil	4	42.9	13.5	87.5	32.4
Natural	4	25.0	9.1	61.6	24.9
χ_{max} (10^{-8} SI)					
Natural	1	2500			
χ (%)					
Natural	1	0.380			

Table A1.2 *Chemistry and magnetic susceptibility of soils and sediments. Summary data for all samples of feature fills.*

	n	Mean	Minimum	Maximum	Std dev.
LOI (%)	180	2.95	1.83	5.14	0.618
Phosphate-P (mg g^{-1})	180	2.37	0.277	11.8	1.62
χ(10^{-8} SI)	180	82.2	9.5	450	66.1
χ_{max} (10^{-8} SI)	29	2780	1720	5160	853
χ_{conv} (%)	29	6.54	0.461	23.3	4.62

Table A1.3 Pearson product-moment correlation coefficients (r) for relationships between the various soil properties for all samples of feature fills[†] (n = 180 for correlations between LOI, phosphate-P and χ; n = 29 for all pairs involving χ_{max} and χ_{conv}).

	Phosphate-P[§]	χ[§¶]	χ_{max}[§¶]	χ_{conv}[§¶]
LOI	0.695**	0.699**	n.s.	0.758**
Phosphate-P[§]		0.789**	n.s.	0.731**
χ[§¶]			n.s.	0.946**
χ_{max}[§¶]				n.s.

[†] Statistical significance: n.s. = not significant (i.e. p≥0.05), * = significant at p≥0.001.

[§] Indicates $\log_{10}$ transformation applied to the data set.

[¶] Using untransformed data sets, which are conventionally used in assessing the relative importance of χ_{conv} and χ_{max} upon χ, the coefficients are as follows: χ with χ_{conv} (r = 0.917, p < 0.001); χ with χ_{max} (r = 0.046, n.s.).

below 4.00% (maximum, 3.87%), with means of 3.30 and 2.80%, respectively. On the whole the LOI values recorded for the feature fills (mean, 2.95%; Table A1.2) are very similar to the subsoil and natural controls. Where LOI exceeds 4.00%, samples may be

considered to have a relatively high organic matter concentration. This could result from the incorporation of topsoil or anthropogenic materials rich in organic matter (e.g. midden deposits) or, perhaps less likely in this environment, the presence of locally much wetter conditions (e.g. in a ditch or area of less permeable substrate) in which organic matter decomposition may have been inhibited. Indeed, ditches and other drainage features may also have favoured plant growth, which would have increased organic matter inputs.

Phosphate-P

The mean phosphate-P concentrations in all three horizons of the control profiles are relatively low, ranging from 0.751 (subsoil) to 0.858 mg g^{-1} (topsoil), with a maximum figure of 1.45 mg g^{-1} in one of the samples of underlying 'natural'. On this basis it seems reasonable to assume that samples of fills with phosphate-P concentrations of <2.00 mg g^{-1} show some degree of phosphate enrichment. With a mean concentration of 2.37 mg g^{-1} for the feature fills (Table A1.2) and with 89 of the 180 samples having figures of <2.00 mg g^{-1} (maximum, 11.8 mg g^{-1}),

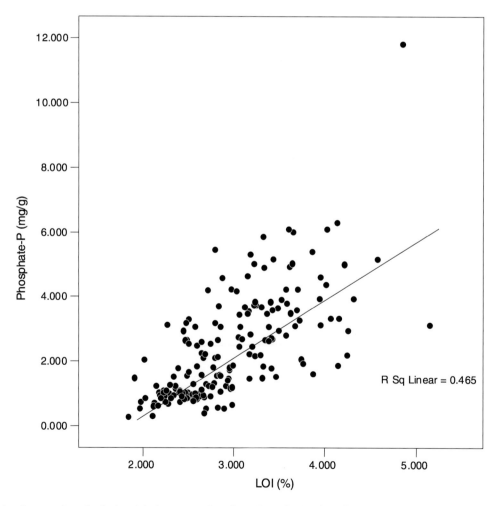

Figure A1.1 Scatterplot of relationship between phosphate-P and LOI for all of the samples of feature fills.

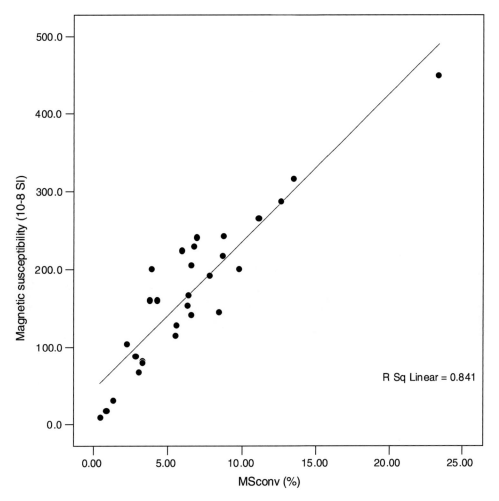

Figure A1.2   Scatterplot of relationship between χ (labelled 'magnetic susceptibility') and χ$_{conv}$ ('MSconv') for all of feature fills.

there is clearly much evidence of phosphate enrichment in the archaeological contexts. Values in the range 2.00–3.99 mg g^{-1} are regarded as being 'enriched', 4.00–5.99 mg g^{-1} as 'strongly enriched', and <6.00 mg g^{-1} as 'very strongly enriched'. While log$_{10}$ phosphate-P exhibits a significant correlation with LOI ($r = 0.695$, $p < 0.001$; Table A1.3), the level of explained variance (expressed in terms of r^2, the coefficient of determination) is relatively low ($r^2 = 0.483$). For illustrative purposes, a plot of the untransformed data is presented in Figure A1.1. There are two implications of this finding. First, phosphate enrichment is associated with sources that were relatively rich in organic matter, though this does not preclude the possibility of a high proportion originating in a largely minerogenic form from bone (as might be the case in an otherwise organic-rich midden deposit). Secondly, the weakness of the relationship suggests either considerable variability in the phosphate:organic matter ratio of the original inputs (e.g. perhaps some materials were more bone-rich) and/or in the degree of subsequent organic decomposition that has occurred (as might be affected by drainage conditions).

χ *(magnetic susceptibility)*

The mean χ values of the control samples are relatively low (Table A1.2), and show a characteristic reduction from the topsoil (49.3 × 10^{-8} SI), through the subsoil (42.9 × 10^{-8} SI), to the underlying natural (25.0 × 10^{-8} SI). χmax was determined for only one control sample (of natural). This gave a moderately high value (2500 × 10^{-8} SI) and correspondingly very low χconv (0.380%) – the latter being indicative of a lack of enhancement. The mean χmax recorded in the feature fill samples (2780 × 10^{-8} SI) is similar to that of the natural, though, as is often the case, there is considerable variability within the data set (range, 1720–5160 × 10^{-8} SI). The feature fills generally display higher and much more variable χ values (mean, 82.2 × 10^{-8} SI; range, 9.5–450 × 10^{-8} SI) than the controls, and many of the χconv values exceed 5.00% (maximum, 23.3%), which is often taken as being indicative of enhancement. Despite the variability in χmax, there is an extremely strong correlation between χ and χconv ($r = 0.917$, $p < 0.001$; footnote of Table A1.3), as is illustrated in Figure A1.2, and no significant relationship between χ and

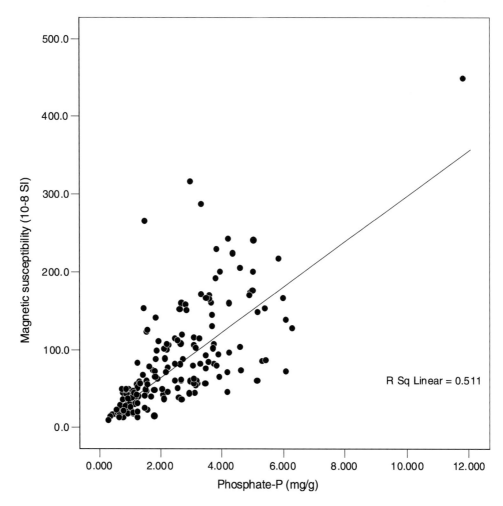

Figure A1.3   Scatterplot of relationship between χ (labelled 'magnetic susceptibility') and phosphate-P for all samples of feature fills.

χmax. The χ data can therefore be safely assumed to provide a good measure of the degree of enhancement in all 180 samples. In the present study, χ values in the range 150–249×10^{-8} SI are regarded as being 'enhanced', 250–349×10^{-8} SI as 'strongly enhanced', and $< 350 \times 10^{-8}$ SI as 'very strongly enhanced'. The critical figures of 150, 250 and 350×10^{-8} SI correspond with χconv values of approximately 5.5, 10.8 and 16.0%, respectively (Fig. A1.2). Overall, there is a significant correlation between $\log_{10} \chi$ and $\log_{10}$ phosphate-P ($r = 0.789$, $p < 0.001$; Table A1.3), the two key anthropological indicators. However, as illustrated in Figure A1.3, the level of explained variance is relatively low ($r^2 = 0.511$ for untransformed data sets). The implication of this is that while some of the samples display clear signs of both χ enhancement (associated with burning) and phosphate enrichment, in many cases one of the two anthropogenic signals is much stronger than the other.

A characterisation of each individual sample in terms of LOI, phosphate enrichment and magnetic susceptibility enhancement is held in the site archive. It is beyond the scope of this report to comment on each individual sample or its specific location. The following sections present a broad overview of the main findings, the samples being placed into 13 groups (A–M: see Fig. 5.7) according to feature type and location.

Comparison of fills from the north-western settlement area with those from elsewhere

From the archaeological evidence the north-western area of the settlement (A on Fig. 5.7) was clearly identifiable as the area of most concentrated human activity. Here, comparisons are made between the chemical and magnetic susceptibility of feature fills in this area and those from the rest of the site in order to establish whether the properties of the fills support the archaeological interpretation. The results, summarised in Table A1.4 (and presented in Figs 5.5 and 5.6), clearly indicate that this is the case. Thus, the fills in the north-western settlement area have significantly higher mean LOI, phosphate-P and χ values than those elsewhere. The differences in phosphate (3.97 mg g^{-1}, cf. 1.75 mg g^{-1}) and χ (122×10^{-8} SI, cf. 66.3×10^{-8} SI) are especially marked. Unfortunately, the χmax values in the north-western region are somewhat higher than in the other areas, and a consequence the difference in the

Table A1.4 Chemistry and magnetic susceptibility of soils and sediments. Comparison of summary data for samples of feature fills from the north-western settlement area and from other areas.

	n	Mean[†]	Minimum	Maximum	Std dev.
NW settlement area					
LOI (%)	46	3.25*	2.26	5.14	0.587
Phosphate-P (mg g^{-1})	46	3.97**	1.55	11.8	1.74
χ (10^{-8} SI)	46	122**	45.0	450	70.7
χ_{max} (10^{-8} SI)	13	3020°	1930	5160	979
χ_{conv} (%)	13	7.03°	2.25	23.3	5.25
Other areas					
LOI (%)	146	2.94*	1.83	8.11	0.792
Phosphate-P (mg g-1)	146	1.75**	0.277	5.15	1.14
χ (10^{-8} SI))	146	66.3**	9.1	317	57.5
χ_{max} (10–8 SI)	17	2570°	1720	4260	683
χ_{conv} (%)	17	5.79°	0.380	13.5	4.27

[†] Results of Mann-Whitney U tests to determine significance of difference in mean values between NW settlement area and other area for each soil property: ° = not significant; * = p<0.05, ** = p<0.001.

mean χ_{conv} values (7.03%, cf. 5.79%) is not statistically significant. Some exceptionally high levels of phosphate-P (maximum, 11.8 mg g^{-1}), χ (maximum, 450 × 10^{-8} SI) and χ_{conv} (maximum, 23.3%) were recorded in the feature fills of the north-western settlement area. In addition, however, high values were also recorded in the other areas, which certainly indicate locations of significant enrichment/enhancement as a result of human activity elsewhere across the site. These are considered in more detail below.

Comparison of different feature types within the north-western settlement area

Table A1.5 presents summary data for the different types of features within the north-western settlement area. Statistical analysis reveals that there is no significant difference in the mean LOI, phosphate-P and χ values between the pit fills and ditch fills (the two principal feature types sampled), which suggests that the materials that accumulated in these two types of feature were broadly similar in character. Unfortunately, the sample size of many of the data sets is too small to permit meaningful statistical analysis. However, it is perhaps interesting to note that the shallower gullies and eaves-gullies have somewhat lower phosphate-P concentrations than the pits and ditches, which could be attributable to midden-type material not being dumped here. Interesting too, is the fact that the single posthole fill sampled shows no sign of phosphate enrichment or magnetic susceptibility enhancement, presumably as a consequence of this fill accumulating after the main

Table A1.5 Chemistry and magnetic susceptibility of soils and sediments. Summary data for samples from different feature types within the north-western settlement area.

	n	Mean[†]	Minimum	Maximum	Std dev.
Pit fill[†]					
LOI (%)	19	3.41	2.46	5.14	0.747
Phosphate-P (mg g^{-1})	19	4.25	1.55	11.8	2.29
χ (10^{-8} SI)	19	128	47.2	450	89.5
χ_{max} (10^{-8} SI)	4	3510	1930	5160	1630
χ_{conv} (%)	4	8.75	2.25	23.3	9.79
Ditch fill[†]					
LOI (%)	19	3.04	2.26	3.86	0.426
Phosphate-P (mg g^{-1})	19	4.11	2.27	5.99	1.16
χ (10^{-8} SI)	19	110	45.0	230	52.1
χ_{max} (10^{-8} SI)	6	2600	2080	3420	445
χ_{conv} (%)	6	6.16	3.26	8.65	1.75
Eaves-gully fill					
LOI (%)	5	3.43	3.05	3.95	0.325
Phosphate-P (mg g^{-1})	5	3.08	2.66	4.60	0.850
χ (10^{-8} SI)	5	136	88.4	205	46.5
χ_{max} (10^{-8} SI)	2	3430	3120	3730	431
χ_{conv} (%)	2	5.43	4.29	6.57	1.61
Gully fill					
LOI (%)	2	3.44	3.17	3.70	0.375
Phosphate-P (mg g^{-1})	2	3.22	2.22	4.22	1.41
χ (10^{-8} SI)	2	160	77.3	243	117
χ_{max} (10^{-8} SI)	1	2780	–	–	–
χ_{conv} (%)	1	8.74	–	–	–
Posthole fill					
LOI (%)	1	2.95	–	–	–
Phosphate-P (mg g^{-1})	1	1.75	–	–	–
χ (10^{-8} SI)	1	73.5	–	–	–
χ_{max} (10^{-8} SI)	–				
χ_{conv} (%)	–				

[†] Mann-Whitney U tests showed that there was no significant difference in mean values of LOI, phosphate-P and χ between pit and ditch fills.

occupation phase (perhaps as a result of natural accumulation).

Comparison of features from different areas outside the north-western settlement area

Outside the north-western settlement area the samples have been placed into twelve groups for the purposes of this report, some being geographical areas and others being specific feature groups (e.g. pit row 3530 and the eastern gullies). Summary data for each of these are presented in Table A1.6, along with the results of Mann-Whitney U tests comparing the mean values for LOI, phosphate-P and χ (for data

Table A1.6   Chemistry and magnetic susceptibility of soils and sediments. Summary data for samples of feature fills from specific areas (B-M: see Fig. 5.7) outside the north-western settlement area.

	n	Mean[†]	Minimum	Maximum	Std dev.
B *Phase 1 settlement*					
LOI (%)	7	3.56°	2.25	4.57	0.780
Phosphate-P (mg g^{-1})	7	2.45*	1.09	5.15	1.34
χ (10^{-8} SI)	7	64.4*	18.7	111	34.7
χ_{max} (10^{-8} SI)	–				
χ_{conv} (%)	–				
C *Enclosure I*					
LOI (%)	6	2.56*	1.83	3.23	0.519
Phosphate-P (mg g^{-1})	6	1.83*	0.277	3.84	1.55
χ (10^{-8} SI)	6	41.6**	9.5	79.2	29.7
χ_{max} (10^{-8} SI)	2	2230	2060	2040	240
χ_{conv} (%)	2	1.88	0.461	3.30	2.01
D *Pit row 3530*					
LOI (%)	7	3.48°	2.01	4.15	0.703
Phosphate-P (mg g^{-1})	7	3.91°	2.06	5.03	1.04
χ (10^{-8} SI)	7	169*	49.3	241	61.4
χ_{max} (10^{-8} SI)	3	3840	3490	4260	389
χ_{conv} (%)	3	5.53	3.76	6.91	1.61
E *Southern roundhouses*					
LOI (%)	10	2.77*	1.90	4.21	0.640
Phosphate-P (mg g^{-1})	10	2.15*	0.635	5.00	1.34
χ (10^{-8} SI)	10	63.7*	13.6	176	55.4
χ_{max} (10^{-8} SI)	1	1720			
χ_{conv} (%)	1	8.43			
F *Enclosure VI*					
LOI (%)	13	2.98°	2.35	3.72	0.408
Phosphate-P (mg g^{-1})	13	2.37*	1.25	3.71	0.880
χ (10^{-8} SI)	13	94.4°	31.5	165	42.6
χ_{max} (10^{-8} SI)	1	3130	–	–	–
χ_{conv} (%)	1	2.82	–	–	–
G *North-eastern area*					
LOI (%)	21	2.92°	2.18	4.31	0.611
Phosphate-P (mg g-1)	21	1.74**	0.762	3.93	0.937
χ (10^{-8} SI)	21	75.3**	37.7	287	56.8
χ_{max} (10^{-8} SI)	3	2220	2150	2270	61.1
χ_{conv} (%)	3	7.39	3.02	12.6	4.84
H *Eastern area*					
LOI (%)	32	2.64**	1.97	4.25	0.477
Phosphate-P (mg g^{-1})	32	1.44**	0.554	3.94	0.857
χ (10^{-8} SI)	32	50.6**	12.6	317	60.0
χ^{max} (10^{-8} SI)	2	2200	2060	2340	198
χ_{conv} (%)	2	11.6	9.76	13.5	2.64
I *South-eastern area*					
LOI (%)	20	2.98°	1.96	4.24	0.557
Phosphate-P (mg g^{-1})	20	1.67**	0.408	4.19	1.04
χ (10^{-8} SI)	20	65.4**	16.4	266	61.6
χ_{max} (10^{-8} SI)	2	2390	2370	2400	21.2
χ_{conv} (%)	2	6.20	1.30	11.1	6.93
J *Phase 5 ditch 4450*					
LOI (%)	3	3.29	2.99	3.58	0.295
Phosphate-P (mg g^{-1})	3	2.62	1.87	3.79	1.02
χ (10^{-8} SI)	3	133	99.0	192	51.5
χ_{max} (10^{-8} SI)	1	2470	–	–	–
χ_{conv} (%)	1	7.77	–	–	–
K *Eastern gullies (NE area)*					
LOI (%)	9	2.27**	2.11	2.43	0.124
Phosphate-P (mg g^{-1})	9	0.876**	0.620	1.07	0.157

Table A1.6 (Continued)

	n	Mean[†]	Minimum	Maximum	Std dev.
χ $(10^{-8}$ SI)	9	38.9**	15.9	49.1	10.3
χ_{max} $(10^{-8}$ SI)	–				
χ_{conv} (%)	–				
L Eastern gullies (E area)					
LOI (%)	3	2.55	2.40	2.66	0.133
Phosphate-P (mg g^{-1})	3	0.971	0.880	1.09	0.108
χ $(10^{-8}$ SI)	3	43.4	39.0	47.3	4.17
χ_{max} $(10^{-8}$ SI)	–				
M Eastern gullies (SE area)					
LOI (%)	3	2.59	2.45	2.74	0.146
Phosphate-P (mg g^{-1})	3	0.925	0.831	1.01	0.090
χ $(10^{-8}$ SI)	3	24.1	18.1	28.0	5.29
χ_{max} $(10^{-8}$ SI)	1	2130	–	–	–
χ_{conv} (%)	1	0.85	–	–	–

[†] Results of Mann-Whitney U tests undertaken on LOI, phosphate-P and χ where $n > 5$ for both data sets to determine significance of difference in mean values between NW settlement area and other area for each soil property: ° = not significant; * = $p < 0.05$, ** = $p < 0.001$.

sets with >5 samples) with those for the north-western settlement area.

As noted above, the samples as a whole display much variability, with some displaying levels of phosphate enrichment and magnetic susceptibility comparable with those in the north-western settlement area. Of the area groupings, pit row 3530 stands out clearly as exhibiting by far the strongest anthropogenic signals. In this case the mean LOI (3.48%) and phosphate-P concentration (3.91 mg g^{-1}) are not significantly different from those recorded in the adjacent north-western settlement area, and the mean χ (169 × 10^{-8} SI) is, in fact, significantly higher. The single pit in the row that contained a burial (context 4144) is strongly enriched in phosphate-P (4.89 mg g^{-1}) and has an enhanced magnetic susceptibility (170 × 10^{-8} SI).

Apart from the relatively high mean χ recorded in Enclosure VI (94.4 × 10^{-8} SI), all of the other groups have mean phosphate-P or χ values that are significantly lower than in the north-western settlement area.

Despite this, the following area groupings have mean phosphate-P concentrations that indicate enrichment (i.e. ≥2.00 mg g^{-1}): the Phase 1 settlement (mean, 2.45 mg g^{-1}), Enclosure VI (2.37 mg g^{-1}), the southern roundhouses (2.15 mg g^{-1}) and the Phase 5 ditch 4450 (2.62 mg g^{-1}). Additionally, one or more samples from the following groups have concentrations in this range: the eastern area, the south-eastern area, the north-eastern area and Enclosure I.

Generally, the evidence for magnetic susceptibility enhancement on the site is not quite so strong as for phosphate enrichment, and even in the north-western settlement area the mean χ (122 × 10^{-8} SI) is less that the figure of 150 × 10^{-8} SI which has been used here as the critical threshold for enhancement in individual samples. Against this background, the

fill of the Phase 5 ditch 4450 stands out as having a high mean χ (133 × 10^{-8} SI), though the sample size is small ($n = 3$) and the maximum is not exceptionally high (192 × 10^{-8} SI). In addition to this area grouping, the following all include at least one sample with a χ value of ≥150 × 10^{-8} SI: eastern area, south-eastern area, north-eastern area, Enclosure VI and the southern roundhouses.

The only area grouping that shows no evidence of phosphate enrichment or magnetic susceptibility enhancement is the eastern gullies. The complete absence of clear anthropogenic signals in any of 15 samples of gully fills would seem to indicate that, unlike the other cut features of the site, infilling occurred naturally rather than resulting from deliberate dumping.

Conclusions

The phosphate and magnetic susceptibility data:

- confirm the archaeological evidence which suggests that the north-western settlement area was an area of more intensive human activity, compared with the rest of the site;
- demonstrate that within the north-western settlement area there is no significant difference in the strength of the anthropogenic signals between the various pit and ditch fills, implying a similar origin for both;
- identify the fills of pit alignment 3530 as clearly showing comparable levels of phosphate enrichment and χ enhancement to those observed elsewhere in the north-western settlement area; and
- establish that at least some of the fills in all the other areas studied (apart from the eastern gullies) show clear signs of phosphate enrichment and/or χ enhancement.

Index

169